TRAVELLERS

NEW ZEALAND

By
NICK HANNA

Written by Nick Hanna, updated by Alex Stewart
Original photography by Paul Kenward

Published by Thomas Cook Publishing
A division of Thomas Cook Tour Operations Ltd
Company registration no. 1450464 England
The Thomas Cook Business Park, 9 Coningsby Road,
Peterborough PE3 8SB, United Kingdom
E-mail: books@thomascook.com, Tel: +44 (0) 1733 416477
www.thomascookpublishing.com

Produced by Cambridge Publishing Management Limited
Burr Elm Court, Main Street, Caldecote CB23 7NU

ISBN: 978-1-84157-992-4

Series Editor: Maisie Fitzpatrick
Production/DTP: Steven Collins

Printed and bound in Italy by Printer Trento

Cover photography: Front L–R: © Layne Kennedy/Corbis; © Bill Ross/Corbis; © Jon Arnold/Jon Arnold Images Ltd
Back L-R: © John Lamb/Stone/Getty; © Ripani Massimo/4-CR

The paper used for this book has been independently certified as having been sourced from well-managed forests and recycled wood or fibre according to the rules of the Forest Stewardship Council.
This book has been printed and bound in Italy by Printer Trento S.r.l., an FSC certified company for printing books on FSC mixed paper in compliance with the chain of custody and on products labelling standards.

Contents

KEY TO MAPS

- ✈ Airport
- 25 [1] Road number
- *196m* ▲ Mountain
- - - - Ferry route
- ☆ Start of walk/tour

Introduction

Although a little further flung than most other travel destinations, New Zealand abundantly repays the effort it takes to get there – as many people are discovering. This beautiful country is now placed firmly on the world tourism map.

Extending just 1,600km (994 miles) from north to south, New Zealand has everything you could possibly want for a completely different kind of holiday.

One of the country's most obvious attractions is the great outdoors: this clean, unpolluted land has 14 national parks, which, along with forest parks and reserves, cover 22 per cent of the nation's 269,000sq km area (103,900sq miles). These parks encompass lakes and rivers swarming with trout, stunning fiords and glaciers, mighty volcanoes and bubbling geysers, golden beaches and bays, and mountains and hills with fern-filled, mossy gorges and tumbling waterfalls. This splendid landscape is ideal for sailing, skiing, hiking, fishing and hunting, while hot-air ballooning and bungee jumping are also favourites with both young and old. There are no native land mammals, but instead, New Zealand has a range of rare and extraordinary birds, making it a worthwhile destination for birdwatchers. Meanwhile, marine mammals such as whales, dolphins and seals flourish in the surrounding seas.

This is the image of New Zealand we know, but less well publicised is a new-found intellectual and cultural confidence which is manifested in literature, film, painting and sculpture, handicrafts, performing arts and even fashion design. Creativity has added a cosmopolitan air to many towns and cities, building on New Zealand's unique blend of Maori and European cultures.

Alongside this cultural outpouring, New Zealand cuisine has also shrugged off its boring image and developed a distinctive style which complements the nation's now famous wines. Once considered an unsophisticated backwater, New Zealand has developed an excellent tourist infrastructure. The relaxed, welcoming attitude of the people of this uncrowded country, christened Aotearoa, or 'Land of the Long White Cloud', by Maori, adds considerably to the enjoyment of visiting it.

New Zealand

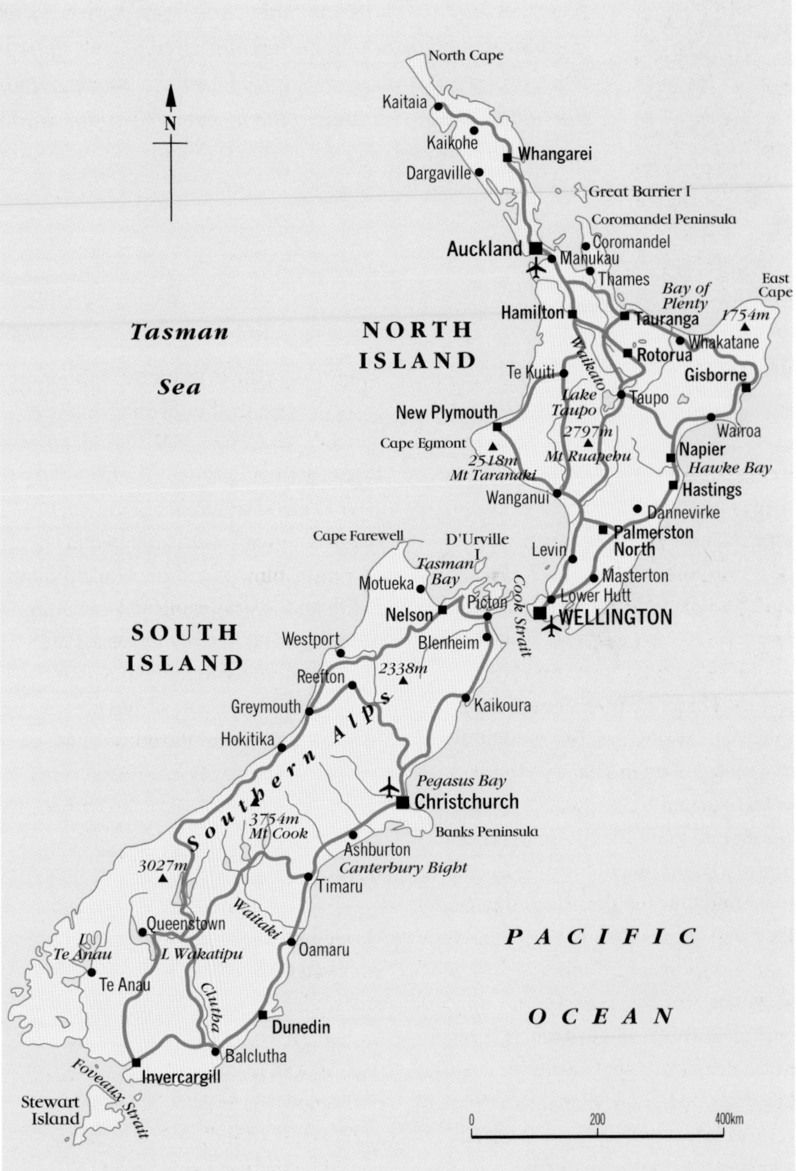
N
North Cape
Kaitaia
Kaikohe
Whangarei
Dargaville
Great Barrier I
Coromandel Peninsula
Coromandel
Auckland
Manukau
Thames
Bay of Plenty
East Cape
Hamilton
Tauranga
1754m
Whakatane
Tasman
Sea
NORTH ISLAND
Rotorua
Waikato
Gisborne
Te Kuiti
Lake Taupo
Taupo
New Plymouth
Wairoa
2797m
Cape Egmont
Napier
2518m
Mt Taranaki
Mt Ruapehu
Hawke Bay
Hastings
Wanganui
Dannevirke
Cape Farewell
D'Urville I
Palmerston North
Levin
Tasman Bay
Masterton
Motueka
Cook Strait
Lower Hutt
Picton
Nelson
WELLINGTON
SOUTH ISLAND
Westport
Blenheim
2338m
Reefton
Kaikoura
Greymouth
Southern Alps
Hokitika
Pegasus Bay
Christchurch
3754m
Mt Cook
Banks Peninsula
Ashburton
3027m
Canterbury Bight
Timaru
Waitaki
Queenstown
PACIFIC
L Te Anau
L Wakatipu
Oamaru
Te Anau
Clutha
OCEAN
Dunedin
Balclutha
Foveaux Strait
Invercargill
Stewart Island
0
200
400km

Land and people

New Zealand lies almost exactly halfway between the Equator and the South Pole. The country comprises mainly two large islands, the North Island and the South Island, the smaller Stewart Island off the southern tip of the South Island, and a scattering of little islands to the south and east of the main landmasses.

The land

The landscapes of New Zealand are dominated by ranges of mountains and hills that run through both islands; there are 223 named peaks of more than 2,300m (7,540ft), the highest being Mount Cook in the South Island, and over 75 per cent of the country lies more than 200m (656ft) above sea level. This rugged topography has given rise to a huge variety of land forms and ecological zones, the only temperate-zone habitat not found here being true desert.

The two main islands are relatively narrow, so no inland location lies more than 110km (68 miles) from the sea as the crow flies.

Climate

New Zealand has an oceanic temperate climate and, due to its isolation from other landmasses, seasonal variations are not extreme. The seasons are the reverse of those in the northern hemisphere (*see* Climate, *pp179–80*). The country's North Island is generally warmer than the South Island.

Population

New Zealand's total population is just over 4.2 million, with 74 per cent (3.1 million) living in the North Island. Twenty-nine per cent of the entire population (1.2 million) lives in the greater Auckland area.

Around 71 per cent of New Zealanders are European in origin, mostly of English or Scottish descent,

THOMAS COOK'S NEW ZEALAND

Thomas Cook first included New Zealand in its Australasia tours in 1880, hailing it as 'the South Pacific Wonderland … undoubtedly the grandest country in the world for the tourist, being so remarkable for wild landscape beauty'. Recognising its potential for natural sights, the company offered excursions in 1881 from Auckland to the 'Hot Lakes' of the North Island ('ten days for Twelve Pounds, inclusive of all charges'), and the first Thomas Cook office opened in the capital in 1889.

with a handful of Irish or Welsh ancestry, and a significant number from Holland. Of the total population, 14 per cent is Maori, and 6.5 per cent is Polynesian from the South Pacific islands (such as Samoa, Tonga and the Cook Islands), who are mostly concentrated in Auckland. Recently, immigration has increased from Asian countries such as Vietnam, Laos, Cambodia, India, China and Taiwan; Asians now account for 8.5 per cent of the population.

The economy

Despite the general lack of flat ground, agriculture and horticulture play a significant role in the economy and, along with the other primary industries (forestry, mining, energy and fishing), account for over 50 per cent of total export earnings (*see also* Sheep, *pp110–11*).

The country has some of the world's largest man-made forests, growing timber (mostly the versatile radiata pine, introduced from California) for use in pulp and paper mills, and for lumber. With a worldwide decrease in the amount of timber available, and the fact that much of New Zealand's 2.1 million hectares (5.2 million acres) of planted forests is now reaching maturity, the country is expected to profit from this resource for many years to come.

Commercial fishing is also an important export earner, with an annual quota system ensuring the sustainable management of fish species within the country's 320km (199-mile) EEZ (Exclusive Economic Zone). Aquaculture (fish farming) is on the increase; there are hundreds of ideal sites in the bays and inlets around the country's 15,000km (9,321-mile) coastline. The increasing popularity of New Zealand's high-quality wines has also meant a boom in demand for the country's winemakers (*see pp166–7*).

New Zealand tourism experienced strong growth in the last decade of the 20th century, with international visitor numbers up by 85 per cent. Strategy 2010, launched in May 2001, maps a path for sustainable tourism growth, and conservatively suggests that by 2010 the country will welcome more than three million international visitors a year, spending over NZ$9 billion.

Cleared of forest during the 20th century, rolling farmlands now support millions of sheep

Hot lakes and volcanoes

The earth's crust is made up of moving plates up to 60km (37 miles) thick. New Zealand marks the boundary of two plates that are moving together. This area forms the southern extremity of the Pacific 'Ring of Fire'. On the North Island, one plate is constantly being forced under another (subducted), and the melting process produces the magma that is extruded through volcanoes. The underground water that meets this molten rock becomes superheated, returning to the surface as hot lakes or geysers. Under the South Island, meanwhile, the plates are forcing each other up, thus producing the mighty peaks of the Southern Alps.

Volcanic activity is largely responsible for shaping the surface of New Zealand, creating some of its most dramatic mountains and lakes.

Volcanic activity is harnessed to provide energy

A geothermal power station

The city of Auckland stands on a series of 50 or more extinct volcanoes, while much of the central North Island was built up into a volcanic plateau by successive eruptions in the distant past.

A fault line runs down the North Island; at its centre is Rotorua, the country's most famous thermal zone, and at its end is White Island, an active volcano 50km (31 miles) offshore in the Bay of Plenty. To the south of Rotorua is the country's largest lake, Taupo, shaped by the violent explosions that began some 250,000 years ago; in the most recent eruption (AD 185) more than 150km^3 (36 cubic miles) of pumice and ash were ejected over vast areas of the North Island. But even this is dwarfed by an eruption that took place 22,600 years ago (dubbed Kawakawa by geologists); new data shows that this is the largest eruption to have taken place in the world in the last 50,000 years.

Maori often used the region's geothermal power, siting their villages on active thermal fields which provided heating in winter and boiling pools for cooking. The energy is still being used; geothermal power stations such as Wairakei (near Lake Taupo) and nearby Ohaaki generate about 7 per cent of the country's electricity needs.

This massive *kauri* in the North Island, Tane Mahuta, is thought to be 2,000 years old

Flora

Many unique species of plants have evolved as a result of New Zealand's isolation from other landmasses for millennia; many of them still survive, despite the effects of over 1,000 years of human settlement. No fewer than 3,400 plant species are endemic, including 1,450 of the 1,650 flowering plants found here.

Forest types

Although only a quarter of the original forests (which once covered 80 per cent of the country) remain today, most of these are protected as national parks, forest parks and reserves. The majority of indigenous trees are evergreens, with only a handful of deciduous species.

In the North Island, the forests are mostly tropical or subtropical in nature, with a dense canopy and an understorey of almost impenetrable shrubs and tree ferns. Climbers and epiphytes (including orchids) flourish in these moisture-laden hothouses. The South Island forests show traces of their sub-Antarctic origin, with less undergrowth, and many species of beech.

Trees

Of particular note are the giant conifers such as the *kauri*, the king of the forests, magnificent trees which can reach heights of up to 60m (197ft), and take 1,500 years to reach full maturity. The first 20m (65½ft) or so of its massive, silvery-grey trunk soars upwards as a clean shaft, unblemished by branches. The fact that the *kauri* was perfect for ships' masts was soon recognised by early colonists; the straight-grained, unknotted wood was highly prized in the 19th century. Thus, most of the original 3 million hectares (7½ million acres) of *kauri* in the North Island were felled by 1860, leaving just 10,000 hectares (24,710 acres) standing today.

Other conifers include the *rimu*, which, like the *kauri*, has a straight, branchless trunk and was an important timber tree. Maori made considerable use of the *totara*, which is easily carved and handy for building canoes and houses; found all over New Zealand, this species can grow to a height of 30m (98ft). Man-made forest plantations are dominated by the *radiata* or Monterey pine, Douglas fir and redwoods.

The most notable of the many flowering trees in New Zealand is the beautiful *pohutukawa*, which grows largely around the North Island coast and flames into scarlet blossom in December – hence its nickname, the 'New Zealand Christmas tree'. Equally attractive are the rich red flowers of the *rata*, the golden-yellow *kowhai* and the snowy-white ribbonwoods.

New Zealand has only one true palm, the *nikau*, which is the world's most southerly growing palm. The cabbage tree looks very much like a palm and adds a tropical air to landscapes everywhere, although in fact it belongs to the agave family.

There are also around 189 species of fern – as well as numerous hybrids – which range from tiny ferns which unfold only on rainy days, to giant tree ferns which grow to a height of more than 15m (49ft).

Alpine plants

Above the forest line, scrub and tussock give way to rolling meadows which are ablaze with alpines during the summer. Gentians, eyebrights, forget-me-nots, giant edelweiss and mountain daisies grow in profusion. Also found here are the world's largest buttercup, the Mount Cook lily and the Chatham Island forget-me-not.

Cushion plants

One of the most curious plants to be found in New Zealand is the vegetable sheep, a shrub which grows in low mounds and is covered in cream-coloured, woolly-looking leaves – hence the name, since from a distance it looks like a resting sheep! Another of the so-called cushion plants is the giant vegetable sheep, which only grows in the highlands around Nelson.

Crimson blossoms on the *pohutukawa* tree

Fauna

It is clear that New Zealand must have split away from the ancient continent of Gondwanaland (present-day Australia, Antarctica, India, Africa and South America) before the appearance of mammals, since none (apart from three species of bat) is endemic to the country. Instead, many unique flightless birds filled the ecological niches elsewhere occupied by mammals, the absence of predators making the country a paradise for them.

Extinct species

But this paradise was not to last: the first Maori settlers brought rats and the Maori dog (now extinct), and Europeans introduced more than 50 species of animals. Captain Cook freed the first sheep, soon followed by pigs, cows, deer, rabbits, cats and possums. Combined with the loss of forest habitat through clearance for agriculture, the effect on land-based birdlife was devastating: 43 species are now extinct, and more than 70 animal and plant species remain threatened despite breeding and conservation programmes.

Among the more spectacular losses were the moas (of which there were once 11 different species, including the largest bird ever to walk on earth, the 4m/13ft tall *Dinornis maximus*) and the New Zealand or Haast's eagle, the largest eagle ever known, with talons the size of a tiger's claws.

Blue penguins nest near Oamaru

Flightless birds

New Zealand's national bird, the kiwi, is the best-known flightless bird. There are three species of kiwi – brown, great spotted and little spotted – all similar in appearance, with vestigial wings, strong legs, and nostrils on the end of a long, flexible beak. Kiwis are nocturnal, and may have evolved thus to avoid being preyed upon by the giant eagles; today, stoats, possums and dogs are their greatest enemies. Population estimates are vague, but earlier optimism has been dispelled and kiwis are now classified as endangered.

More easily visible is the cheeky *weka*, a mischievous member of the rail family, which may often be seen strutting around campsites stealing food or shiny objects. You are unlikely to see the brilliant-hued *takahe* in the wild; once thought to be extinct, a small colony of these birds was discovered in Fiordland in 1948, but the total population still numbers only 250 nationally, with around 150 in Fiordland.

Other birdlife

Other native species include the *kaka*, a forest parrot, and its cousin the *kea*, which is renowned for its destructive habits – hikers sometimes find their boots and even tents pecked to pieces by this fearless and intelligent bird. The unusual *kakapo* has long, hair-like feathers growing from the base of its bill, which it uses to find its way around at night; fewer than 100 adult individuals of this highly endangered species are known to exist. The early 2002 breeding season saw the successful hatching of another 23 chicks, boosting numbers by nearly 40 per cent.

In rural areas you might hear a small native owl, the morepork, whose cry gave rise to its common name, and on forest walks the melodious songs of both the *tui* and the bellbird. The large and strikingly coloured native pigeon or *kereru* is found over most of the country; it feeds on shoots and berries.

New Zealand's black stilt, or *kaki*, is the world's rarest wading bird. These slender, red-legged birds were once widespread, but there are now only a few left in the wild near Twizel in Mackenzie Country. The white-bodied pied stilt is, however, common and can be found throughout wetland areas.

Reptiles

Among the range of small reptiles native to New Zealand is the extraordinary *tuatara*, which has the longest unbroken ancestry of any living animal and whose predecessors date back to the Triassic period, some 200 million years ago. It has a ridge of spines along its back, and can grow to be 24cm (9½in) long. Often erroneously referred to as a lizard, the nocturnal *tuatara* lives on around 30 isolated, offshore islands, and is fully protected.

The kiwi is now an endangered species due to predation by stoats, possums and dogs

Ecotourism

New Zealand has 150 species of fern

New Zealand's 'clean, green' image draws many thousands of visitors to the country, and yet the very presence of tourists may be threatening fragile areas as it has done in many other parts of the world. With a tourism strategy aiming to increase international visitor numbers to 3.2 million per year by the year 2010, can the environment withstand the impact?

Already some major natural attractions (such as the Waitomo Caves, Mount Cook National Park, and the Fox and Franz Josef glaciers) are close to capacity at peak times of the year, their facilities rapidly becoming inadequate in coping with visitor numbers. Many of the more popular three- to five-day walking tracks (The Great Walks) are also overcrowded, with insufficient space in overnight huts. Milford Sound is almost as busy as the Grand Canyon, with a constant procession of 'flightseeing' aeroplanes and helicopters drowning out the commentaries on the boats below.

Fortunately, many of these problems have been identified and strategies defined which will ensure that tourism develops on a sustainable basis. The tourism industry has produced its own 'Code of Environmental Principles', and most operators are aware that their resource base (nature itself) is their most important asset.

The tourism strategy is to 'Welcome Visitors', 'Protect our Environment' and 'Celebrate our Culture'. The Department of Conservation manages – more successfully than most such organisations in the world – more than 30 per cent of the country's land area in national parks, forests and reserves.

Westland's rainforest, South Island

Most importantly, New Zealand took a significant step in the right direction with the introduction in 1991 of the Resource Management Act, which enshrined in law the sustainable management of the environment (including the nation's cultural and historic heritage). This landmark legislation has been hailed as the leading edge of environmental planning, and other countries (including the USA) are now looking to New Zealand in an attempt to emulate its policies for tourism and nature conservation. It seems that here, at least, is one country where ecotourism may turn out to be more than just an empty buzzword.

History

Around AD 950	The Polynesian explorer Kupe discovers New Zealand, which he names Aotearoa ('Land of the Long White Cloud').
1350	Overpopulation forces many Polynesian islanders to set sail for Aotearoa in a fleet of large canoes.
1642	The Dutch explorer Abel Janszoon Tasman sights land at Hokitika on 13 December.
1769	Captain James Cook arrives on board the *Endeavour* on 9 October at Gisborne.
1790	Sealers, whalers and timber traders arrive. Maori exchange their traditional war clubs for firearms and inter-tribal wars take on a new, bloodier, dimension.
1814	The Reverend Samuel Marsden of the Anglican Church Mission Society sets up the first mission station, gradually making converts and trying to halt cannibalism. The first settlers arrive.
1817	Britain extends New South Wales legislation to New Zealand.
1832	The first British Resident, James Busby, arrives from Australia, but his efforts to promote law and order and to protect the Maori are ineffective.
1839	Captain William Hobson is appointed Lieutenant Governor to persuade Maori chiefs to relinquish their sovereignty to the British Crown.
1840	Hobson negotiates the controversial Treaty of Waitangi, which is signed on 6 February at Waitangi in the Bay of Islands. The treaty is later inked by another 500 chiefs.
1840–48	Numerous organised settlements are established, notably Wellington, Wanganui, Nelson, New Plymouth, Christchurch and Dunedin.
1843	The first skirmishes of Land Wars between Maori and settlers.

1852	The first gold strikes are made in the Coromandel; gold rushes bring in thousands of prospectors in the next 15 years. The first large-scale sheep stations are established.
1860	The Land Wars escalate, lasting almost two decades in the North Island. The Maori, despite their impressive tactics, are overwhelmed by the better-equipped colonial armies. Vast areas of Maori land confiscated.
1865	Capital moved from Auckland to Wellington.
1867	Maori gain the vote; the first four Maori members are elected to Parliament.
1882	First cargo of frozen meat sails to Europe.
1893	New Zealand is the first sovereign state to give women the vote.
1907	New Zealand becomes an autonomous dominion within the British Empire.
1947	New Zealand becomes an independent member of the Commonwealth.
1973	Preferential trading links with Britain end with Britain joining the EEC.
1975	The Waitangi Tribunal set up to hear Maori claims as specified under the Treaty of Waitangi.
1987	The Labour Party initiates a nuclear-free policy, and the USA excludes the country from the ANZUS defence pact.
1990	The National Party ousts Labour.
1996	New Zealand gets its first woman prime minister.
1999	Another woman prime minister takes over as head of Labour-led coalition.
2003	Auckland hosts America's Cup (yachting).
2005	Formation of the Maori Party.
2006	Major General Jerry Mateparae becomes the first Maori to be appointed Chief of Defence.
2008	New Zealand hero Sir Edmund Hillary dies.

Politics

New Zealand is a sovereign state with a democratic government based on the British parliamentary system, except that there is no Upper House. The legislative body, the House of Representatives, currently comprising 120 members, is elected for a three-year term. The Queen is the titular head of state, represented in New Zealand by a Governor-General.

The Muldoon muddle

Post-war politics in New Zealand were dominated by the National Party and, in particular, by its now-discredited leader, Sir Robert Muldoon. His interventionist regime controlled everything from subsidies to prices and pay, almost bankrupting an economy which was at the same time reeling from rising oil prices and the loss of protected markets when Britain joined the EEC.

Radical reforms

In 1984 Muldoon was thrown out and replaced by a Labour Party administration (led by the charismatic David Lange, who died in 2005) whose sweeping reforms included privatisation, deregulation and the removal of subsidies. This experiment in free-market economics, focused principally on agriculture and industry, reduced government deficit by the end of the 1980s, but the electorate balked at the high cost (principally an unemployment rate of over 9 per cent), and in 1990 Labour lost power to the National Party under the Right Honourable James Brendan (Jim) Bolger.

Stealing their rivals' ideological clothes, the National Party took the axe to the labour and financial markets, and government spending – 'the user pays' became a way of life. New Zealand is now reaping the benefits of these reforms, with falling inflation and a growth rate that continues to exceed predictions.

Constitutional changes

In 1993, following a referendum on constitutional change, the electorate voted to adopt MMP (Mixed Member Proportional) representation, a system which gives smaller parties a say in Parliament. The first MMP elections were held in 1996; National and Labour shared the majority of the vote, but the balance of power was retained by the newly formed New Zealand First, a Maori-dominated party. The

Maori voice is now being heard in Parliament as never before.

Land rights

The issue of land rights has dominated Maori politics since the Land Wars of the 19th century. The problem originated with the Treaty of Waitangi in 1840, which comprised two texts, in English and in Maori, each differing significantly in the translation. In the English text, Maori ceded 'sovereignty', but in the Maori text they gave the British only the right of governance. The wordings also differ on the issue of land ownership.

A century and a half of frustration over the alienation of Maori from their land came to a head in 1975 when Maori civil rights campaigner Whina Cooper, then 80 years old, captured the public imagination with her 'great march' on Parliament, drawing 5,000 supporters along the 1,100km (683½-mile) route. Later made a Dame, she was the most influential Maori woman of the 20th century, known as 'the Mother of the Nation'. She died in 1994.

The Waitangi Tribunal was set up in 1975 as the official forum for resolving grievances. The same year, the government proposed an all-embracing settlement encompassing all land seized, stolen or taken by unfair means in the country. Potential cost to the Crown: NZ$1 billion over the next ten years.

The current view is that the Waitangi Tribunal is a permanent commission of inquiry – a forum to address contemporary issues affecting Maori. From its inception more than 1,100 claims have been registered with the Treaty office.

The government's stated aim is to have all claims settled by the year 2012, although it is acknowledged that it could take until 2020 to achieve this.

New Zealand's capital, Wellington

Culture

Whether they arrived by canoe, boat or aeroplane, all New Zealanders can trace their ancestry to immigrant stock, the legacy of which is a strongly pragmatic streak in the nation's character. Kiwi ingenuity and a 'let's fix it' attitude apply as much to topical political issues as to broken-down farm machinery. These traits – combined with an innate sense of fairness and a strong sense of principle – are an integral part of the national identity.

Just beer, rugby and racing?

The popular image of New Zealanders is that their interests focus around just three things – beer, rugby and racing. The first needs no explanation. As for the second, it might be more accurate to say simply that New Zealanders love sport, for although the country's national rugby team, the All Blacks, has a devoted following, so do many other sports, from aerobics to yachting. Horse-racing is a particular passion, and many towns and communities have a racetrack just outside town.

While there is a great deal of truth in this image, it also belies a cultural sophistication which is less well known. Despite the country's small population, music and live theatre flourish.

There is also a strong strand of talent in opera: New Zealand opera singers include the late Oscar Natzke and Inia Te Wiata (both basses), as well as Sir Donald McIntyre, Dame Malvina Major and Dame Kiri Te Kanawa, to name only the best known.

New Zealand's artists embrace styles as diverse as those of Colin McCahon, a pioneer modernist, and Ralph Hotere, who draws on Maori and Pacific Island motifs for inspiration. Contemporary Maori art – particularly carving – has become a significant movement.

Perhaps the best-known New Zealand writer was Katherine Mansfield, but a new generation has now risen to international prominence, starting with Keri Hulme (whose novel *The Bone People* marked a fresh direction in Maori writing), Patricia Grace and Witi Ihimaera.

The film industry is also thriving, with Jane Campion's Oscar-winning *The Piano*, followed soon after by the release in 1995 of Lee Tamahori's *Once Were Warriors*, a raw, violent story about contemporary urban Maori life, based on Alan Duff's book. New Zealander Russell Crowe, who won the Oscar for Best Actor in 2000 for his performance in *Gladiator*, is now a famous Hollywood star.

Wellington is home to Peter Jackson and the production team of JRR Tolkien's saga, the *Lord of the Rings* trilogy, which won 17 Oscar awards altogether. All three films were shot over a 15-month period in 1999–2000 at various 'Middle Earth' locations around the country. Numerous companies in New Zealand offer tours of all the locations.

A Maori carving

The kiwis

As well as being the name for the national bird, the word kiwi is widely used to describe New Zealanders themselves.

In the money markets it is also a nickname for the New Zealand dollar, and Americans use it as an abbreviation for kiwifruit (although no Kiwi would use it in this way).

Pakeha is the Maori word for a Kiwi of European descent, and is widely used. Interestingly, Maori had no collective name for themselves before the coming of the Europeans, and it was only later on that they used the word *maori* to refer to themselves – in their language, it means 'usual' or 'normal'.

New Zealanders are often self-deprecating when it comes to their own achievements – except when they beat their nearest neighbours, Australia, on the rugby or cricket field.

'Oz' is generally regarded with friendly rivalry and derision, and in much the same way people in the South Island (to which they refer jokingly as 'the mainland') complain that North Islanders ignore them politically and – almost as bad – prefer to go overseas for their holidays rather than visit them.

Maori arts and crafts

Weaving and tattoos

The early Maori used seal and dog skins to stay warm in Aotearoa's relatively cool climate but, more importantly, they developed the use of flax as the main source of material for clothing. Flax fibres were twisted into patterns to create fabrics, a form of hand-weaving that produced exceptionally fine work; cloaks were also decorated with feathers, dyed strands or fur.

Tattooing (*moko*) was an important part of an individual's identity and status, and warriors would often be tattooed not only all over their faces but on their thighs and buttocks as well. Women's tattoos extended only over the chin. The process was long and extremely painful, with designs actually cut into the flesh with a chisel before soot was rubbed into the pattern.

Maori cultural heritage includes superb craftsmanship

Carving

Carving was used to decorate almost everything from adze handles to musical instruments, reaching its highest form in the decoration of *whare runanga* (meeting-houses) and food storage houses. Master carvers enjoyed high status in the community.

The most common motifs are the *manaia* (a bird-like, half-human figure) and *hei-tiki*. Usually called simply *tiki*, the significance of the latter, small figurines that are sold widely today as charms, has now been lost. However, you should not buy one for yourself; it should be a gift.

Music and dance

Dance was an integral feature of Maori life, signalling important events or ceremonial occasions within the tribe. Traditionally, songs and dances were accompanied by flutes (made from whalebone and wood), and, as drums were unknown, the rhythm was marked only by foot stomping and the slapping of hands on the chest and thighs. Later, Maori also took to the guitar and adapted Victorian melodies to their own poetic songs.

Haka is a generic term applied to all rhythmic dances, although today it is usually applied to the vigorous, shouted dances performed by men, such as the *haka taparahi* and the *peruperu* (war dance). *Peruperu* dancers use fearsome facial gestures (staring eyes and protruding tongue) to signal to potential enemies: 'You look good, and I am going to eat you!'

The national rugby football team, the All Blacks, uses *haka* choruses to great effect at the start of international matches. The intricate *poi* dance, in which flax balls attached to string are swirled in time to music, is performed only by women.

Many forms of traditional Maori art, such as carving, survive today

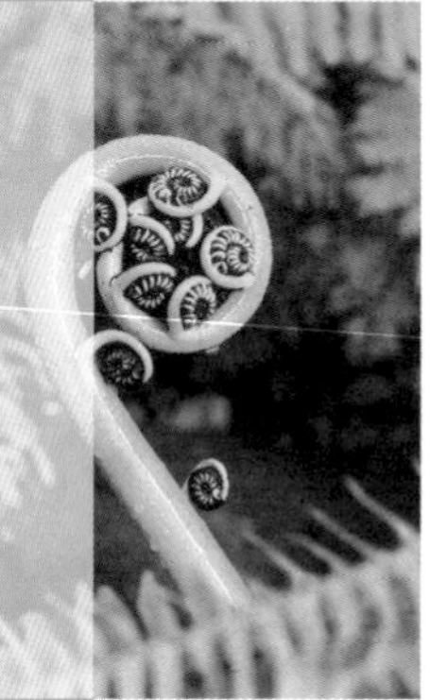

Impressions

New Zealand has such an incredible range of action-packed attractions that deciding where to go and what to see may be daunting. However, it is a fairly compact country, and you can do an enormous amount in a relatively short space of time if you set your mind to it. Since many activities are weather-dependent, you should not structure your trip too tightly; a flexible itinerary will help you make the most of the endless repertoire of things to do.

Planning your itinerary

A hit list of the best New Zealand has to offer might include the following:

Aerial sightseeing – ballooning (Christchurch), ski-plane landings (Mount Cook), helicopter flights (Mount Tarawera from Rotorua, Fox and Franz Josef glaciers, Mount Cook).
Beaches – Bay of Islands, Bay of Plenty, East Cape, Coromandel, Waiheke Island, Abel Tasman National Park.
Birdwatching – Cape Kidnappers, Farewell Spit, Hauraki Gulf, Mount Bruce National Wildlife Reserve, Paparoa National Park, Stewart Island, Taiaroa Head (Otago Peninsula).
Cruising – Hauraki Gulf, Bay of Islands, Marlborough Sounds, Fiordland.
Dramatic scenery – almost everywhere, but particularly the Mount Cook National Park, Fox and Franz Josef glaciers and Fiordland.
Museums – the Auckland Museum, the National Maritime Museum, Kelly Tarlton's Underwater World and the Antarctic Encounter (Auckland); the Museum of New Zealand, Katherine Mansfield Birthplace (Wellington); the International Antarctic Centre and the Canterbury Museum (Christchurch); the Otago and Settlers Museum (Dunedin).
Thrills and spills – black-water rafting (Waitomo), jet-boating and white-water rafting (almost everywhere), bungee-jumping (Queenstown, Lake Taupo and Rangitikei).
Wildlife – swimming with dolphins (Bay of Islands and Whakatane), whale-watching (Kaikoura), seal- and penguin-watching (Otago Peninsula).
Volcanic activity – Rotorua, Tongariro National Park, White Island.

Getting around

Despite the wild, rugged nature of much of New Zealand, the distances between places of interest or activities aren't overwhelming because the country has a well-developed transport system. Travelling around by public transport or by car is quick and easy.

By air

Air New Zealand, Qantas and Origin Pacific Airways provide scheduled services between major cities, towns and resorts. Smaller airlines and helicopter companies offer scenic tours and link services to smaller centres.

By rail

Tranz Scenic provides several different inter-city and scenic rail services. One of the most popular rail routes for visitors is the TranzAlpine Express (*see pp124–5*).

By coach

There is an extensive network of coach services linking most towns and cities.

Mount Cook in the Southern Alps, South Island

InterCity Coachlines and Newmans Coach Lines are the main operators (*see p186*). Several companies offer 'alternative' coach services, particularly popular with young travellers, which provide stops at places of interest and a casual, friendly atmosphere; this is a great way to meet people as well as to get to know the country. Bus and coach services within towns and cities are also good.

By car

The flexibility and independence which a rental car provides makes it by far the most attractive option for touring New Zealand. For short periods rental cars are fairly expensive, but generous discounts can often be negotiated for longer-term rentals of a month or more. A car and tent is a good combination; alternatively, consider hiring a camper van if you are travelling with your family.

New Zealand has an extensive network of sealed (tarmacked) roads, but some backcountry roads are still unsealed, and in some areas there may be restrictions for rental cars. On the whole, driving is a pleasure, despite several Kiwi peculiarities – such as one-way, single-lane bridges on some main roads – of which you should be aware. (For more details on internal travel, *see pp182–3.*)

Information

One of the great things about travelling around New Zealand is the amount of detailed information available. Much of this is channelled through numerous information centres, coordinated by Tourism New Zealand, which forms the Visitor Information network (*see p189*, and *www.newzealand.com*). The friendly, helpful staff at the centres provide impartial, up-to-date information on everything from bus travel to bungee-jumping.

A complementary service is offered by the Department of Conservation (DOC), which runs equally efficient and helpful visitor centres in national parks and at major natural attractions. The DOC visitor centres often incorporate high-quality displays on the local environment.

Meeting Kiwis

New Zealanders are renowned for their friendliness and hospitality, and have an outgoing, relaxed attitude towards visitors. Apart from the usual courtesies, there are no particular pitfalls to beware of – with the possible exception of comparing them unfavourably with Australians!

One of the best ways of meeting people and finding out more about the Kiwi way of life is to spend a few days in a homestay or farmstay (*see pp173–4*). These range from the cheap and cheerful to the highly sophisticated.

Maori etiquette

All Maori tribes, many sub-tribes and community groups, and even universities and schools still have their *marae*

All Blacks prop Kees Meeuws

(courtyard/square/plaza – *see p69*). The protocol governing *marae* is highly formalised, and it is very important that you seek permission before entering the *whare runanga* (meeting-house) on any *marae*, and walk around the *marae* rather than across it; footwear must be removed before going inside a *whare runanga*. It is more than likely, however, that you will be part of an organised tour, in which case you will be told what to do.

The Maori greeting *kia ora*, which means both 'good health' and 'welcome', accompanied by pressing noses, is answered with the same words.

Smoke-free zones

New Zealand is a health-conscious nation and smoking is on the decline (it has the lowest rate of tobacco consumption of any developed country). Smoking is banned on all public transport and, since 2004, in all indoor workplaces, including restaurants, bars and clubs.

What to bring

Almost any item you may require, from camera film to contraceptives, is easily obtainable in New Zealand, and despite the relatively small market base and a Goods and Service Tax (GST) of 12.5 per cent, you will find that many goods are priced similarly to those in Britain.

It is also worth noting that the weather can be highly variable from one area to the next: one day you might be comfortable in a T-shirt and shorts, the next you might be better off in a sou'wester! The best advice is to come prepared for highly changeable conditions.

In a country that is so geared towards the outdoors, dress is casual, but if you plan to sample any of the more up-market restaurants in the cities it is a good idea to pack some smart clothes, as many establishments set minimum dress codes.

Sandflies and sunburn

New Zealand has neither dangerous mammals nor snakes, but, as if to make up for this total lack of hazards, it does have the ubiquitous sandfly. These vicious insects were noted even by Captain Cook, who wrote in his journal on 11 May 1773, at Dusky Sound: 'The most mischievous animal here is the small black sandfly which are exceeding numerous and are so troublesome that they exceed everything of the kind I have ever met with, wherever they light they cause a swelling and such an intolerable itching that it is not possible to refrain from scratching and at last ends in ulcers like the small pox.'

A Maori legend has it that the gods who created Fiordland were so pleased with their work that they sat back to relax and admire it; seeing this, the goddess of life and death, Hinenui te pou, created *te namu*, the sandfly, to goad them back to work. Apply insect repellent, and if you are bitten, try to refrain from scratching for 30 minutes – the itching will go away.

The other vital precaution to take is against sunburn. The clarity of the air in New Zealand allows more harmful ultraviolet rays to reach ground level than elsewhere, a situation that has intensified with the growing hole in the ozone layer over the Antarctic. Outside, wear sunglasses and/or a hat, as well as plenty of sunblock, even on overcast days. Travellers arriving from winter in the Northern Hemisphere are particularly susceptible to sunburn unless adequately protected.

Mount Aspiring near Wanaka, South Island

Auckland and Northland

The majority of visitors to New Zealand arrive in Auckland, the country's largest and most dynamic city. You should plan to spend at least a few days here, orientating yourself and exploring the city's many attractions before setting off further afield.

A logical starting point from Auckland is to head up towards Northland, the irregularly shaped, 240km (149-mile) long peninsula that juts out at an odd angle from the North Island's top corner. Stretching out towards the Equator and bisecting the 35th parallel, Northland revels in a mild subtropical climate which has earned it the nickname of the 'winterless North'.

Northland has a rich historical legacy. It was here that the first Polynesian explorers settled, later to be followed by the Europeans on their whaling ships. Ancient legends, tribal battles and warfare between the Maori and European colonists are all woven into the fabric of Northland. The main resort area in Northland is the scenic Bay of Islands, with 800km (497 miles) of coastline facing 150 or so offshore islands.

There are no resorts on the islands themselves; most accommodation surrounds the bustling town of Paihia, which copes with its annual summer influx of over 70,000 visitors. Alongside Paihia is Waitangi, the site of the 1840 treaty signing which forms such a pivotal role in the country's history. Just to the north of the Bay of Islands are the orchards of citrus and kiwifruit that surround the township of Kerikeri. On the west side of the peninsula at Waipoua, nature's own work is magnificently visible in the form of the impressive *kauri* trees in the forests.

From Paihia it's a long journey up to one of the most isolated spots in New Zealand, Cape Reinga. In Maori legend, this was the starting point for an even longer journey: it was from here that the spirits set off for the ocean voyage to Hawaiki, the ancestral homeland.

Auckland

The country's largest city is sprawled across the narrowest point of the North Island. Auckland is almost completely surrounded by water: to the south and west, Manukau Harbour opens out into the Tasman Sea; to the north and east,

Waitemata Harbour gives on to the Hauraki Gulf and, eventually, the Pacific.

The second most noticeable feature about Auckland is the volcanic cones which randomly dot the city. At one time there were more than 50 volcanoes here, and when the district was most heavily populated by Maori tribes in the mid-18th century nearly every single one of them was home to a fortified settlement, or *pa*. Intertribal warfare brought this prosperous period to a close at the end of that century, and by the time Auckland was chosen as the new capital after the Treaty of Waitangi in 1840, the region was almost deserted.

Eventually, 49 of these volcanic cones were used for landfill; the most prominent of those that remain, including Mount Eden and One Tree Hill, provide spectacular viewpoints over the city. If you are visiting on a weekend, the panorama will reveal a flotilla of yachts cruising the harbour waters. Not for nothing is Auckland known as the 'City of Sails' – reputedly there are more boats per person here than in any other city in the world.

Despite Auckland's urban sprawl, the proximity of vast stretches of coastline means that deserted coves and surfing beaches are never more than a short drive (or sail) away.

The city can justifiably claim to be the most sophisticated and cosmopolitan in the country, with a wide range of cultural activities, busy boutiques and scores of excellent restaurants and bars. The high-rise Sky Tower houses the country's second casino, the Skycity Casino.

As the main international gateway for New Zealand, Auckland is the initial entry point for many visitors, and a major export centre. In recent years the city has also become a focal point for Pacific Islanders, who have flocked here in search of work or to pursue higher education. As New Zealand builds on historic links and ties itself to other far-flung islands in the South Seas, Auckland has cast itself in the role of 'hub of the Pacific'.

With 29 per cent of the country's population (1.2 million people) living within a 40km (25-mile) radius of the heart of the city, you might think it would seem crowded, but Aucklanders have always preferred low-density housing, and even the humblest home has its own garden – hence the sprawling

Downtown Auckland

Auckland and Northland

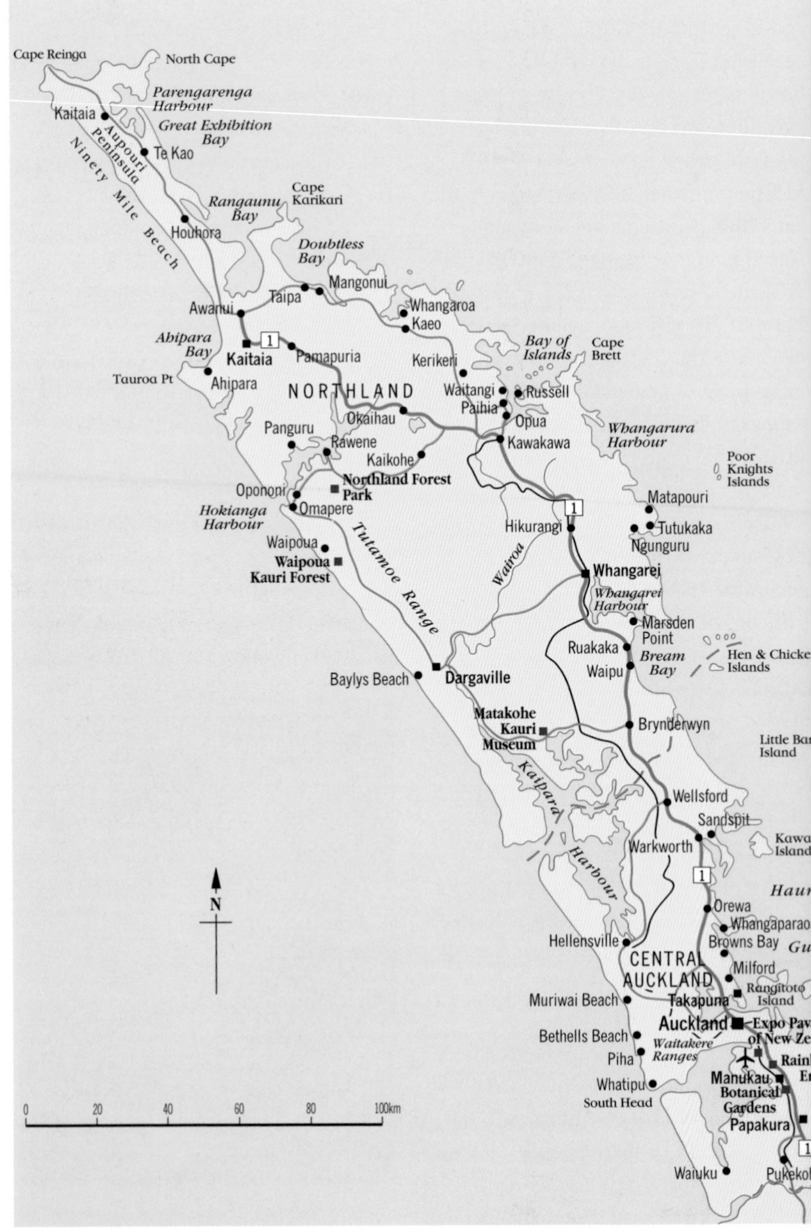

suburbs. For the visitor, this has its drawbacks as, with the exception of the downtown area, it is not an easy city to get around without transport. Unless you have hired a car, the best options are the **Auckland Explorer Bus** (*www.explorerbus.co.nz*), a hop-on-hop-off tour visiting 14 of Auckland's attractions, with full commentary, leaving from the Ferry Building at the bottom of Queen St, or the **Stagecoach Link** (*www.stagecoach.co.nz/thelink*), which also visits major attractions and leaves regularly from Britomart, the substantial urban renewal project and transport centre linking train, bus and ferry services in downtown Auckland. The **City Circuit** (*www.stagecoach.co.nz/citycircuit*) is a free bus service that takes in most of the central sights and attractions. You can buy anything from single journey tickets to Discovery Day Passes or 7-day and monthly passes for buses, ferries and rail.

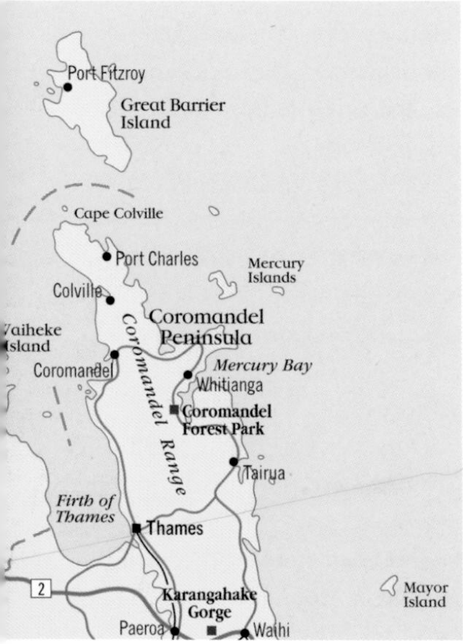

For information on bus, ferry and rail services in Auckland, visit the Britomart Kiosk, or call the MAXX Contact Centre. Tel: (09) 366 6400, or toll-free 0800 103 080. www.maxx.co.nz

Auckland Domain and Museum

The Domain is Auckland's biggest public park, 80 hectares (198 acres) of rolling lawns, gardens, and the splendid subtropical conservatory called the Wintergardens. At the centre is the Auckland Museum.

Originally opened in 1929, the Greek Revival-style building has undergone an ambitious restoration and exhibition renewal programme. With its extensive collections, amassed since 1852, the three-storey museum provides an excellent introduction to the peoples of the Pacific and New Zealand, and the flora, fauna and geography of the area. It also houses some of the world's finest collections of Maori Treasures (*taonga*).

The museum covers 9,000sq m (97,000sq ft), with two vibrant 'Discovery Centres' for children, a cafeteria, a 'must visit' museum store and two interactive information centres. A Maori cultural group performs three times daily, at 11am, noon and 1.30pm (with a 2.30pm show January–March), and tickets can be purchased in advance. Entrance to the museum is free, though a donation is suggested.

Auckland Museum. Open: daily (except Christmas Day & Anzac Day morning) 10am–5pm. Tel: (09) 309 0443. www.aucklandmuseum.com. Wintergardens. Open: Nov–Mar Mon–Sat 9am–5.30pm, Sun 9am–7.30pm; Apr–Oct daily 9am–4.30pm. Free admission. Buses: 312 & 532 from Queen St, The Link from Britomart, & the Explorer Bus from the Ferry Building.

Auckland Zoo

Linked to MOTAT 1 (*see opposite*) by a tramway, the zoo houses the usual exotic creatures as well as native species such as the kiwi. On weekends and holidays the keepers give regular talks at various enclosures.
Motions Rd, Western Springs. Tel: (09) 360 3819. www.aucklandzoo.co.nz. Open: daily (except Christmas) 9.30am–5.30pm. Admission charge.

City Art Gallery

The gallery is divided between two buildings. The Heritage Gallery, on the corner of Wellesley and Kitchener streets, houses traditional works of art, including those of the country's best-known artist, C F Goldie (1870–1947), who specialised in Maori portraits. The New Gallery contains modern pieces.
Heritage Gallery. Tel: (09) 379 1349. www.aucklandartgallery.govt.nz. Open: daily (except Christmas Day & Good Friday) 10am–5pm. Guided tours. Free admission (charge for special shows). New Gallery. Corner of Wellesley & Lorne sts. Free admission.

Kelly Tarlton's Antarctic Encounter and Underwater World

Kelly Tarlton was a famous underwater explorer; his vision led to the building of the Underwater World. He died in 1985, seven weeks after seeing his dream come true, but his legacy has turned out to be one of the country's most popular tourist attractions. The main feature of this underground aquarium is a circular acrylic tunnel with a moving walkway which carries you through large tanks teeming with fish, stingrays and several species of shark. It is also possible to take a thrilling underwater guided tour and swim with the sharks.

Underwater World was extended to include the Antarctic Encounter in 1993. Inside, there is a replica of the hut used by Sir Robert Scott on his last, ill-fated expedition in 1910–12. Then you board a Sno-Cat to 'experience' the Antarctic; this includes a simulated (and disorientating) white-out, a mock Orca whale which rises from the depths to devour a seal, and a real penguin colony.
23 Tamaki Drive, Orakei Wharf, Orakei, approximately 6km (4 miles) from the city centre. Tel: (09) 528 0603, or toll-free 0800 805 050. www.kellytarltons.co.nz. Open: daily summer 9am–9pm – last admission 8pm; winter 9am–6pm – last admission 5pm. Buses: 756 & 757 from Britomart, or the Explorer Bus from the Ferry Building. Admission charge.

Mount Eden and One Tree Hill

The top of Mount Eden (at 196m/643ft, Auckland city's highest volcanic peak) presents a fabulous panorama of the city. This strategic point was once an important *pa* (fortified settlement), occupied soon after the landing by Polynesians in 1350; ancient terracing is visible around the summit.

One Tree Hill offers another (less spectacular) viewpoint. One Tree Hill was an even bigger *pa* than Mount Eden, and terracing is also evident here. Sadly, the tree was removed in 2000.

Mount Eden lies off Mount Eden Rd. Buses: 274 from Britomart, or the Explorer Bus (summer only) from the Ferry Building.

One Tree Hill lies off Manukau Rd. Bus: 522 from Britomart.

Museum of Transport and Technology

This museum is spread over two sites alongside the Auckland Zoo. The main site, MOTAT 1, contains exhibits such as vintage machinery, a historic beam engine and a hands-on science centre.

MOTAT 2 also has the only Solent Mark IV flying boat left in the world.

805 Great North Rd, Western Springs. A tramway links MOTAT 1 with the zoo. Tel: (09) 815 5800 or toll-free 0800 668 286. www.motat.org.nz. Open: daily (except Christmas Day) 10am–5pm – last admission 4.30pm. Admission charge. Buses: 137 from Britomart, or the Explorer Bus (summer only) from the Ferry Building.

New Zealand National Maritime Museum

This museum is a celebration of the country's maritime heritage, and the seagoing traditions of the South Pacific. It seems almost a shame to label this dynamic enterprise with the dusty tag of 'museum', so skilfully have traditional-style displays been woven together with workshops (including one which runs boat-building and restoration courses, as well as others housing sailmakers, riggers and wood-carvers). There is also the marina itself, sailing trips aboard an old steam launch, and historic exhibits, such as the reconstruction of a steerage cabin

Mount Eden is the highest volcanic peak in Auckland, and offers spectacular views over the city

Auckland environs

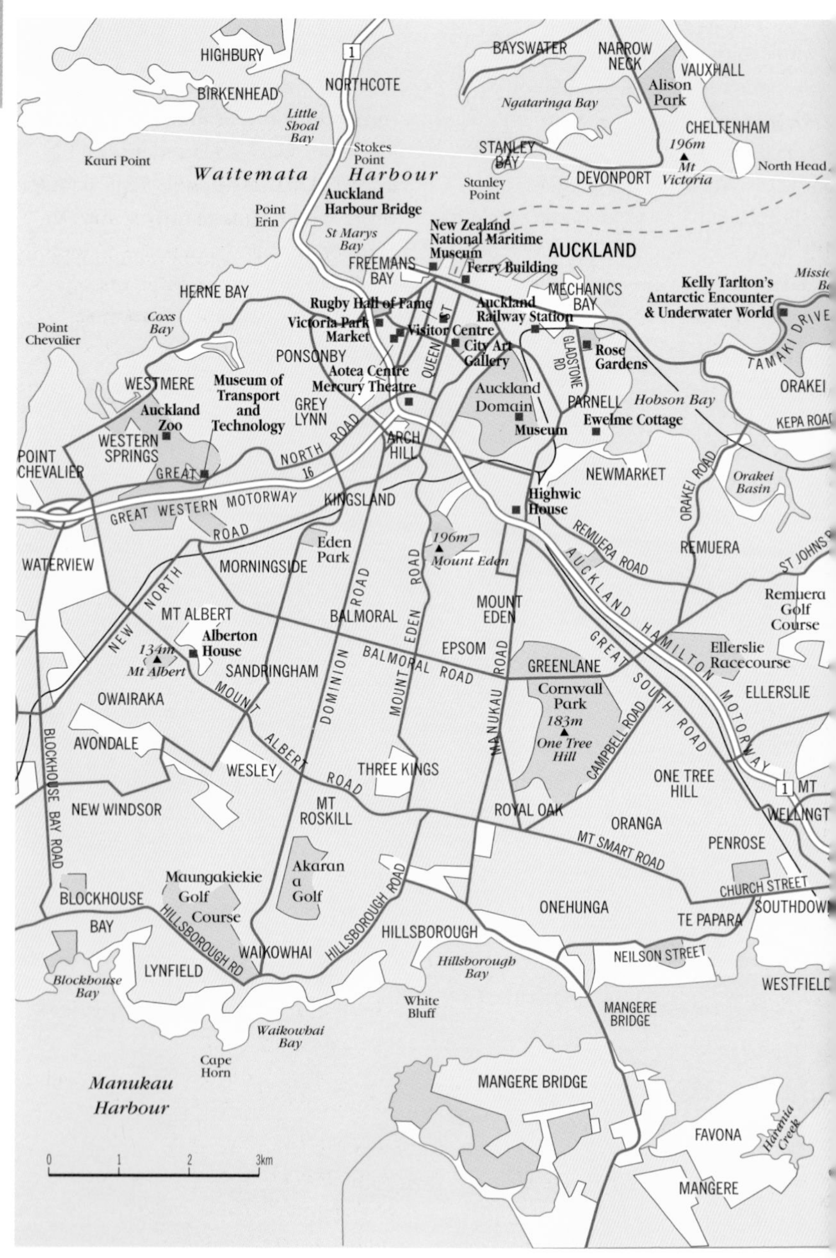

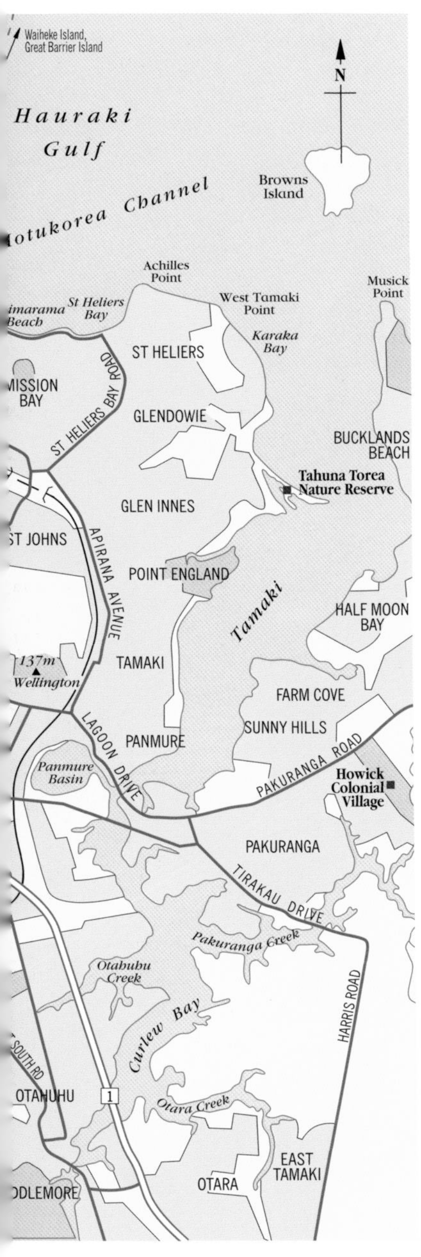

on an early immigrant ship which sways and creaks convincingly as you explore its interior.

In addition, there is an outstanding collection of Pacific canoes, historic yachts and coastal vessels, and an intriguing passenger-shipping database where descendants of early immigrants can look up the names and dates of the ships their ancestors arrived on.

A 12-minute film reconstructs **Te Waka**, the last great migratory voyage which brought the Maori to Aotearoa, showing how they survived, and how they navigated using the sun, stars and birds. *Corner of Quay & Hobson sts. Tel: (09) 373 0800. www.nzmaritime.org. Open: daily (except Christmas Day) summer 9am–6pm; winter 9am–5pm. Admission charge.*

Parnell

Parnell is a trendy, gentrified suburb, full of galleries, boutiques and restaurants, wine bars and pubs. At its heart is Parnell Village, a Victorian-style arcade of shops and restored houses. *30-minute walk from downtown, or take bus 532 or The Link from Britomart, or the Explorer Bus from the Ferry Building.*

Victoria Park Market

This is a large complex with a wide range of stalls, cafés and bars. *Corner of Victoria St West & Wellesley St. Tel: (09) 309 6911. www.victoria-park-market.co.nz. Open: daily 9am–6pm. Free admission. Buses: The Link from Britomart, or the Explorer Bus from the Ferry Building.*

Historic houses

Several historic homes survive in Auckland such as Ewelme Cottage

New Zealand has a wealth of historic buildings ranging from the earliest surviving building, Kemp House in Kerikeri (*see p47*), to old lighthouses and pioneer cottages. Auckland itself has several historic houses which can be visited conveniently in a single day.

Highwic

This is one of New Zealand's finest houses in the timber Gothic style. Built by Alfred Buckland in 1862, it was designed in the early English style with steep slate roofs, vertical boarding, dormers and latticed casement windows. The house was expanded several times to accommodate Buckland's family (twice married, he fathered 20 children) and servants. The earlier part of the house is far less ornate and of simpler proportions than later additions, which reflect the High Victorian style with their excessive ornamentation, heavily embroidered furnishings and dark walls. Highwic remained in the Buckland family until 1978.

Alberton

Built in 1863, Alberton was the home of Allan Kerr Taylor (1832–90), who made his fortune in farming and gold-mining. This grandiose mansion is unusual because of its fairy-tale towers and decorative verandas. The interior is typically Victorian.

Ewelme Cottage

When Ewelme Cottage was built in 1863–4, the district of Parnell consisted mostly of open fields. Today, the house stands surrounded by others in what is now a busy inner-city suburb, but it still embodies the feel of the pioneer lifestyle. Designed by a clergyman and his wife, Vicesimus and Blanche Lush, Ewelme was built using local kauri wood and is shingle-roofed. It was lived in by the Lushes' descendants until 1968; nearly all the furniture and personal effects are original. Several rooms in Ewelme were used as sets for the Oscar-winning film *The Piano* directed by Jane Campion.

Highwic *40 Gillies Ave, Epsom. Tel: (09) 524 5729.*
Alberton *100 Mt Albert Rd, Mt Albert. Tel: (09) 846 7367.*
Ewelme Cottage *14 Ayr St, Parnell. Tel: (09) 379 0202.*
Highwic and Alberton *open: Wed–Sun 10.30am–noon & 1–4.30pm.*
Ewelme Cottage *open: Fri–Sun 10.30am–noon & 1–4.30pm. All are closed Christmas Day & Good Friday. Admission charge.*
These houses are just three of the many properties in the country owned or administered by the Historic Places Trust (*Pouhere Taonga* in Maori), which also helps with the protection of Maori heritage sites. UK National Trust members enjoy reciprocal rights. For more details, contact: New Zealand Historic Places Trust, *PO Box 2629, Wellington or 2 Durham Street East, Auckland. Tel: (09) 307 1538. www.historic.org.nz*

AUCKLAND ENVIRONS

Beaches

There is a good selection of beaches along the coastline near Auckland and around the harbour. Travelling eastwards, Tamaki Drive runs along the shoreline, past several fine beaches such as Mission Bay, Kohimarama and St Heliers. On the North Shore, there are many good beaches between Devonport and Long Bay, some of the more popular of these being Takapuna, Milford and Browns Bay, with Orewa further north. The West Coast is dominated by rolling surf off the Tasman Sea; some of the better-known surf beaches are Bethells, Whatipu, Piha and Muriwai. (Care must be taken at all times on this coast.)

Great Barrier Island

The largest of the Gulf islands, Great Barrier has a population of slightly more than 1,000 people spread over 285sq km (110sq miles) with wilderness areas and beautiful beaches to explore. The wildest areas are in the northern section, which has many rare bird and plant species. Excellent hiking trails and campsites make this a walkers' paradise, while fishing, diving and kayaking are all possible around the extensive coastline. The island has a handful of guesthouses and hostels in addition to the DOC campsites. To get to Great Barrier, the following options are available:

Fullers Ferries run seasonal sailings from the Downtown Ferry Terminal, 99 Quay St. Tel: (09) 367 9111. www.fullers.co.nz.

The SeaLink Passenger and Car Ferry Service runs at least five times a week, and every day in summer, from the Viaduct Basin. Tel: (09) 300 5900. www.sealink.co.nz.

Great Barrier Airlines operates daily out of Auckland Airport. Tel: (09) 275 9120, or toll-free 0800 900 600. www.greatbarrierairlines.co.nz.

Mountain Air flies the Great Barrier Express daily out of Auckland Airport. Tel: (09) 256 7025, or toll-free 0800 222 123. www.mountainair.co.nz.

For general information, contact the Great Barrier Island Visitor Information Centre. Tel: (09) 367 6009. www.greatbarrier.co.nz

Hauraki Gulf

Nestling between the mainland and the Coromandel Peninsula to the east, the Hauraki Gulf is a popular yachting area. Most of it lies within the **Hauraki Gulf Maritime Park**, which encompasses more than 50 islands. Some of these islands can be reached on day-trips, while others are more remote, and require additional time and energy to explore. Most of them are, however, serviced by regular ferries or light aircraft. A selection of the more popular islands includes the following:

Kawau Island

Tucked into the coastline above Auckland, Kawau's main attraction is the historic **Mansion House**; originally built by a mine manager, it was restored by Sir George Grey (one of the country's early governors) in the 1860s.

The house and gardens are open to the public. Elsewhere on Kawau there are old copper mines, walking tracks, and secluded beaches and picnic spots.
360 Discovery Cruises depart from Auckland or Gulf Harbour. The trip includes 2 hours' cruising from Auckland, 2½ hours ashore to explore and an optional barbecue lunch on a 60-min, fully commentated cruise around the bays of Kawau Island.
360 Discovery Cruises Ticket Office, Pier 4, Quay Street, Downtown Auckland. Tel: (09) 307 8005, or toll-free 0800 888 006. www.360discovery.co.nz.
Mansion House. Open: daily 9.30am–3.30pm. Tel: (09) 422 8882. www.doc.govt.nz. Admission charge.

Rangitoto Island

Rangitoto emerged from the sea around 600 years ago, and is one of Auckland's youngest volcanoes. There are walking tracks across the intriguing volcanic landscape, and lava caves and fern groves to discover.

The island has the country's largest remaining forest of *pohutukawa* trees (*see p11*), and more than 200 species of native trees and flowering plants. There are terrific views from the 259m (850ft) summit (allow an hour each way).
Fullers Ferries depart three times a day from Auckland and Devonport, and also run the Rangitoto Volcanic Explorer Tour, which includes a guided tour of the island. Tel: (09) 367 9111. www.fullers.co.nz.
The Auckland DOC (Department of Conservation) Visitor Information Centre in the Ferry Building, Quay St, has walking maps. Tel: (09) 379 6476. www.doc.govt.nz

Waiheke is just one of several islands in the Hauraki Gulf which can easily be visited from Auckland

Waiheke Island

Waiheke is one of the closest islands to Auckland. Its many attractions – fine beaches, bush-walking tracks, vineyard trails, good restaurants, and a thriving arts and crafts community – make it a popular weekend getaway. Another reason for the island's popularity may be that it is reputed to be an average 5°C (41°F) warmer than the mainland! It also offers mountain biking, horse-riding and kayaking around the coast.
Waiheke Island Visitor Information Centre, 2 Korora Road, Artworks, Oneroa, Waiheke Island. Tel: (09) 372 1234. www.waihekenz.com.
Fullers Ferries ply up to 19 times a day from Auckland (journey time 35 minutes), and offer island bus tours as well. Tel: (09) 367 9111. www.fullers.co.nz.
The island's scheduled bus service connects with ferry arrivals and departures.

Walk: Devonport

This is an easy walk which takes you through the historic settlement of Devonport, with a short ferry ride across the harbour from central Auckland. The walk takes in fine views of the Hauraki Gulf and its islands.

Allow 2 to 3 hours.

Take a Fullers Ferry from the Downtown Ferry Terminal. (For a timetable call (09) 367 9111.) On leaving the Devonport Wharf building, turn left along Queen's Parade. Turn right at the end, down Spring St, to the Navy Museum.

1 The Royal New Zealand Navy Museum

This small museum has a rich collection of items relating to New Zealand's naval heritage, with a huge array of medals, models and memorabilia from various campaigns. There are also ships in bottles, a cat-o'-nine-tails, figureheads and armaments.

Tel: (09) 445 5186. www.navymuseum.mil.nz. Open: daily (except Christmas Day, Boxing Day & Good Friday) 10am–4.30pm. Guided tours available on request. Free admission.

Retrace your steps and turn left up Victoria Rd. Notice the elegant shop façades that have stood for over a hundred years.

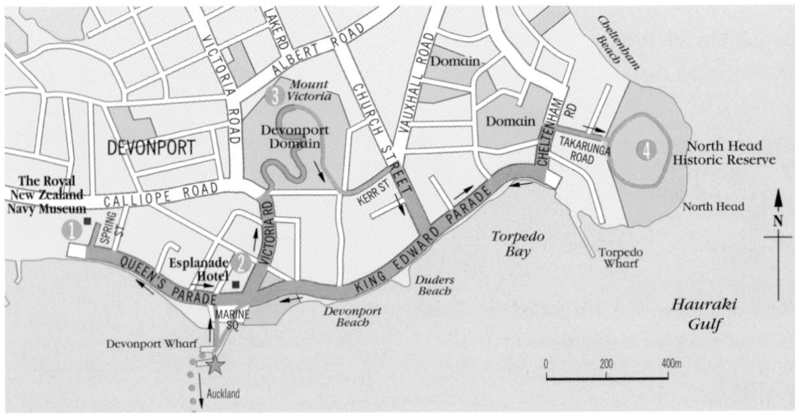

View of Auckland from Mount Victoria

2 Victoria Road

This main thoroughfare is lined with bookshops, craft galleries, outdoor cafés, and antique and souvenir shops. On the corner, commanding the seafront, is the Esplanade Hotel. Built in 1902, it was modelled on the popular English seaside hotels of the era.

At the end of Victoria Rd, on the corner with Kerr St, keep going up the path which leads to the top of Mount Victoria, an extinct volcanic cone with the outline of ancient Maori fortifications clearly visible around the summit.

3 Mount Victoria

From Mount Victoria, which is 196m (643ft) high, there are 360-degree views over Hauraki Gulf and its islands and back across the city and its harbour. An orientation table at the summit enables you to identify the surrounding local landmarks; on a clear day the views extend as far as Great Barrier Island and out to the Coromandel Peninsula.

The outlines of terraces and pits can be distinguished on the hill top, principally on the northern and eastern elevations.

Follow the path back down the east side of the hill. Turn right at the end of Kerr St to enter Church St. At the seafront, turn left on to King Edward Parade and follow the road round past the playing fields up Cheltenham Rd, turning right up Takarunga Rd.

4 North Head Historic Reserve

North Head, like Mount Victoria, was a strategic *pa* (fortified settlement) due to its commanding views across any potential routes of attack. It became a military post in the late 19th century, when fears of a Russian invasion in 1885 prompted the building of gun batteries; one of these housed an unusual 'disappearing gun' which recoiled underground after firing – it is just one of the defences that can still be seen today.

The whole hillside is riddled with ancient guns, searchlights, a network of old tunnels, and other fortifications, most of which can be explored with the aid of a torch.

Open: daily 6am–10pm. Free admission.

Follow the road back along the seafront to return to Victoria Rd and the ferry terminal.

Devonport Visitor Centre 3 *Victoria Rd. Tel: (09) 446 0677. www.northshorenz.com. Open: daily 10am–4pm.*

Bay of Islands

This is one of New Zealand's most historic regions, and it is also one of the most popular resort areas of the North Island. Paihia, Waitangi and Russell are the three most important towns on the bay.

Paihia and Waitangi

Paihia, the main hub for excursions and accommodation in the Bay of Islands, is a busy resort that offers the visitor many opportunities for boat trips, diving, swimming and yachting. Excursions to swim with dolphins are also popular, and Paihia is a major centre for deep-sea fishing.

Just over 2km (1 mile) from Paihia on the north side of the Waitangi River is the 506-hectare (1,250-acre) **Waitangi National Reserve**, at the centre of which is the historic Waitangi Treaty House. The Treaty House was the setting for the first signing of the Treaty of Waitangi (1840). The house itself, one of the country's oldest surviving buildings, was completed in 1834 and was the home of James Busby, the first British Resident. The interior has been partially restored. Outside the house, overlooking the Bay of Islands, a huge flagpole stands on the site where the treaty was signed. To one side is an unusual *whare runanga* (meeting-house), each of its 28 carved interior wall slabs representing a different group of tribes. A short walk away, on Hobson's Beach, is an impressive *waka* (war canoe); the 37m (121ft) long *Ngatokimatawhaorua* was built for the 1940 Centennial celebrations of the signing of the treaty. At the entrance to Waitangi National Reserve is a well-equipped visitor centre with half-hourly audiovisual presentations on the Treaty.

Waitangi National Reserve. Tel: (09) 402 7437. Open: daily, summer 9am–6pm; winter 9am–5pm. Admission charge.

Russell

Russell's first outside settlers were ex-convicts and sailors who deserted from the whaling ships which stopped here in the early 19th century. By 1840, it was the largest European settlement in the country and a notorious frontier town, with no less than 40 'grog shops' and brothels. The missionaries called it the 'hell-hole of the Pacific'.

Today, Russell is a tranquil township where life revolves around big-game fishing, messing about in boats, and a handful of historic attractions. Prime among the latter is **Christ Church**, the oldest surviving church in the country. The church still bears the marks of musket balls from an attack in 1845, and the churchyard contains many historic graves.

Just across from the church is the **Russell Museum**, containing a wide range of memorabilia relating to maritime history and the early settlers, as well as a remarkable one-fifth scale reproduction of the *Endeavour.*

A key feature of the town is an unusual building known as **Pompallier**

House (named after the first Catholic bishop of the South Pacific), an elegant two-storey house built by French missionaries for their printing presses. It is New Zealand's oldest surviving industrial building and has been restored to its former role as a printing and book-binding works. You can buy the beautiful volumes made here at a small shop on site.

A short walk or drive up the hill above town brings you to Flagstaff Hill, with panoramic views of the Bay. It was here that Hone Heke, a Maori leader, chopped down the flagstaff – a symbol of the hated British settlers – four times in the 1840s.

Christ Church is on the corner of Church & Robertson sts.
Russell Museum, 2 York St. Tel: (09) 403 7701. www.russellmuseum.org.nz. Open: daily, Jan 10am–5pm; Feb–Dec 10am–4pm. Admission charge.
Pompallier House, The Strand. Tel: (09) 403 9015. Open: daily (except Christmas Day) Dec–Apr 10am–5pm; May–Nov 10am–4pm. Admission charge.
Ferries depart at regular intervals throughout the day from Paihia wharf to Russell (crossing time 10 minutes).

Christ Church in Russell is the oldest church in New Zealand

Cape Reinga

Cape Reinga is the most northerly point in New Zealand which can be reached by road. (From Cape Reinga you can see North Cape, to which there is no public access and which lies, in fact, 5km (3 miles) further north.) From the Cape Reinga promontory there are spectacular sea views, especially of waves sometimes 10m (33ft) high crashing over Colombus Reef, just offshore where the Pacific Ocean and Tasman Sea meet.

An integral part of all Cape Reinga tours is a trip back down the west side of the peninsula along **Ninety Mile Beach**. In fact, the beach is 90km (56 miles) long (the misunderstanding is attributed to a French explorer who merely marked '90' on his chart, subsequently interpreted as miles by the English).

On the east side of the peninsula, most tours also stop off at Houhora, where there is an extensive and well-displayed old collection of Victoriana, stuffed birds, shells and Maori exhibits at the **Wagener Museum**, as well as an early pioneer house, the **Subritzky Homestead**, next door.

Cape Reinga is 115km (71½ miles) northwest of Kaitaia. Day-trips operate from Kaitaia and Paihia. It is better to go from Kaitaia, since the round-trip tour from Paihia is 500km (310½ miles).
Wagener Museum and Subritzky Homestead, Houhora.
Tel: (09) 409 8850. Open: daily 8.30am–4pm. Admission charge.

Doubtless Bay

The first landing here was by the legendary Polynesian explorer Kupe in AD 950. In 1769, the *Endeavour* arrived here and the lookout boy shouted 'Land on three sides, Sir.' Cook replied 'Doubtless, a bay', and the name stuck. It has beautiful beaches (at **Cable Bay**, **Cooper's Beach** and **Taipa**) and is fast becoming a holiday-home centre. At the eastern end of Doubtless Bay is the laid-back waterfront community of **Mangonui**, a former *kauri* export depot.

Approximately 30km (18½ miles) from Kaitaia.

Hokianga Harbour

The deep inlet of Hokianga Harbour on the western coastline of Northland presents one of those strange contrasts in landscape which are typical of New Zealand: on the southern spur of the harbour is deep forest, while the northern head consists of a single enormous sand dune rising up above the water. The harbour was in use in the early 19th century, but later developments passed it by, and it is now a peaceful area where the main activities are fishing, boating, and lazing on the beach. The two main settlements are **Omapere** and **Opononi**.

70km (43½ miles) north of Dargaville & 80km (49½ miles) northwest of Whangarei.

Kaitaia

Northland's second-largest town after Whangarei, Kaitaia has no special

attractions, but it is a useful base for visiting Cape Reinga to the north.
155km (96 miles) northwest of Whangarei.

Kerikeri

Thanks to its fertile volcanic topsoil, the Kerikeri district is one of the richest agricultural areas in Northland and produces quantities of citrus fruit in the orchards that lie hidden behind the tall hedges lining the roadside. This small community has developed into a centre for pottery and handicrafts.

Kerikeri was the site of the country's second mission station, established here by the Reverend Samuel Marsden in 1819. The wooden **Kemp House**, built in 1822, stands above the picturesque Kerikeri inlet alongside the **Stone Store**, the oldest stone building in New Zealand (completed in 1836); the latter is still in use as a shop today, and has a small museum on its first floor. Just across the bridge over the inlet is **Rewa's Maori Village**, a full-scale replica of an old Maori fishing village.
Kerikeri is 22km (13½ miles) north of Paihia.
Kemp House. Tel: (09) 407 9236. Open: daily (except Christmas Day) Nov–Apr 10am–5pm; May–Oct 10am–4pm.
Stone Store Museum. Tel: (09) 407 9236. Open: daily (except Christmas Day) Nov–Apr 10am–5pm; May–Oct 10am–4pm.
Rewa's Maori Village. Open: daily summer 9am–5pm; winter 10am–4pm. Admission charge for all three.

The Kerikeri Basin, with two of New Zealand's oldest houses

Matakohe Kauri Museum

Kauri logging was one of the most important industries in Northland at the turn of the 20th century, reaching its peak between 1870 and 1910. This excellent museum traces the history of *kauri* logging, and displays include old milling equipment, a bushman's shanty, and some gigantic *kauri* planks, the size of which (up to 8m/26ft long and over 2m/6½ft wide) brings home exactly why this timber was so valuable.

Adjoining rooms show the end result in the form of a re-created settler's house with *kauri* panelling and some fine pieces of *kauri* furniture. The museum also houses a huge collection of *kauri* gum in raw and worked form; this amber-coloured resin was once hugely popular as a craft medium.

In the adjoining shop you can pick up small souvenirs made from swamp *kauri* (preserved tree trunks excavated from the swamps) which has been carbon-dated at around 44,000 years old.

26km (16 miles) from the Brynderwyn junction on Highway 1 (signposted). Tel: (09) 431 7417. www.kauri-museum.com. Open: daily (except Christmas Day) Nov–Apr 8.30am–5.30pm; May–Oct 9am–5pm. Admission charge.

Waipoua Kauri Forest

In the Maori creation myth, Tane Mahuta, Lord of the Forest, brought light to the world by thrusting his feet upwards to separate Rangi (the Sky Father) from Papa (the Earth Mother). It is easy to imagine how this cosmology originated when you stand beside the awesome trunk of New Zealand's largest tree, named after Tane Mahuta, in the Waipoua Forest. Its height is impressive

An old log hauler outside the Kauri Museum in Matakohe

(over 50m/164ft) but it is really the girth (nearly 14m/46ft around) that gives such a powerful impression of strength and longevity.

Tane Mahuta is just one of several massive *kauri* in the forest, all easily accessible by boardwalk from the main road (Highway 12) which runs through the forest. Nearby are Te Matua Ngahere (Father of the Forest – the oldest *kauri* in the forest, about 2,000 years old), the Four Sisters (a grove of four graceful *kauri* growing close together), and the Yakas Kauri (a 30-minute walk from the road).

Waipoua and the neighbouring forests of Mataraua and Waima together make up the largest remaining tract of native forest in Northland, and are home to threatened species such as native forest parrots (*kakariki* and *kaka*) and the North Island brown kiwi. There are a number of marked walking trails through the forest, ranging from one to six hours in duration; information and route maps are available from the DOC Waipoua Visitor Centre.

Waipoua is 2km (1 1/3 mile) off Highway 12, around 50km (31 miles) northwest of Dargaville.
Waipoua Visitor Centre, River Road, Waipoua Forest. Tel: (09) 439 3011. Open: daily summer 8.30am–5.30pm; winter 8.30am–4pm. Free admission.

Whangarei

Northland's only city, Whangarei, faces an extensive, sheltered harbour – one of the deepest in New Zealand – and the

The Whangarei Falls, a picturesque spot outside the city

country's only oil refinery. Points of interest include **Claphams Clock Museum**, with more than 1,000 clocks and watches, and **The Quarry**, which has a range of weaving, hand-dyed clothing and ceramics.

The **Whangarei Falls**, 6km (3 1/2 miles) outside town on the Ngunguru road, is a popular picnic spot. The 25m (82ft) high cascade tumbles into a pool and there is a pretty walk down through woodlands to the base, with another path continuing across a bridge and up the other side again. You can swim in the pool above the falls.

Whangarei is 169km (105 miles) north of Auckland.
Claphams Clock Museum, Quayside, Town Basin. Tel: (09) 438 3993. www.claphamsclocks.co.nz. Open: daily 9am–5pm. Admission charge.
Northland Craft Trust at The Quarry, Selwyn Ave. Tel: (09) 438 1215. Open: daily 8am–5pm. Free admission.

Early explorers

In legends passed down from generation to generation, it was the great Polynesian voyager Kupe who discovered New Zealand, landing in the far north of the country around AD 950. He came from a homeland known to the Maori as 'Hawaiki', which is now thought to have been one of the Society Islands in East Polynesia. Kupe circled the islands, naming this new country Aotearoa, 'Land of the Long White Cloud'. He saw no inhabitants, and eventually returned to Hawaiki with the sailing instructions which would enable others to follow.

Around 200 years later, Chief Toi and his grandson, Whatonga, landed in Aotearoa after a series of mishaps. Strangely, they found the land inhabited (a fact for which we have no explanation), and stayed to intermarry with the peoples already there.

In the 14th century, a number of other canoes set off to look for Aotearoa, to ease overpopulation in the Society Islands. At least 12 named canoes are known to have arrived, and even today many Maori tribes are known by the name of the canoe from which they claim descent.

Europeans had long speculated on the existence of an undiscovered landmass in the southern hemisphere, and in 1642 the Dutch East India Company ordered Abel Janszoon Tasman to look for this missing continent.

The rocky outcrop known as Kupe's Sail on the Palliser Bay coast

Maori seafarers discovered New Zealand some 800 years before Captain Cook

On 13 December he became the first European to set eyes on the country when he spied land near Hokitika. He sailed north and reached Golden Bay, but after a brief skirmish with the Maori he put back to sea.

In 1768, the English Captain James Cook sailed in the *Endeavour* to Tahiti, where he opened the 'secret instructions' that ordered him to proceed to New Zealand. The *Endeavour* arrived in Gisborne on 9 October 1769, but after a hostile encounter with the Maori two days later, Cook was forced to sail away again.

Apart from the initial misunderstanding at Gisborne, Cook found the Maori friendly and helpful, and his accounts of this rich, fertile land and its hospitable people created a great deal of interest in Europe.

Central North Island

The central North Island has a variety of landscapes and destinations. Lying across the Hauraki Gulf from Auckland, the Coromandel Peninsula was more popular with city-dwellers than tourists, but that's changing now that its superb beaches, laid-back lifestyle and rugged scenery are becoming better known.

Coromandel's east coast merges into the Bay of Plenty. Here, too, the beaches are a major attraction (particularly for 'surfies'), and the seas offshore are renowned for big-game fishing. Beyond the Bay of Plenty's coastal resorts are the wild and sparsely populated coastlines of the East Cape, leading round into Poverty Bay and Gisborne, the most easterly city in the country. The Hawke's Bay region, south of Gisborne, is well known for its wines and sunshine. The seaside city Napier and the neighbouring Hastings are famous for their Art Deco architecture.

Volcanic activity is never far away in the North Island, and Lake Taupo was created by massive eruptions in the past. The main geothermal area lies slightly to the north of Taupo, focused on the city and the lake of Rotorua.

To the south of Lake Taupo, the volcanic belt reaches its southernmost point beneath the peaks of the Tongariro National Park. No tour of the central North Island is complete without a visit to the Waitomo Caves.

Bay of Plenty

Mount Maunganui

The Mount Maunganui resort lies on the east side of Tauranga Harbour, straddling a narrow peninsula. The Mount itself overlooks the township and its beaches. Walking trails take you around the 232m (761ft) high Mount (once an important *pa*, or fortified settlement), and to the hot salt-water pools at its base. The long, sandy, oceanside beach is popular with swimmers, surfers and body-surfers.

Mt Maunganui Hot Salt Water Pools, Adams Ave, Mount Maunganui. Tel: (07) 575 0868. Open: Mon–Sat 6am–10pm; Sun & public holidays 8am–10pm.

Tauranga

The city of Tauranga lies at the western end of the Bay of Plenty, and is a busy commercial centre, its prosperity based on the citrus trees and kiwifruit that grow in the fertile areas inland, and

A giant kiwifruit near Te Puke

Tauranga Harbour, the largest port in the country for exports.

Tauranga was the scene of bloody battles during the Land Wars (most notably, the Battle of Gate Pa). During the fighting the local missionary, Archdeacon Brown, tended the wounded of both sides.

You can visit the house which Brown completed in 1847, called **The Elms Mission House**. The garden, planted in the 1830s, is one of the oldest in the country, and contains a picturesque library and a reconstruction of the original tiny chapel.

The city's other main historical attraction is **The Historic Village**, with its many relocated and restored old buildings. Here you can browse craft shops selling everything from woodcraft and hand-spun woven garments to leadlight ornaments and hand-painted gifts, or just relax over coffee and cake in the beautiful surroundings.

Back in the city centre, don't miss the Te Awanui war canoe resting in its shelter at the top end of the Strand. Built entirely from *kauri* wood, this replica is often paddled out into the harbour during ceremonial occasions.

Tauranga is 88km (54½ miles) north of Rotorua.

The Elms Mission House and Library, Mission St. Tel: (07) 577 9772. www.theelms.org.nz. Open: Sat, Sun, Wed & public holidays 2–4pm. Admission charge. Garden open daily. Free admission.

The Historic Village, 17th Ave West, Gate Pa. Tel: (07) 571 3700. www.thehistoricvillage.co.nz. Free admission.

Te Puke

Te Puke is dubbed the 'kiwifruit capital of the world'; the first kiwifruit vines were planted here in 1937. Learn all about this fuzzy fruit at **Kiwi360**, a horticultural theme park offering rides through the orchards, heli-tours of the grounds and the beautiful Te Puke coastline, and, for the kids, a magic castle, funhouse mirrors, a giant dragon maze and super-slide, among other things. There is also a Kiwi360 café and souvenir shop.

Te Puke is 31km (19 miles) southeast of Tauranga.

Kiwi360, Box 541, Te Puke, on the main Rotorua-Tauranga Rd (Highway 2), 6km (3½ miles) south of Te Puke. Tel: (07) 573 6340. www.kiwifruitcountry.co.nz. Open: daily (except Christmas Day) 9am–6pm. Admission charge.

Whakatane

At the opposite end of the Bay of Plenty to Tauranga is Whakatane, another popular holiday base with a long, sweeping beach over the headland at Ohope. In the town itself is the diminutive **Whakatane Museum and Gallery**, displaying Maori tools, cloaks, flaxwork, weapons and ornaments that belonged to the descendants of the Polynesians who landed here in the Mataatua canoe around AD 1350. Whakatane is noted for its deep-sea fishing, and is the main access point for White Island (*see below*), just offshore.

Whakatane is 100km (62 miles) southeast of Tauranga.

Whakatane Museum and Gallery, 11 Boon St. Tel: (07) 306 0505. www.whakatanemuseum.org.nz. Open: weekdays 10am–4.30pm; Sat, Sun & public holidays 11am–3pm. Admission charge.

White Island

White Island is an active volcano that smoulders 50km (31 miles) offshore. Sulphur deposits were mined here from the 1870s until 1934. You can see the abandoned workings alongside the active craters, sulphur vents, boiling pools and huge gannet colonies.

Scenic flights to White Island are operated by Vulcan Helicopters, PO Box 10, Waimana. Tel: toll-free 0800 804 354. www.vulcanheli.co.nz. All-day cruises and walking tours are operated by White Island Tours. Tel: (07) 308 9588. www.whiteisland.co.nz

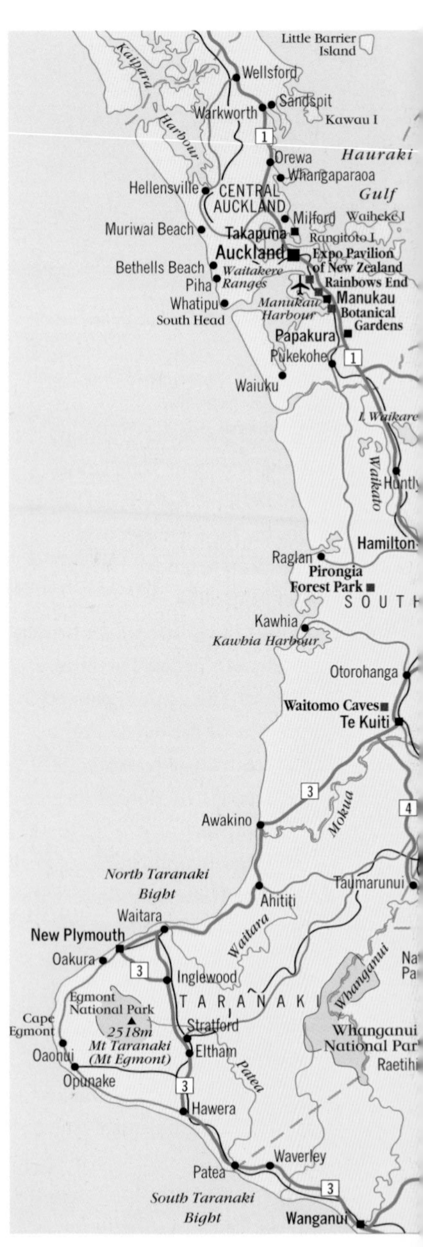

Central North Island

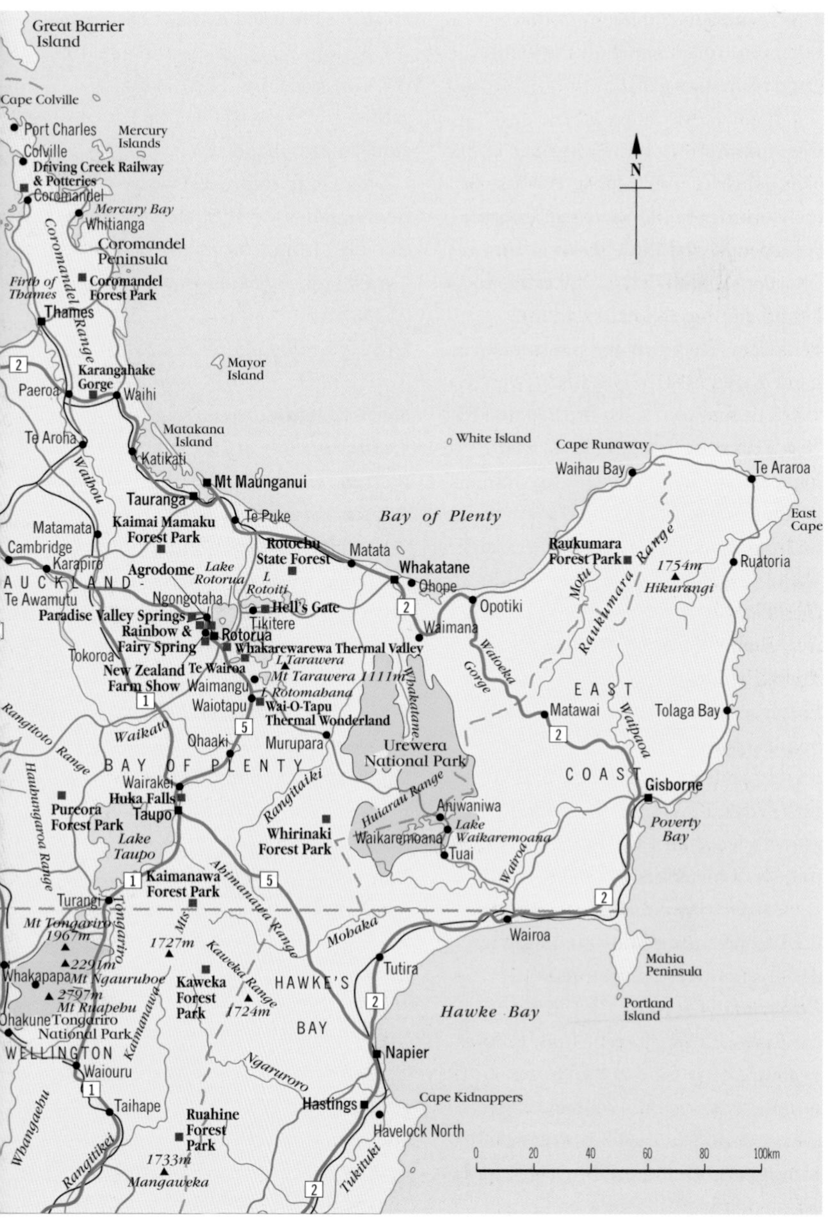

Coromandel Peninsula

Colville

This is the last settlement in the northern Coromandel on the scenic Cape route (*see p75*).

Coromandel

This delightful township at the base of the Coromandel Range is a magnet for craftspeople and those seeking 'alternative' lifestyles, as well as the focus of anti-mining campaigns in the peninsula. The town and peninsula were named after HMS *Coromandel*, which called in for *kauri* spars in 1820. In 1852 New Zealand's first gold finds were made here, and 300 prospective miners flooded in from Auckland. However, the boom proved premature, and it wasn't until the late 1860s that viable gold reefs were discovered. Those first gold strikes were made at Driving Creek, now the site of the **Driving Creek Railway and Potteries**. The narrow-gauge railway, built by potter Barry Brickell to bring clay down from the hills to his kilns, now serves a dual purpose as a tourist attraction with the 'station' lying in the middle of his potteries yard.

Near Driving Creek, the methods used to separate gold from quartz are demonstrated at the restored **Coromandel Stamper Battery**, one of the first such works to be built in New Zealand. Early mining tools, rock samples and various colonial artefacts are on display in the **Coromandel Mining and Historical Museum**, in the original School of Mines building. Most of the craft workshops around Coromandel welcome visitors; their locations are listed in *The Coromandel Art & Craft Trail* leaflet, available from the Visitor Centre. There is also a garden trail around five beautiful gardens just outside the township.

There is an impressive grove of *kauri* trees on Highway 309, around 15km (9 miles) from Coromandel.

Coromandel is 55km (34 miles) north of Thames.

Driving Creek Railway and Potteries, 3km (2 miles) north of town. Tel: (07) 866 8703. www.drivingcreekrailway.co.nz. Trains run daily at 10.15am & 2pm all year; in summer, also at 12.45pm & 3.15pm. Admission charge.

Coromandel Stamper Battery, 2km (1 1/3 mile) north of town. Tel: (025) 2464 898. Open: summer daily 10am–5pm; weekends only in winter. Admission charge.

Coromandel Mining and Historical Museum, Rings Rd. Tel: (07) 866 8598. Open: summer daily 10am–4pm; weekends only in winter. Admission charge.

Coromandel i-SITE Visitor Centre, 355 Kapanga Rd. Tel: (07) 866 8598. www.coromandeltown.co.nz. Open: Mon–Sat 9am–5pm; Sun 10am–2pm.

Thames

Thames was built on the exploitation of gold and *kauri* in the late 19th century, and used to be one of the largest towns in New Zealand, with a population of 18,000 and over 70 working gold mines in the vicinity. It is now the principal gateway and shopping centre for the Coromandel Peninsula. The gold bonanza days are recalled in the **Historical Museum**, while the nearby **Mineralogical Museum** has one of the largest collections of minerals and fossils in the country. **Goldmine Experience** runs tours through the Gold Mine and Stamper Battery just outside Thames. Alternatively, details of a walk along Rocky's Goldmine Trail are available from the town's Visitor Centre.

Thames is 119km (74 miles) southeast of Auckland.

Historical Museum, corner of Pollen & Cochrane sts. Tel: (07) 868 8509. Open: daily 1–4pm. Admission charge.

Mineralogical Museum, corner of Brown & Cochrane sts. Tel: (07) 868 6227. Open: daily summer 11am–4pm; winter 11am–3pm. Admission charge.

Goldmine Experience, corner of SH25 & Moanataiari Creek Rd. Tel: (07) 868 8514. www.goldmine-experience.co.nz. Open: summer daily 10am–4pm; winter weekends and public holidays 10am–4pm. Admission charge.

Thames i-SITE Visitor Centre, 206 Pollen St. Tel: (07) 868 7284. www.thamesinfo.nz. Open: Mon–Fri 8.30am–5pm; Sat, Sun & public holidays 9am–4pm. Closed: Christmas Day.

Whitianga

Whitianga is a busy summer resort town in Mercury Bay on the peninsula's east coast. The resort is renowned for its fishing (particularly game fishing, which peaks during February and March), watersports and beaches. There are numerous good swimming beaches nearby, plus the novelty of **Hot Water Beach** at the mouth of the Tauwaiwe River to the south, where you can dig your own spa pool in the sand.

From Whitianga's wharf, ferries ply back and forth to **Ferry Landing**, site of the original settlement on the other side of the Narrows, from where you can walk or cycle to a number of beaches and lookout points over Mercury Bay.

Whitianga is 95km (59 miles) north of Thames.

Cattle graze the lowland slopes of the Coromandel Ranges

East Cape

The East Cape coastline encompasses some of the most dramatic and unspoiled scenery in the North Island. For many years the rugged **Raukumara Range** – which runs down the centre of the cape – made transport difficult, and the Maori who lived here were left in peace. Even though a 334km (207½-mile) coastal road from Opotiki to Gisborne has since been built, the region remains quiet and laid-back, with small Maori communities dotted along the coast.

Gisborne

This is the first city in New Zealand to see the sun rise every day; its other claim to fame is as the site of Captain Cook's first landfall on 9 October 1769. Cook's men unfortunately mistook the Maori *haka* (challenge) as an attack, and promptly shot the reception committee; further misunderstandings led to several more Maori deaths before the *Endeavour* sailed away. Cook named the spot Poverty Bay 'because it afforded us not one thing we wanted'.

Poverty Bay was, in fact, a complete misnomer, since the fertile plains around Gisborne are dotted with market gardens, maize fields and vineyards (*see pp166–7*). Cook's landing site is marked by an obelisk on the north side of the Turanganui River, and his statue gazes landwards from the top of Titirangi Hill above the port.

Near the town centre on the riverbank is the award-winning **Tairawhiti Museum**, which includes a number of interesting *taonga* (treasures) in its changing displays on various aspects of Maori culture and colonial history.

Behind the main museum is the **Te Moana Maritime Museum**, housed inside the bridgehouse of *The Star of Canada*, wrecked on the beach in 1912.

Gisborne is 216km (134 miles) northeast of Napier.

Tairawhiti Museum, Kelvin Rise, 18–20 Stout St. Tel: (06) 867 3832. www.tairawhitimuseum.org.nz. Open: Mon–Sat 10am–4pm; Sun & public holidays 1.30–4pm. Closed: Christmas Day & Good Friday. Admission charge.

Hamilton

This prosperous city, a centre for the rich farmlands of the Waikato district, sits on New Zealand's longest river, the Waikato. Behind Hamilton's gleaming new buildings lie several scenic riverside parks. You can also cruise along the Waikato on the old paddle-steamer, the **MV *Waipa Delta*.**

The **Waikato Museum** houses an extensive collection of artefacts from

Statue of Captain Cook in Gisborne

the local Tainui people, including the war canoe *Te Winika*, built in 1836, and contemporary Tainui carvings, a large collection of historic photographs, and excellent displays of modern art.

Hamilton is 126km (78 miles) south of Auckland.

The MV Waipa Delta *cruises daily for lunch, tea & dinner. For information & booking, tel: toll-free 0800 472 3353. www.waipadelta.co.nz.*

Waikato Museum, corner of Grantham & Victoria sts. Tel: (07) 838 6553 or (07) 838 6606. www.waikatomuseum.org.nz. Open: daily (except Christmas Day & Boxing Day) 10am–4.30pm. Free admission.

Hastings

Hastings, sister town to Napier (*see pp60–61*), sits in the centre of New Zealand's warmest and driest region, Hawke's Bay (not to be confused with the bay itself, called Hawke Bay). This area is known as 'Wine Country' and has earned the reputation as a leader in gourmet, locally-grown food and award-winning wines, its red wines being particularly celebrated on the world stage. Food and wine trails are popular, either self-driven or on tours run by local operators by coach, limousine, bicycle or horse and cart. The Hawke's Bay Farmers Markets, held at the Hawke's Bay Showgrounds in Hastings on Sunday mornings (and on Tennyson St in Napier on Saturday mornings), are a great way to sample and buy the many 'local only' goods. The yearly festival, Harvest Hawke's Bay, is one of New Zealand's biggest and brightest celebrations of wine and food and takes place in February with events around Hastings and Napier.

One of Hastings' main attractions lies just outside town at the family-oriented **Splash Planet**, a 23-hectare (57-acre) park with castles, pirate ships, train rides and other amusements.

Beyond Hastings at the southernmost extremity of Hawke Bay is **Cape Kidnappers**, one of the few mainland nesting sites for the striking Australian gannet, which congregates here in large numbers between late October and late April. You can visit the gannet colonies from September/October to April/May.

Hastings is 236km (146½ miles) southwest of Gisborne. For details and bookings of food and wine tours, contact Hastings i-SITE Visitor Centre, corner of Russell & Heretaunga sts. Tel: (06) 873 5526 or toll-free 0800 429 537. www.hawkesbaynz.com. Open: Mon–Fri 8.30am–5pm, Sat & Sun 9am–5pm.

Splash Planet: Grove Rd. Tel: (06) 873 8033. www.splashplanet.co.nz. Open: Nov–mid-Feb daily 10am–5.30pm; mid-Feb–Mar Sat & Sun 10am–5.30pm. Admission charge. For information on the gannet colony, contact the DOC Centre, 59 Marine Parade, Napier. Tel: (06) 834 3111. Open: Mon–Fri 9am–4.15pm. Gannet-viewing tours operated by: Gannet Beach Adventures. Tel: toll-free 0800 426 638. www.gannets.com. Gannet Safaris. Tel: toll-free 0800 427 232. www.gannetsafaris.co.nz

Napier

Lying at the southern end of Hawke Bay, Napier would have remained a humdrum seaside resort had it not been for the events of 3 February 1931, when a massive earthquake measuring 7.9 on the Richter scale levelled most of the township, killing 258 people. The survivors set about rebuilding with unprecedented vigour, and within two years a completely new town had risen from the rubble. The architects adopted Art Deco or Spanish Mission styles (in vogue in America at the time), and the result is a town with a wealth of classic, 1930s-style features that have been carefully preserved to this day. The best way to explore Napier's Art Deco heritage is on a guided walking tour or by taking a stroll through the streets using the booklet *Art Deco Walk*, available for $4 from the Art Deco Shop, or the Napier Visitor Centre.

The story of the earthquake is related in an audiovisual exhibit at **Hawke's Bay Museum**, which also has a good selection of decorative arts from the 1930s, and a well-designed exhibition of carvings from the Ngati Kahungunu peoples of the east coast.

Napier's seafront esplanade, Marine Parade, is a broad avenue lined with Norfolk pines; it has several attractions, all within a few minutes' walk of each other, including **Marineland**, where you can get up close to fur seals, penguins and dolphins, and the **National Aquarium of New Zealand**, where sharks, stingrays, eels, trout, sea

An Art Deco window in Napier

horses, turtles, octopus and hundreds of other sea life and fish species are on display. If you're after expansive sea views while relaxing in warm bubbles, **Ocean Spa Napier** offers open-air hot pools, including a 25m (82ft) lap pool, two leisure pools and toddlers' pool, as well as outdoor and private indoor spas, steam room, sauna, sun bed and massage facilities.

Napier is 216km (134 miles) southwest of Gisborne.

Guided walking tours leave from the Art Deco Shop, 163 Tennyson St. Tel: (06) 835 0022. www.artdeconapier.com. Open: daily 9am–5pm.

Hawke's Bay Museum and Art Gallery, 9 Herschell St (corner of Marine Parade). Tel: (06) 835 7781. www.hawkesbaymuseum.co.nz. Open: daily (except Christmas Day) 10am–6pm. Admission charge.

Marineland, 290 Marine Parade. Tel: (06) 834 4027. www.marineland.co.nz. Open: summer Mon & Thur 10am–4.30pm, Tue, Wed & Fri–Sun 10am–5.30pm; winter daily 10am–4.30pm. Admission charge.
National Aquarium, 546 Marine Parade. Tel: (06) 834 1404. www.nationalaquarium.co.nz. Open: daily 9am–5pm – last entry 4.30pm. Admission charge.
Ocean Spa Napier, 42 Marine Parade. Tel: (06) 835 8553. Open: Mon–Sat 6am–10pm; Sun & public holidays 8am–10pm. Admission charge.
For further information contact the Napier i-SITE Visitor Centre, 100 Marine Parade. Tel: (06) 834 1911. www.hawkesbaynz.com. Open: weekdays 8.30am–5pm; weekends 9am–5pm; extended hours over summer.

Otorohanga

This small town on the way to the Waitomo Caves (*see p73*) is worth a stop for the **Kiwi House and Native Bird Park** (just off the main road). Here there is a nocturnal house with brown kiwis, a water-bird section, and a huge, walk-in aviary with a variety of native forest birds such as the *kea, tui* and *kaka.*
Otorohanga is 60km (37 miles) south of Hamilton on Highway 3.
Kiwi House and Native Bird Park, Alex Tefler Drive. Tel: (07) 873 7391. www.kiwihouse.org.nz. Open: daily Sept–May 9am–4.30pm; June–Aug 9am–4pm. Admission charge.

Rotorua

Rotorua is at the centre of what is known as the Taupo Volcanic Belt, which runs from the Tongariro National Park in the south to White Island in the Bay of Plenty. Volcanic activity is, however, most evident in Rotorua: even if you don't notice the steam escaping from back gardens, road drains or rocky patches, your nose will certainly warn you of the ever-present hydrogen sulphide – it smells like rotten eggs – which wafts over the city.

The area was first inhabited by the Te Arawa tribe in the 14th century after they had made their way inland from the point at which their canoe beached in the Bay of Plenty. They used the boiling volcanic pools for cooking and heated their houses *(whare)* naturally by building them on warm soil. During the 19th century the Te Arawa were usually at war with neighbouring tribes. Once the local feuds ceased in the 1870s, tourists came in for cures in the thermal waters, and Rotorua took off as a spa town.

The first building in the resort was the Tudor-style **Bath House**, built in 1908 at the centre of Government Gardens on the shores of the lake. It houses **Rotorua Museum**, winner of 'Best Heritage Attraction' at the 2000, 2001 and 2002 New Zealand Tourism Awards. The museum offers a range of changing exhibitions and events. Of its several excellent permanent exhibitions, two are particularly interesting: *Tarawera Te Maunga Tapu* (Tarawera,

A Sacred Mountain), which tells the story of Tarawera Mountain and the fatal eruption on 10 June 1886 (*see* Te Wairoa Buried Village, *p66*), and *Nga Taonga o Te Arawa* (The Treasures of the Arawa People), which includes superb, unusual carvings and important artefacts.

Nearby is the **Polynesian Spa**, voted as one of the top ten medical/thermal spas in the world in 2004 and 2005 by Condé Nast Traveller. There are over 30 hot mineral pools, including adults-only pools, private spas and a large, high-alkalinity pool for families. A full range of luxurious spa therapies is on offer in the Lake Spa Retreat, and there is a café and specialist gift shop.

Renovated to celebrate the Millennium, the **Blue Baths**, in a magnificent Spanish Mission-style building adjacent to the Bath House, have been meticulously restored, re-opening 68 years after the date they were first opened. Bathe in the thermally heated waters, then take tea in the elegant Tea Rooms upstairs. The old changing rooms house an exhibition on the history of the building and the Baths.

From a quay further along, on the lakeside, explore Lake Rotorua and Mokoia Island by paddle-steamer, cruise boat, jet hydrofoil, floatplane or helicopter. A short walk past the quay is **Ohinemutu Marae**, a Maori village which was once the main settlement on the lake before the spa town developed. The main attractions are a Tudor-style Anglican church, **St Faith's** – its graveyard contains many important tombs – and a richly carved meeting-house, Tamatekapua, opposite the church, named after the captain of the *Arawa* canoe.

The Bath House in Rotorua's Government Gardens now houses Rotorua Museum

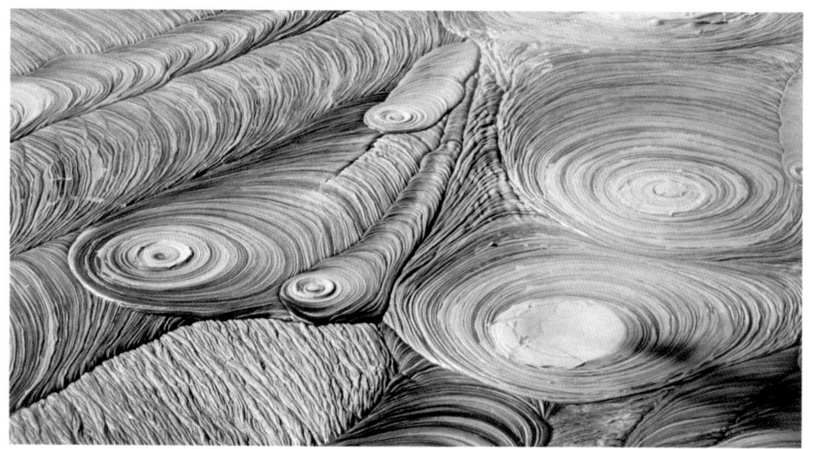
Bubbling geothermal mud, Rotorua

For fantastic views over Rotorua, take the **Skyline Skyrides** gondola up to the summit of Mt Ngongotaha, where you can enjoy fine dining in the restaurant, a tasty snack in the café, an exhilarating ride on the Sky Swing, or a thrilling downhill race on the Luge. For this and the other main attractions outside the city centre (*see Rotorua environs*), you can join a tour or shuttle bus if you don't have your own vehicle. The Visitor Centre is a regular pick-up and drop-off point for buses and tours, as well as being the depot for national bus and coach services.

Rotorua is 221km (137 miles) southeast of Auckland.
Rotorua Museum, Government Gardens. Tel: (07) 349 4350. www.rotoruamuseum.co.nz. Open: daily 9.30am–5pm. Admission charge.
Polynesian Spa, Hinemoa St. Tel: (07) 348 1328. www.polynesianspa.co.nz. Open: daily 8am–11pm (last pool entry 10.15pm, spa therapies 9am–8pm). Admission charge.
Blue Baths, Government Gardens. Tel: (07) 350 2119. www.bluebaths.co.nz. Open: Mon–Fri 10am–7pm; Sat & Sun 10am–8pm. Museum open: daily 10am–5pm. Admission charge.
Skyline Skyrides, Fairy Springs Rd. Tel: (07) 347 0027. www.skylineskyrides.co.nz.
Rotorua i-SITE Visitor Centre, 1167 Fenton Street. Tel: (07) 348 5179. www.rotoruanz.com. Open: daily summer 8am–6pm; winter 8am–5.30pm.

Rotorua environs

Agrodome and New Zealand Farm Show

Both of these locations offer a similar type of experience – essentially a one-hour show about sheep. If you thought sheep were too boring to merit such

coverage, then think again! The shows are highly entertaining, and as well as explaining the differences between up to 19 different varieties of sheep on display, there is a sheep-shearing demonstration, a mock sheep auction, lamb-feeding and plenty of audience participation. Both offer farm tours and horse treks; the Agrodome also hosts a range of extreme sports, such as bungee, skydiving, helicopter flights and jet-boating, among others.
Agrodome, Western Rd, Ngongotaha, is 7km (4 miles) northwest of Rotorua city centre on SH5. Tel: (07) 357 1050. www.agrodome.co.nz. Shows: daily 9.30am, 11am & 2.30pm. Admission charge.
New Zealand Farm Show, Fairy Springs Rd, Ngongotaha, is 5km (3 miles) north of Rotorua city centre on Highway 5. Tel: (07) 348 8683. Shows: daily 10.30am, 11.45am, 1pm, 2.30pm & 4pm. Admission charge.

Hell's Gate and Wai Ora Spa

In 1934, the Irish playwright George Bernard Shaw visited Hell's Gate and is reputed to have said: 'Hell's Gate, I think, is the most damnable place I have ever visited, and I'd willingly have paid ten pounds not to have seen it.' Quite why this sensitive soul was so upset by a few boiling sulphur cauldrons is perhaps a matter for theologians, but children (and probably adults too) will love the walk through Hell's Gate, where they can wonder at the bubbling pools, sulphurous jets of steam, boiling whirlpools, mud volcanoes and 'plopping liquids' in this 20-hectare (49-acre) reserve. Notices warn of the dire consequences of stepping off the path – temperatures in some pools reach 115°C (239°F). After enjoying Rotorua's most active geothermal field, you can self-indulge here with mud baths, spas and mud therapies at the Wai Ora Spa.
Tikitere, Rotorua, 16km (10 miles) from the city centre on Highway 30. Tel: (07) 345 3151. www.hellsgate.co.nz. Open: daily 8.30am–8.30pm. Admission charge.

Paradise Valley Springs

Similar in concept to Rainbow and Fairy Springs but less crowded, Paradise Valley Springs also has trout pools, native flora and fauna, including a wetlands area for New Zealand waterfowl, and other animals on display, including a pride of lions, and cubs which can be patted and photographed. Lions' feeding time is at 2.30pm daily.
Paradise Valley Rd, 11km (6½ miles) from the city centre, signposted off Highway 5. Tel: (07) 348 9667. www.paradisev.co.nz. Open: daily 8am–6pm – last entry 5pm. Admission charge.

Rainbow Springs

The Springs, first opened to the public in 1898 and some of the most powerful natural springs in the region, are now part of a massive tourist complex which includes trout pools, native flora and fauna, and a nocturnal kiwi house. Hundreds of rainbow trout swim upstream from Lake Rotorua to spawn in the Rainbow Spring pools, and these are supplemented by juveniles reared in hatchery pools here. The pools are shaded by ferns and tree ferns.

The complex includes displays of animals introduced to New Zealand (such as deer, Himalayan thar, and the massive 'Captain Cooker', a pig species brought here by Cook over 200 years ago), and native birds (like the *kea* and the *kaka* parrots), New Zealand wood pigeons (*kereru*), the mellifluous *tui* and the Paradise duck. It also serves as a conservation and breeding centre for protected species such as kiwis and the endangered *kokako.* A souvenir shop, a restaurant and the adjoining Rainbow Farm complete the facilities.

Rainbow Springs, Fairy Springs Rd, Auckland Highway, is 5km (3 miles) north from the city centre on Highway 5. Tel: (07) 350 0640 or toll-free 0800 724 626. www.rainbowsprings.co.nz. Open: daily 8am–9pm (later during summer). Admission charge.

Te Puia and the Whakarewarewa Thermal Valley

'Whaka' (as most people call it) is the closest of the major thermal reserves to Rotorua city centre, best known for its twin geysers which spout at regular intervals. The first (and smallest) of these is the **Prince of Wales Feathers**, which reaches a height of around 12m (39ft) and always precedes the eruption of its neighbour, **Pohutu** (Maori for 'splashing'), which can reach 20–30m (66–98ft), playing sometimes for 20 minutes or more. Nearby are

Rainbow trout swim upstream to spawn in the clear waters of Rainbow Springs

silica formations, boiling pools and a Maori village.

Within the reserve is the **New Zealand Maori Arts and Crafts Institute**, set up in the 1960s to revive the dying art of Maori woodcarving and weaving. You can see Maori carvers and weavers at work inside the institute, and finished pieces are placed in the institute gallery. The valley's *marae* (meeting place) is the venue for the midday cultural performance, Kapa Haka, and the evening cultural experience and *hangi* (traditional meal cooked on hot rocks), Mai Ora. Both run daily and can be booked on site.

Hemo Rd, Rotorua, 3km (2 miles) from the city centre. Tel: (07) 348 9047. www.tepuia.com. Open: daily summer 8am–6pm, winter 8am–5pm. Admission charge (includes guided tour and Maori concert).

Te Wairoa Buried Village

In the mid-19th century, Rotorua was famous not only as a spa centre but also for its fabulous Pink and White Terraces, a celebrated attraction of fan-like silica formations on the shores of Lake Rotomahana, usually visited by canoe from the Maori village of Te Wairoa.

However, on the morning of 10 June 1886, Mount Tarawera (previously thought to be dormant) exploded, burying the villages of Te Wairoa, Moura and Te Ariki in nearly 3m (10ft) of ash, lava and mud. More than 150 people died, and the famous Pink and White Terraces were obliterated forever.

Parts of Te Wairoa have since been excavated, including the hut of the local *tohunga* (priest), who predicted the disaster and remained buried alive here for four days. Other remnants include the old Rotomahana Hotel, and an unusual stone storehouse with carvings on the lintel – very rare in New Zealand, since Maori seldom carved in stone. There is a new museum complex which contains fascinating displays, as well as a waterfall trail.

15km (9 miles) east of the city centre, on Tarawera Rd. Tel: (07) 362 8287. www.buriedvillage.co.nz. Open: daily Nov–Mar 9am–5pm; Apr–Oct 9am–4.30pm. Admission charge.

Waimangu Volcanic Valley

This multi award-winning site is another impressive volcanic area, with all the different attractions visible on a pleasant, downhill walk to Lake Rotomahana (around an hour one way; a free bus carries you back up again).

The main sights include the **Frying Pan Lake**, which is the world's largest hot spring, the former site of the Waimangu Geyser, and the **Inferno Crater**, which contains a steaming, pale blue lake.

14km (8½ miles) south of Rotorua on Highway 5, signposted off the main road, then a further 6km (3½ miles). Tel: (07) 366 6137. www.waimangu.co.nz. Open: daily 8.30am–5pm (Jan till 6pm). Admission charge.

Wai-O-Tapu Thermal Wonderland

Billed as the country's 'most colourful thermal area', Wai-O-Tapu ('Sacred Waters') is worth the journey out from Rotorua city if only to see how natural chemicals have rendered an incredible range of tints and hues in thermal zones such as the **Champagne Pool** and the **Artist's Palette**.

Nearby is the **Lady Knox Geyser** which is 'soaped' every day at 10.15am (the soap acts to disperse the upper layers of water, thus allowing the super-heated steam to burst through from the reservoir below); even so, the performance of the geyser is unpredictable. If there is enough water in the reservoir, Lady Knox can reach heights of around 20m (65ft) and play for an hour; if not, it might only fizzle briefly to a height of around 5m (16ft). *27km (16½ miles) south of Rotorua on Highway 5, signposted off the main road. Tel: (07) 366 6333. www.geyserland.co.nz. Open: daily 8.30am–5pm – last admission 3.45pm. Admission charge.*

A colourful pool at Wai-O-Tapu

The **Tarawera Legacy** combines a visit to Rotorua Museum, Te Wairoa and Whakerewarewa. For reservations, *tel: (07) 349 3463 or toll-free 0800 924 426. www.taraweralegacy.co.nz*

Taupo and Lake Taupo

The resort town of Taupo enjoys a spectacular setting on the shores of Lake Taupo, New Zealand's largest lake (600sq km/380sq miles) which lies at the geographical heart of the North Island. From Taupo town, looking across the lake, you can see the distant peaks of the Tongariro National Park. This busy tourist centre has a wide range of attractions, from fishing trips to lake cruises, bungee-jumping and visits to geothermal areas.

This enormous, water-filled crater was formed by a series of massive eruptions which began around 250,000 years ago. Taupo's violent past is, however, masked by the tranquil lake waters which draw thousands of fishermen each year to what is claimed to be one of the best trout fisheries in the world.

(*cont. on p70*)

Maori society

Traditional Maori society was organised into the *whanau* (extended family groups), the *hapu* (sub-tribes, made up of several *whanau*), and the *iwi* (tribes). The *whanau* were ruled over by *kaumatua* and *kuia*, the male and female elders, who were in turn subject to the *ariki* (chiefs) of the *hapu* and the word of the *tohunga*, the priests who were entrusted with the secrets of tribal lore.

Every facet of Maori life was regulated by the dual concepts of *tapu* ('sacred', from which we derive 'taboo') and *mana* (which relates to prestige, pride and dignity). Any slight to one's *mana* had to be met with *utu* (retribution), a social code that gave rise

Meeting-house and *marae*, Banks Peninsula

to incessant intertribal conflict – although this was only seasonal, and war didn't take place when the *kumara* (sweet potato) crops needed attention.

The constant fighting meant that principal villages were often located on hill tops and were fortified; many hills still bear the distinctive terracing which marks the ramparts and ditches surrounding *pa* (hill forts).

At the centre of all villages was the *marae*, an open courtyard which served as a focal point for community life. Facing the *marae* was the *whare runanga* (meeting-house), which was often elaborately carved to represent the spirits of famous ancestors and contained tribal artefacts that were revered as treasures.

Religion and legends

An important part of Maori cultural heritage is their vast store of imaginative and colourful legends, which were passed down from generation to generation. Maori mythology reveals a depth of thought and religious feeling which is closely tied in with their animist beliefs and reverence for nature. Traditionally, Maori worshipped many gods and goddesses, although, unlike other Pacific peoples, they also believed in a 'supreme being', Io. This concept made it much easier for them to adapt to Christianity in the 19th century, which many did.

A traditional Maori greeting

Language

Spoken fluently, the Maori language is highly allegorical and riven with ancestral and spiritual references, but usage has fallen away in recent years. A campaign is on for greater use of Maori in everyday life. Te Reo Maori is now being taught in language classes in schools.

The shores of Lake Taupo, New Zealand's largest lake

Taupo's geothermal heritage is more evident in the thermal pools, such as **AC Baths**, just outside of town, which has several mineral pools and private spas. Similar facilities are available at the **Taupo Hot Springs**, hidden in a wooded valley off the Taupo-Napier highway.

Lounging around in hot pools is one way of using up geothermal heat, but at the **Wairakei Geothermal Power Station** it generates up to 1,550GWh (gigawatt hours) of power per year for the national grid. Completed in 1958, this was the second geothermal power station in the world. The construction of the power station destroyed the original **Wairakei Terraces** and geysers, and work was begun in 1996 to redevelop these. You can now do self-governed tours or book guided tours of the Wairakei Terraces Walkway and learn about the Maori history of the area, visit therapeutic, multicoloured, or red mud pools, and a geyser. You can book tickets at the Visitor Centre for a Maori cultural evening that includes a concert and *hangi* (traditional meal cooked in the ground), and a tour of the Terraces and a Maori village with carvers, weavers, tattooists and musicians at work. You can also book guided visits to the power station's geothermal field.

Other geothermal phenomena in the vicinity include the **Craters of the Moon** mud pools, which are run by the Department of Conservation free of charge.

Hot water is also put to good use at the **Wairakei Prawn Farm**, where you can round off a tour of the prawn ponds by enjoying a meal in the grillhouse afterwards.

From the nearby jetty you can speed up the Waikato River on the *Huka Jet*, which takes you right to the spectacular **Huka Falls**. Alternatively, you can walk to the falls along the Huka Falls Road.

Elsewhere along the river you can go rafting or enjoy spectacular views while jumping off a 45m (148ft) high cantilever platform above the water at **Taupo Bungee**. There are many options for lake cruises, most of which visit contemporary Maori rock carvings on the lake's shore; the most popular ships are the *Barbary* (a 1920s wooden racing yacht once owned by Errol Flynn) and the *Ernest Kemp*, a replica steam ferry. If you prefer modern transport, enjoy a cruise on the *Cruise Cat* catamaran, which offers daily sailings and can be privately chartered.

Taupo is 84km (52 miles) southwest of Rotorua.
AC Baths, Spa Rd. Tel: (07) 376 0350. www.acbaths.co.nz. Open: daily (except Christmas Day) 6am–9pm. Admission charge.
Taupo Hot Springs and Health Spa, 1km (1/2 mile) along the Taupo-Napier highway. Tel: (07) 377 6502. www.taupohotsprings.com. Open: daily 7.30am–9.30pm. Admission charge.
Wairakei Visitor Centre, 9km (5 1/2 miles) north of Taupo on SH1. Tel: (07) 378 0913. www.wairakeiterraces.co.nz. Open: daily Oct–Mar 9am–5pm; Apr–Sept 9am–4.30pm.
Craters of the Moon, 5km (3 miles) north of Taupo. For details, contact Taupo i-SITE Visitor Centre (tel: (07) 376 0027). Open: daily dawn–dusk. Free admission.
Wairakei Prawn Farm, Huka Falls Rd. Tel: (07) 374 8474. www.prawnfarm.co.nz. Open: from 9am. Tours: daily, on the hour 11am–4pm. Admission charge. Evening reservations for restaurant recommended.
The Huka Jet. *Tel: (07) 374 8572 or toll-free 0800 485 2538. www.hukajet.co.nz. Departs: daily (except Christmas Day) every half-hour Oct–Apr 8.30am–5pm; May–Sept 9am–4pm.*
Taupo Bungee, 202 Spa Road. Tel: (07) 377 1135 or toll-free 0800 888 408. www.taupobungy.co.nz. Open: daily (except Christmas Day) 9am–5pm; extended hours in summer depending on bookings (typically 9am–7pm).
The Barbary, *Taupo Boat Harbour. Tel: (07) 378 3444. www.barbary.co.nz. Departs: daily 10.30am & 2pm; extra 5pm cruise in summer.*
The Ernest Kemp, *Taupo Boat Harbour. Tel: (07) 378 3444. Departs: daily 10.30am & 2pm; extra 5pm cruise in summer.*
Cruise Cat Scenic Cruises, Taupo Boat Harbour. Tel: (07) 378 0623 or toll-free 0800 825 825. Departs: Mon–Sat 10.30am & 2pm; Sun brunch cruise departs 10.30am.

For further information and bookings for rafting and boat trips, contact the Taupo i-SITE Visitor Centre, 30 Tongariro Street. Tel: (07) 376 0027. www.laketauponz.com

Tongariro National Park

Created in 1887, Tongariro was New Zealand's first national park. The three main peaks in Tongariro are **Ruapehu** 2,797m (9,177ft), the highest peak on the North Island, **Ngauruhoe** 2,291m (7,516ft), the most active of the three, with a symmetrical cone, and **Tongariro** 1,967m (6,453ft), the oldest volcano. The first tourists began arriving in 1901. The famous Chateau Tongariro, one of New Zealand's best-known hotels, was completed in 1929. Skiing began in the 1930s. All three volcanoes have erupted during the last century; there is an early warning system, and evacuation plans are posted on hotel walls.

The main access points to the park are Ohakune, Turangi and Whakapapa Village. Ohakune has the best selection of

Lake Taupo with Mount Tongariro in the distance

motels, restaurants and other amenities, while Turangi is handy for walking tracks in the northern section of the park. Chateau Tongariro and the main DOC Visitor Centre (with audiovisual displays on volcanic activity and the Maori heritage) are at Whakapapa Village.

The National Park is primarily a service centre and stop on the main trunk railway line. There is excellent walking throughout the park, from short 30-minute rambles over volcanic features to the more demanding Round the Mountain Track; details available from the DOC centre.

Whakapapa is 354km (220 miles) from Auckland, 341km (212 miles) from Wellington.
DOC Visitor Centre, Whakapapa. Tel: (07) 892 3729. www.doc.govt.nz. Open: daily Apr–Oct 8am–5pm; Nov–Mar 8am–6pm.

Urewera National Park

This is the third-largest national park in New Zealand, covering just under 213,000 hectares (526,300 acres) of untamed forests in the Urewera Range, and is the largest untouched stretch of native forest in the North Island, with more than 650 types of native flora. Urewera shelters many notable species, including *kaka* and *kakariki*, plus the New Zealand robin, New Zealand falcon and rifleman. Deer, possums and pigs are actively hunted. At the centre of the park is the magnificent **Lake Waikaremoana** ('Lake of Rippling Waters'), almost entirely surrounded by bush, except on the south side, which is dominated by the dramatic **Panekiri Bluff**. Following the shoreline for most of its 51km (31½-mile) length, the Lake Waikaremoana Track takes three to four days to walk, and is one of the most popular in the North Island. Information on short walks is available from the visitor centre at Aniwaniwa.

Waikaremoana and Aniwaniwa are accessible via SH38, which runs from Wairoa on Hawke's Bay through to Murupara (to join SH5 near Rotorua).

Aniwaniwa Visitor Centre, SH38, Aniwaniwa. Tel: (06) 837 3803. www.doc.govt.nz. Open: daily 8am–5pm.

Waitomo Caves

The Waitomo Caves are usually ranked as one of the great natural wonders of New Zealand, primarily thanks to the presence of a particular type of glow-worm (*Arachnocampa luminosa*).

The larvae of the glow-worm cling to cave roofs, spinning a delicate thread which they use to ensnare insects that are attracted to their light. The glow-worms are found in the main cave, **Waitomo.** Here, after the usual tour, you board a boat for a short trip down the underground river to the Glow-worm Grotto. The effect is magical: thousands of glow-worms suspended on the cave roof above appearing like twinkling stars on a clear night. In peak season 1,500 people descend daily into the Waitomo Cave, so try to come either early in the morning or late in the afternoon if you don't want to find yourself on a tourist conveyor belt. The second main cave is the **Aranui**. It doesn't have glow-worms, but it is still worth visiting for its delicate limestone formations.

The only way to see the third cave, **Ruakuri**, is by black-water rafting: you descend into the cave system and float along on your back, propelled by the current and supported by a rubber tyre. Ruakuri also has glow-worms, and there are plans to open it up to more general access to ease overcrowding in the main caves. Near the Waitomo Cave is the award-winning **Museum of Caves**, with giant fossils, cave crawls, and multi-media shows and displays about glow-worms.

On the road out to Waitomo, it is worth stopping at the **Ohaki Maori Village**, a replica Maori village complete with *wharetohutohu* (nursery/learning houses), *wharepunis* (sleeping houses) and *pataka* (food-storage houses).

Waitomo Caves are 150km (93 miles) from Rotorua, signposted off SH3.
Guided tours for Waitomo Cave depart daily every half hour 9am–5pm (5.30pm in summer); Aranui Cave tours depart 10am, 11am, 1pm, 2pm & 3pm, more frequently in busy times.
Ruakuri Cave Tours depart daily 9am, 10am, 11.30am, 12.30pm, 1.30pm, 2.30pm & 3.30pm. Booking essential.
Tickets for all caves available at Waitomo Cave, Te Anga Rd. Tel: (07) 878 8227. www.waitomocaves.co.nz.
Museum of Caves, Waitomo Cave Village. Tel: (07) 878 7640. www.waitomo-museum.co.nz. Open: daily summer 8.45am–7.30pm; winter 8.45am–5pm. Admission charge.
Ohaki Maori Village. Open: daily 10am–8pm. Admission charge.
Black-water Rafting, 585 Caves Rd, SH37, Waitomo Cave. Tel: (07) 878 6219 or toll-free 0800 228 464. www.blackwaterrafting.co.nz.
Waitomo Adventures Ltd, Waitomo Caves Rd. Tel: (07) 878 7788 or toll-free 0800 924 866. www.waitomo.co.nz

Tour: Coromandel

This route follows the beautiful west coast of the Coromandel Peninsula up to remote Fletcher Bay, where the road ends. It passes deserted beaches – where you can stop for a swim – then runs alongside the peninsula's rugged, forested hills. The last section of the journey (north of Colville) is along gravel roads, so if you have a hired car you may need to check insurance restrictions.

Allow a whole day, one way.

From Thames, follow the coast road (SH25) north to Tapu. Just past Tapu is Te Mata Beach.

1 Te Mata Beach

The Coromandel has yielded a wider variety of gemstones than anywhere else in the country, and Te Mata Beach is a particularly good place to look for large specimens of carnelian agate. Elsewhere, you might come across jasper, amethyst, chalcedony and petrified wood on the peninsula's numerous beaches.

Continue until the road climbs a bluff to the Mount Moehau lookout.

2 Mount Moehau

Beneath you is the wide sweep of Coromandel Harbour, with the Moehau Range rising up ahead towards the middle of the peninsula. The highest point is Mount Moehau, 892m (554ft); the mountain is a sacred Maori site and the burial place of Chief Tamatekapua, captain of the *Arawa*, one of the early canoes carrying immigrants from Hawaiki which arrived here around 1350. The range is

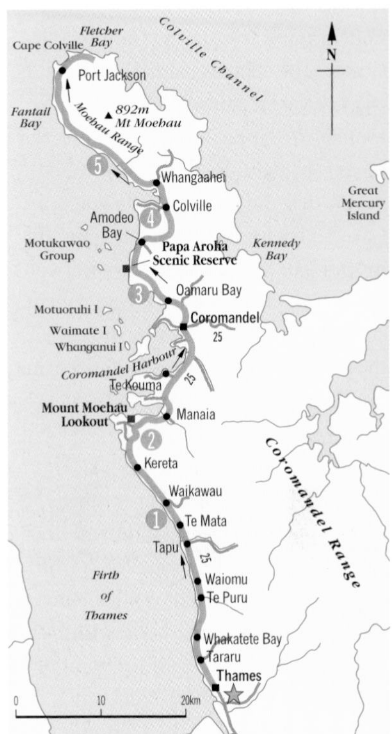

also home to a rare native frog, *Leiopeima archeyi*, although you may well have to trek part of the way up Mount Moehau for a chance to spot this small, primeval creature.
Descend into Coromandel (see p56) and follow the signs for Colville.

3 Beaches and bays

The road winds up over a hill before descending into Oamaru Bay (where there is a campsite), and then continues on to the **Papa Aroha Scenic Reserve**, a small area of native bush on the headland. A 20-minute amble through the reserve's typical coastal forest of *pohutukawa*, *puriri* and *kohekohe* takes you to a quiet little beach.
Colville lies a further 12km (7½ miles) from Papa Aroha.

4 Colville

Once a major centre for *kauri* milling, this small community on Colville Bay is now surrounded by farmland and arts and crafts communities. This is your last chance to stock up on picnic supplies or stop for refreshments before tackling the Cape road.
A short distance further on, the road divides – take the left fork which is signposted to Port Jackson.

5 The Cape road

The road hugs the shoreline most of the way up the coast from here, passing between the gnarled trunks of ancient *pohutukawa* trees; in summer their bright red blossoms hang from boughs over the beaches and rocks. Passing the campsite at **Fantail Bay**, the road becomes more and more tricky – which is why this is known as one of the most hair-raising roads in the North Island – but the views become increasingly spectacular until, just after the big beach at Port Jackson, you finally arrive at Fletcher Bay. This cove has a campsite, good fishing, and, if you are feeling energetic, the option of a short hike over the headland to the 150m (492ft) high Needles.
Return to Thames along the same road.

The beautiful Coromandel coastline with its white sand beaches

Wellington and Taranaki

The Taranaki region, on the west coast of the North Island, is dominated by snowcapped Mount Taranaki/Egmont. The eruptions of this now-dormant volcano have covered the surrounding lands with fertile ash. This, and the high rainfall on Taranaki's slopes, have created lush pastures, which have been put to good use by the many local dairy herds that produce some of the country's finest cheeses.

This region has not always been so peaceful, for it was here that the Land Wars of the 1860s between *pakeha* and Maori erupted, and some of the bloodiest engagements took place in these surroundings.

From Taranaki's upper slopes there are sweeping panoramas across to the fuming cones of the Tongariro National Park and out along the coastline. On the mountain's north side, the city of New Plymouth spreads along the coast, its vast offshore reserves of natural gas creating energy for the national grid. The city is also renowned for its extensive displays of rhododendrons and azaleas, and surfers and board-sailers are drawn to the rolling breakers that crash in off the Tasman Sea on to the beaches nearby.

Heading south from Taranaki you soon come to the mighty Whanganui River, the longest navigable river in the country. Steamers, jet-boats and other assorted craft offer rides upstream from the riverside city of Wanganui, which also has a good museum and art galleries. Inland lies Palmerston North, a thriving agricultural centre forming the crossroads between Taranaki, Wellington and central North Island.

If you cross the Tararua Range south of Palmerston North, you reach the rolling plains which descend to the Pacific Ocean. These form the dairy and sheep pastures of the Wairarapa, with the regional centre, Masterton, playing host to the annual 'Golden Shears' international sheep-shearing competition. In contrast to the untold numbers of sheep surrounding them, just a handful of some of the rarest and most endangered bird species in the country are nurtured and protected at the Mount Bruce National Wildlife Centre, just north of Masterton, a must for wildlife enthusiasts.

South of Masterton, the vineyards of Martinborough are fast gaining a reputation for their fine wines, while eastwards the sea beats mercilessly on the rugged, inhospitable Wairarapa

Wellington and Taranaki

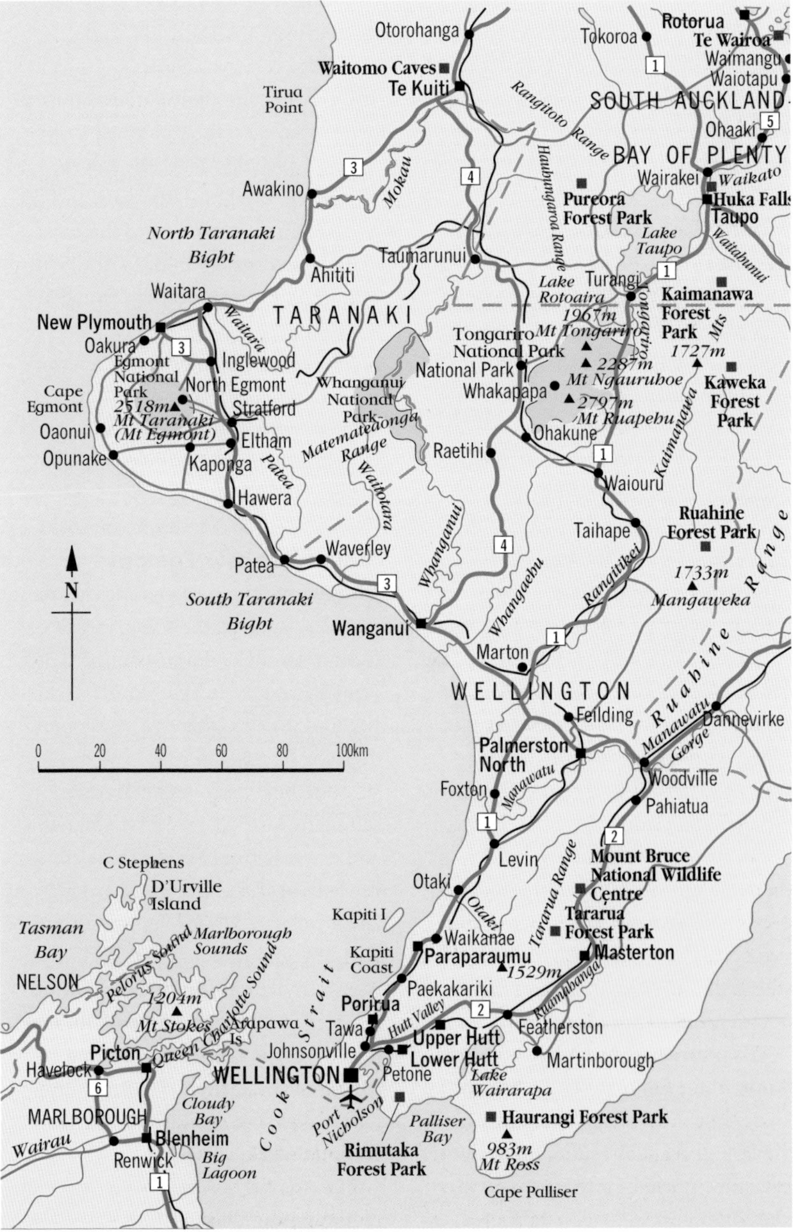

coastline. Heading south again across the Rimutaka Range, you reach the dormitory cities of Upper Hutt and Lower Hutt. These eventually merge into the outskirts of Wellington, the nation's capital, set amidst steep hills overlooking the vast harbour.

Mount Bruce National Wildlife Centre

The National Wildlife Centre consists of numerous aviaries which have been built around native bush on the slopes of Mount Bruce. The centre plays a crucial role in ensuring the survival of some of the most threatened and endangered species in New Zealand.

The centre was established in 1958 in an attempt to captive-breed the *takahe,* a bird which was thought to be extinct until the dramatic discovery of a small colony in Fiordland in 1948. Today, the centre offers the opportunity for visitors to see some of the rarest species in the world, many of which cannot be seen anywhere else since they only live on offshore islands.

Apart from the *takahe* (of which there are now less than 220 left), you may see the *kokako*, saddlebacks and stitchbirds from the bush, rare black stilts from wetland areas, and the nocturnal morepork forest owl.

The centre has the largest nocturnal house in the country, where brown kiwis have been bred successfully for the last 30 years. Breeding programmes have now started for the great spotted and little spotted kiwis. The heated burrows with one-way windows maximise your chances of seeing the elusive and rare lizard-like *tuatara* (*see p13*).

Currently, the centre focuses on six priority species: the Campbell and Auckland Islands' teals, the shore plover, the stitchbird, the *kaka* and the *kokako*. The latter is one of the most endangered species in the world, with only eight known breeding females alive today.

30km (18½ miles) north of Masterton on SH2. Tel: (06) 375 8004. www.mtbruce.org.nz. Open: daily (except Christmas Day) 9am–4.30pm. Admission charge.

Mount Taranaki/Egmont

Dominating the surrounding dairyland for miles around, the solitary peak of Mount Taranaki rises up on the North Island's west coast like a lonely sentinel. Because it adjoins the sea, it even has its own weather system and is often shrouded in cloud – Abel Tasman, sailing by in 1642, missed it altogether and it was left to Captain Cook to name it when he sighted the peak in 1770. Cook called it Mount Egmont (after the Earl of Egmont, then First Lord of the Admiralty) and, although it has since reverted to its Maori name of Taranaki, it now goes under the joint name Mt Taranaki/Egmont. The surrounding national park is still known as **Egmont National Park**.

The mountain is rich in Maori mythology and legend. Taranaki has always been considered *tapu* (sacred) by the Maori, who used to travel up the surrounding river valleys to collect red ochre and bury the bones of their chiefs and *tohungas* (priests) in secret caves on its slopes.

Taranaki is an unpredictable mountain, sunny and clear one minute, treacherous and windswept the next. Many climbers have lost their lives here, but this is still one of the country's most frequently climbed peaks – largely thanks to the local alpine club's open invitation climbs, which allow up to 600 people to reach the summit in a day.

On a clear day there are magnificent views from the Taranaki summit across to Tongariro and out over the Tasman Sea. The peak can be climbed in a single day. Always consult park staff about conditions.

Mount Taranaki

The main visitor centre is at North Egmont, where there is a comprehensive exhibition centre, and details on routes and mountain huts.

Even if you are not tempted to take on a major climb, it is worth the effort driving out here on a fine day and taking one of the marked trails which lead through the surrounding *kamihi* and *totara* forest.

North Egmont Visitor Centre, Egmont Rd, 26km (16 miles) from New Plymouth, signposted off SH3 from Inglewood. Tel: (06) 756 0990. www.doc.govt.nz. Open: daily peak 8am–4.30pm; Dec–Feb 7am–6pm; off peak 8am–4pm.

New Plymouth

Midway between Auckland and Wellington on the west coast is New Plymouth, an energy-production centre. Oil drilling began here in 1865, but was eclipsed by the discovery of vast natural gas reserves in the offshore Kapuni field in 1962 and the Maui field in 1969.

Among the parks in the city centre, the best known is **Pukekura Park**, with 49 hectares (121 acres) of lakes, streams, rolling lawns, native and exotic trees, fern gullies and flowers. It also contains a children's playground, cricket ground, fountain and waterfall, a historic band rotunda and the Bowl of Brooklands, a natural amphitheatre where national and international concerts are regularly held. From December to February the park hosts the fantastical Festival of Lights. The beautiful 3.6-hectare (9-acre) landscaped grounds of the **Tupare Gardens**, on the edge of New Plymouth, are also well worth a visit. A half-hour drive out of the city takes you to the **Pukeiti Rhododendron Trust** (ablaze with rhododendrons and azaleas in Sept–Nov), a 320-hectare (791-acre) rainforest property with easy walking tracks. On the way, visit **Hurworth**, a pioneer cottage built by Harry Atkinson, an immigrant, and prime minister of New Zealand for four terms of office.

The city's **Govett-Brewster Art Gallery** is home to the Len Lye Collection. Len Lye, a New Zealander (died 1980), was an acclaimed writer-painter, but in Taranaki he's known for his kinetic sculptures, particularly 'wind wands', which have achieved cult status.

The biggest Taranaki cultural project, **Puke Ariki**, is located in the city centre on the foreshore, the site of an ancient Maori *pa* (fortified settlement). The museum showcases the history and culture of the region's peoples.

New Plymouth is a convenient base for visiting Mount Egmont/Taranaki (*see pp78–9*). It has excellent surfing and windsurfing beaches, and a seal colony in the **Sugar Loaf Marine Park**, just past the power station.

New Plymouth is 180km (112 miles) southwest of Waitomo, 160km (99 miles) northwest of Wanganui.
The main entrance to Pukekura Park and Brooklands is on Fillis St, a 10-minute walk from the city centre. Open: daily 7.30am–7pm (till 8pm in summer). Free admission.
Tupare Gardens, 487 Mangorei Rd. Tel: (06) 765 7127. Open: daily 9am–5pm. Admission charge.
Pukeiti Rhododendron Trust, Carrington Rd. Tel: (06) 752 4141. www.pukeiti.org.nz. Open: daily 9am–5pm (Apr–Aug 10am–3pm). Admission charge.
Hurworth Cottage, 906 Carrington Rd. Tel: (06) 756 8606. Open: weekends 11am–3pm. Admission charge.
Govett-Brewster Art Gallery, 40 Queen St. Tel: (06) 759 6060. www.govettbrewster.com. Open: daily (except Christmas Day & Good Friday) 10am–5pm. Free admission (donations encouraged).
Puke Ariki, 1 Ariki St. Tel: (06) 759 6060. www.pukeariki.com. Open: Mon–Fri 9am–6pm (until 9pm Wed); Sat & Sun 9am–5pm.
Sugar Loaf Marine Park seal colony trips are organised by Chaddy's Charters, Ocean View Parade. Tel: (06) 758 9133.

Wanganui

This bustling city, at the mouth of New Zealand's longest navigable river, has been an important supply route to the interior since the first Maori settlement. Now, jet-boats and paddle-steamers, not canoes, carry passengers upstream on scenic trips. Sail upriver on the 1899 **PS *Waimarie***, an original coal-fired riverboat, restored as a Millennium project for the people of Wanganui.

Daily scheduled 2pm cruises, as well as lunch, dinner and barbecue cruises that sail with a minimum of 30 people, depart from the Riverboat Centre in the middle of the city.

Running through the heart of Wanganui down to the river is Victoria Avenue; most of the city's attractions lie within a few minutes' walk of this busy shopping thoroughfare. Just off Victoria Avenue is **Wanganui Regional Museum**, New Zealand's largest regional museum, with an excellent collection in its Maori Court; the centrepiece is the historic war canoe *Te Mata-O-Hoturoa* of the 1870s (bullets are embedded in its hull). The museum also has the skeleton of a giant moa and colonial artefacts.

The nearby **Sarjeant Art Gallery** houses New Zealand and British works as well as contemporary art. Wanganui has numerous parks (including a deer park, the Virginia Lake Scenic Reserve, and the Riverland Family Park), St Paul's, a church with Maori carvings at Putiki and an unusual, 1919 elevator tower on Durie Hill (opposite side of the riverbank), with sweeping views.

Wanganui is 192km (119 miles) north of Wellington and 160km (99 miles) southeast of New Plymouth.

For PS Waimarie *cruise bookings, contact the Riverboat Centre, 1A Taupo Quay. Tel: (06) 347 1863 or toll-free 0800 783 2637. www.riverboat.co.nz. Open: Mon–Sat 9am–4pm; Sun & public holidays (except Christmas Day) 10am–4pm.*

Regional Museum, Watt St. Tel: (06) 349 1110. www.wanganui.com. Open: daily (except Christmas Day & Good Friday) 10am–4.30pm.

Admission charge.

Sarjeant Art Gallery, Queen's Park. Tel: (06) 349 0506. www.sarjeant.org.nz. Open: daily (except Christmas Day & Good Friday) 10.30am–4.30pm. Free admission (donations encouraged).

For other attractions, river trips and bookings, contact the Wanganui i-SITE Visitor Centre, 101 Guyton St. Tel: (06) 349 0508. Open: weekdays 8.30am–5pm, weekends 10am–2pm.

Canoeing on the Whanganui River

Wellington

According to Maori legend, the explorer Kupe was the first to discover Wellington's harbour. When the first Europeans arrived in 1840 the local Maoris welcomed them, hoping that they would provide protection against hostile neighbouring tribes. Wellington was the first of the several settlements set up by the London-based New Zealand Company, and it quickly became a successful trading post. Although Governor Hobson initially chose Auckland as his capital, it was too far away from the rapidly increasing population of the South Island, and a commission eventually chose Wellington as the new capital in 1865.

As the administrative capital and a rapidly growing business centre, the city's main disadvantage was the lack of flat land for building, so land reclamation (helped along by a huge earthquake which partially raised the sea bed in 1855) began in the harbour, a process that continues today. Squeezed in by the hills that surround it, Wellington is thus a very compact city and, unlike Auckland, easy to get around on foot. The lack of space means that many workers commute in from outlying suburbs and cities, such as Porirua and Lower and Upper Hutt to the north.

Dubbed the 'windy city', Wellington is noted for the winds that can whistle through Cook Strait. These can reach speeds of over 100kph (62 mph) and are funnelled by the high-rise blocks into a fearsome maelstrom in the city centre. Blowing mostly in the spring and autumn, these enervating winds are, on the positive side, credited with blowing away smog and putting backbone into the Wellingtonian character!

While Wellington remains at heart a city of government bureaucrats, diplomats and international business, it is also striving to create a role for itself as the events and cultural capital of the country. The city is home to the Museum of New Zealand, four professional theatre companies, the New Zealand Symphony Orchestra and the Royal New Zealand Ballet. It hosts the biennial New Zealand International Festival of the Arts, just one of numerous festivals that take place here. An ever-expanding range of nightspots, cafés and restaurants has also added to the vibrancy of the capital in recent years.

At the heart of Wellington's renaissance are the massive improvements to Lambton Harbour, just a few steps from the core business and shopping area along Lambton Quay. Old wharf buildings and sheds have been imaginatively renovated, and the star attraction of the development is the Museum of New Zealand (Te Papa Tongarewa) which opened early 1998. Housed in a huge purpose-built building, the museum covers every aspect of New Zealand's land, life and loves, and will take at least a morning to browse around.

The country's capital also offers Frank Kitt's Park, Lagoon Beach (featuring water sculptures and boardwalks), dockside restaurants, apartments and shops, and a new marina.

Botanic Gardens

See p88.

Brooklyn Wind Turbine

Opened in 1993, this 31m (102ft) high wind turbine generator on a hill above the suburb of Brooklyn is part of an

Wellington

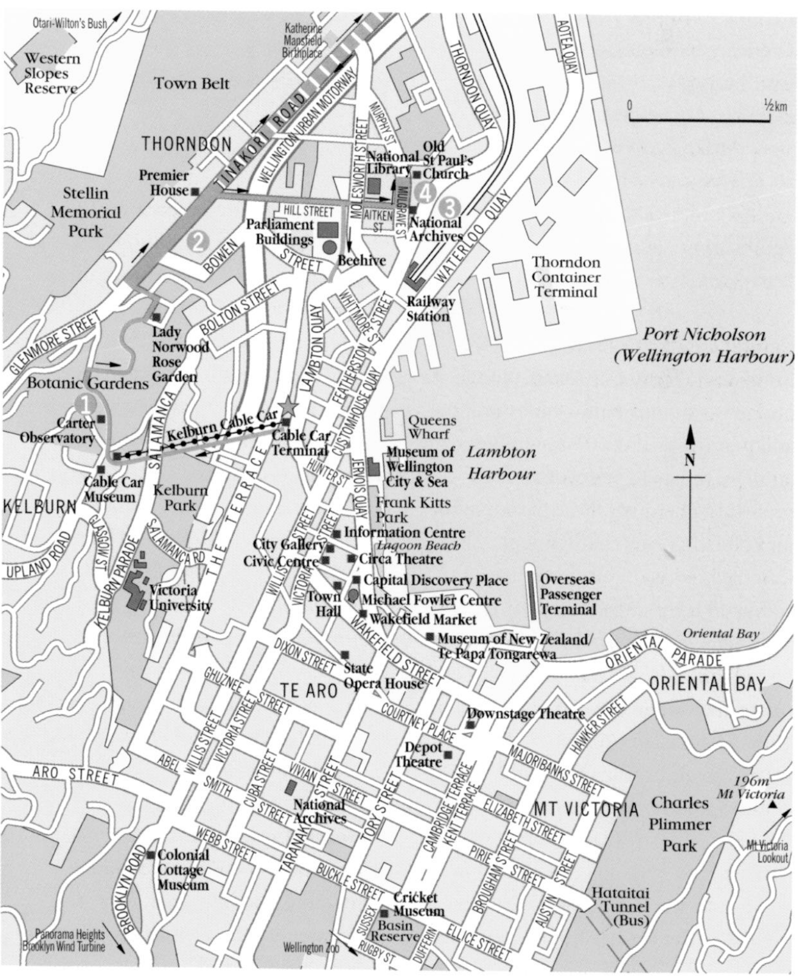

experiment to see whether the 'windy city' really is windy enough to generate its own electricity. The graceful, Danish-designed turbine, small by today's standards, can generate up to 225kW (302hp) – enough to power around 80 homes – on a blustery day.

Information boards (with a digital read-out of the energy being generated) are next to the car park at the top. There are fabulous views from the site – even Mount Victoria looks like a mere molehill way below in the distance. *Signposted off Brooklyn Rd, about a 20-minute drive from downtown. Tel: (04) 381 1200. Access road open: daily summer 8am–8pm; winter 8am–5pm. Free admission.*

Capital Discovery Place

In the Civic Square under the 'city to sea' bridge is a unique hands-on exhibition and performance centre for children and families: there are performances by professional visiting theatre companies for children, or by children themselves. Creativity is encouraged in a fully equipped television studio where Children OnTV is produced, and in SoundHouse New Zealand, a video and sound engineering suite.
Civic Square. Tel: (04) 913 3720. www.capitale.org.nz. Open: daily 10am–5pm. Admission charge.

City Gallery

Since 1993 the City Gallery has been housed in the former Public Library overlooking Civic Square, a cavernous building with ample space for the many stimulating exhibitions hosted each year. The extensive programme covers art, architecture, design, photography and the moving image, and exhibitions are usually of a very high standard. With at least three or four main exhibitions running at any one time, it is always worth looking in to see what's on.
Civic Square. Tel: (04) 801 3952 (recorded info) or (04) 801 4153 (general info). www.citygallery.org.nz. Open: daily (except Christmas Day) 10am–5pm. Free admission.
Free Weekend Exhibition Tours: Sat & Sun 1pm. Free admission, except for visiting exhibitions.

The 'windy city' generates power from this experimental turbine above Brooklyn

Colonial Cottage Museum

This is central Wellington's oldest remaining building, built by a carpenter, William Wallis, for his family in 1858. The house is furnished

in period style and displays give an indication of the difficulties in settling in the colonial days.
68 Nairn St. Tel: (04) 384 9122. www.colonialcottagemuseum.co.nz. Open: Boxing Day–mid-Feb, daily 10am–4pm; mid-Feb–24 Dec, Sat & Sun noon–4pm. Closed: public holidays. Admission charge.

Katherine Mansfield Birthplace

Born in an unassuming two-storey wooden house in 1888, Katherine Mansfield became one of the world's best-known short-story writers and New Zealand's most famous author.

Mansfield left the country when she was 19, but many of her best stories (such as *Prelude, The Aloe* and *A Birthday*) were based on her childhood memories of this house, which is now an award-winning tourist attraction.

The house has been carefully restored and furnished with period antiques – even the wallpaper has been re-created from fragments found here. Videos, tapes and photographs evoke Mansfield's short but eventful life.

The notes which you will be given on entry link the different rooms and settings to events in her stories.

The garden has also been replanted in its original Victorian design.
25 Tinakori Rd, Thorndon, a 10-minute walk from the railway station. Tel: (04) 473 7268. www.katherinemansfield.com. Open: daily (except Mon, Christmas Day & Good Friday) 10am–4pm. Admission charge.

Kelburn Cable Car

Built in 1902, the cable car (now with modern Swiss cars) glides upwards past Victoria University of Wellington for a five-minute ride to Kelburn suburb and the Botanic Gardens (*see p88*).

Also check out the **Cable Car Museum** (*1a Upland Rd; tel: (04) 475 3578*) in the winding house at the Kelburn end.
Cable Car Lane, off 280 Lambton Quay. Tel: (04) 472 2200.

A trip on Wellington's cable car is a good way to gain an overview of the city

www.wellington.com/cablecar.
Open: weekdays 7am–10pm, Sat 8.30am–10pm, Sun & public holidays 9am–10pm. Cars depart every 10 minutes. Closed: Christmas Day. Single or return fares.
Cable Car Museum, top of the cable car at Kelburn. Tel: (04) 475 3578. Open: daily 9am–5pm. Closed: Christmas Day. Free admission.

Mount Victoria Lookout

The Maori name for this hill on the southeastern edge of the harbour basin was Matai-rangi, which means 'To Watch the Sky', indicating that it was probably once used as a lookout point. The panorama of the city and harbour from here has been somewhat overshadowed by the Brooklyn Wind Turbine (*see pp83–4*).
Mount Victoria is signposted from Oriental Bay and Courtenay Place and can also be reached via Constable St and Alexandra Rd. Otherwise, buses run (Mon–Fri only) from the railway station.

Wellington viewed from Mount Victoria Lookout

Museum of New Zealand/ Te Papa Tongarewa

Magnificently situated in its new, purpose-built home on the stunning Wellington waterfront, Te Papa is a gateway for visitors to discover and understand the rich history of New Zealand. This exciting museum allows visitors to travel through time to visit New Zealand in the past and future, using a combination of displays and leading-edge technology. See how earthquakes, cyclones and volcanoes have shaped the landscape. Experience the eruptions of Mount Ruapehu. Discover how New Zealand's native plants and animals, many of them unique, have adapted to their environments. Uncover a 'dinosaur' and explore some of the oldest rock formations to be seen in the country.

Within the building, high above the harbour, is Te Marae, a fully functioning *marae,* and its focal point, Te Hono ki Hawaiki, a *wharenui* (meeting-house).
Cable St. Tel: (04) 381 7000.
Open: daily 10am–6pm (Thur until 9pm). Free admission.

Museum of Wellington City & Sea

This is now located in the wonderfully restored **Bond Store** dating from 1892 within the old harbour area of the city. The museum leads visitors through a fascinating journey of discovery about Wellington's land, sea and people, their past, present and future, using traditional museum techniques, holographs, interactive exhibits and a huge cinema screen.

Maori legends are told with holographic special effects, and in 'A Century Ago', you can experience life as it was for Wellingtonians at the beginning of the 20th century.

The Bond Store, Queens Wharf alongside Jervois Quay. Tel: (04) 472 8904. www.museumofwellington.co.nz. Open: daily (except Christmas Day) 10am–5pm. Tours available. Free admission.

National Archives

See p89.

Old St Paul's Church

See p89.

Otari-Wilton's Bush

This 105-hectare (259-acre) park is a sanctuary entirely devoted to the cultivation and preservation of indigenous plants, and contains the largest such collection in the country. There are picnic areas, rock gardens, 100 hectares (247 acres) of native forest, an 800-year-old *rimu*, more than 10km (6 miles) of walking tracks, a treetop canopy walkway, and an information centre. The gardens are rich in native bird life; you may see *tui*, fantails, grey warblers and kingfishers flitting from tree to tree.

Wilton Rd, Wadestown. A 20-minute bus ride from the city centre.
Tel: (04) 499 1400. Open: daily dawn–dusk. Information Centre open: daily 9am–4pm. Free admission.

Parliament Buildings

The old Parliament building, which once laid claim to being the largest all-wood building in the world, burned down in 1907. The building was replaced with the current Italianate-style building which houses the two debating chambers; it has recently undergone extensive renovation to make it earthquake-proof.

Next door is the unmistakeable **Beehive** (which houses the executive wing of government), designed by Sir Basil Spence and completed in 1981. You can tour the Parliament building and visit the Public Gallery in the debating chamber.

Corner Molesworth St & Lambton Quay. Tel: (04) 471 9503. Free guided tours on the hour weekdays 10am–4pm, Sat 10am–3pm, Sun noon–3pm. Closed: Christmas Day & Boxing Day, 1 & 2 Jan, 6 Feb & Good Friday.

Wellington Zoo

See native flora and fauna, as well as more exotic wildlife, on display at the zoo. The zoo's recently built nocturnal house, Te Ao Maahina (The Twilight), has the look and feel of a nocturnal native forest, through which you can walk and see free-roaming kiwis as well as *tuatara*, geckos and moreporks.

Danniell St, Newtown, 4km (2½ miles) from the city centre. Tel: (04) 381 6750. www.wellingtonzoo.com. Open: daily (except Christmas Day) 9.30am–5pm – last entry 4.15pm. Admission charge. Bus: 10 from the railway station.

Walk: Wellington

This walk encompasses several of the more interesting historic sights in Wellington's centre, as well as the extensive Botanic Gardens. It is an easy walk, largely because the cable car takes you to the top of the hill – after that it is a continuous descent. For route, see map on p83.

Allow around 2 hours (plus time to visit the birthplace of Katherine Mansfield).

Start at Kelburn Cable Car terminal on Lambton Quay (see p85). When you disembark at the top, turn right immediately into the Botanic Gardens.

1 Botanic Gardens

The 25-hectare (62-acre) gardens have more than the usual variety of plantings, ranging from native bush to herb gardens, exotic fern gardens, and a circular rose garden. At the summit of the hill is the **Carter Observatory**, the Astronomy Centre of New Zealand, which has a planetarium, astronomy displays, and hands-on computer programmes and telescope viewings. Wander down the hill, passing the Education and Environment Centre, ending up at the Lady Norwood Rose Garden at the bottom, and leaving via the Centennial Entrance on the north side.

Botanic Gardens: Tel: (04) 499 1400. Open: daily dawn–dusk. Free admission. Carter Observatory: Tel: (04) 472 8167. www.carterobs.ac.nz. Open: summer, Sun–Tue 10am–5pm, Wed–Sat 10am–late; winter Mon–Thur 11am–4pm, Fri & Sat 11am–late. Donations encouraged.
Telescope Viewing Wed–Sat 10pm (weather permitting). Booking essential.
Turn right and walk down Tinakori Rd.

2 Thorndon

Tinakori Road is the main artery of Thorndon, a suburb where the first Europeans settled in the 1840s. There are some charming old wooden houses on either side, many now converted into up-market shops, bistros and cafés. Just past the junction with Upton Terrace is **Premier House**, which served as the prime minister's residence from 1875 until 1937 and is once again the official residence of the prime minister.
Continue to the bottom of Tinakori Rd to visit Katherine Mansfield's birthplace (see p85); allow an extra 40 minutes to see the house, then return to the Hill St turn-off. Turn down Hill St, and continue on to the junction with

Mulgrave St. Directly opposite is the National Archives building.

3 National Archives

Inside the National Archives, turn right for the air-conditioned vault where the Treaty of Waitangi and several dozen other important historical documents are stored. The Treaty itself looks rather torn and battered (it travelled around the country for several months until the 213 signatures necessary for its implementation were collected), but it is the genuine article.

10 Mulgrave St. Tel: (04) 499 5595. www.archives.govt.nz. Open: weekdays 9am–5pm, Sat 9am–1pm. Free admission.

Turn right out of the National Archives and walk straight ahead to Old St Paul's Church.

4 Old St Paul's Church

Designed by parish vicar and architect Rev Frederick Thatcher in 1866, this all-wood church was built entirely using native timbers and is a marvellous example of the Gothic Revival style adapted to wood.

The soft lighting and dark timber of the panelling, pews and soaring arches exude a sense of warmth and serenity alongside numerous brass plaques in honour of local parishioners.

This lovely church was scheduled for demolition to make way for a new cathedral, but in 1966 it was handed over to the Historic Places Trust. Now it is used for music and drama events and special services.

34 Mulgrave St. Tel: (04) 473 6722. www.oldstpauls.co.nz. Open: daily 10am–5pm. Closed: Christmas & Good Friday. Guided tours by arrangement. Free admission.

Go back down Aitken St (opposite the National Archives) and then left through the courtyard in front of the Parliament Buildings and the Beehive (see p87), crossing Bowen St back to Lambton Quay.

Old St Paul's is a delightful wooden building in the heart of modern Wellington

Nelson and Marlborough

It doesn't take long to cross the often turbulent Cook Strait on the inter-island services from Wellington to the South Island, but once you pass the first headland there is still an hour's journey ahead before you reach the port of Picton. This massive inlet is part of the Marlborough Sounds, and a popular holiday area. There are plenty of boats to ferry you to isolated spots within the Marlborough Sounds Maritime Park to go birdwatching or camping.

At the head of Queen Charlotte Sound is Picton, the gateway to the South Island for ferry passengers. If you have plenty of time, the surrounding scenery is best appreciated by hiking along the Queen Charlotte Walkway; alternatively, an hour's drive or so along the coastline, on the Queen Charlotte Drive to Havelock, provides wonderful views of this beautiful area.

South of Picton lies Blenheim, the administrative centre of the Marlborough region and centre of a flourishing wine industry. Marlborough's benevolent climate is partly due to the protection offered by the Kaikoura Mountains to the south. The coastal town of Kaikoura, on the other side of this range, is a magnet for ecotourism thanks to the year-round presence of mighty sperm whales and other marine life.

Protecting Marlborough on its western flank, the Richmond Range marks the boundary with the neighbouring region of Nelson, known for its thriving horticulture and fruit-growing, its glacial valleys, forest parks and rushing rivers. Nelson city is the focal point of the region; the many sheltered bays and beaches nearby are popular for family camping holidays. To the south, the twin lakes of Rotoroa and Rotoiti sit high up in the Nelson Lakes National Park, surrounded by forests which are crisscrossed with walking and hiking tracks. Hunting and fishing opportunities abound.

West of Nelson, the highway skirts Tasman Bay, before climbing steeply over Takaka Hill to descend into Golden Bay. The last sleepy outposts in this remote corner of the South Island come alive in the summer months as people flock to the beaches, or set off from here on famous trails such as the Heaphy Track and the Abel Tasman Coastal Walk. Curving round the top of Golden Bay, Farewell Spit is a 30km (18½-mile) long sand bar (mostly accessed on 4WD tours) where thousands of wading and wetland birds nest in the summer months.

Nelson and Marlborough

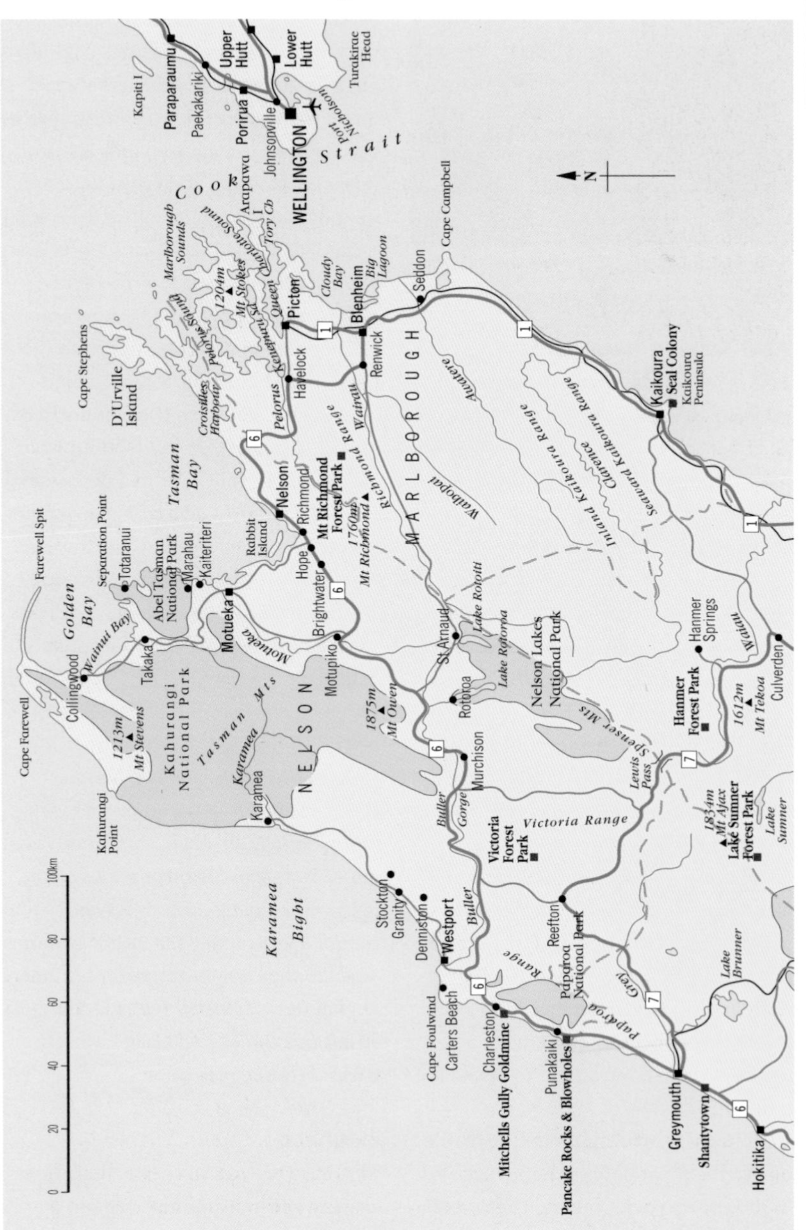

A blaze of colour in one of Blenheim's many gardens

Abel Tasman National Park

This is one of the smallest national parks in New Zealand; it covers just 22,350 hectares (55,230 acres), and was named in honour of Abel Tasman on 19 December 1942, the 300th anniversary of his visit. In fact, Tasman's landfall here wasn't a happy one: his canoes were attacked by the local Maori, four men were killed, and he left quickly. French explorer Dumont d'Urville had better luck in January 1827, and, having befriended the locals, charted the coastline here.

Permanent European settlers arrived during the 1850s, logging the forests and quarrying for granite. Shipwrights also moved in, taking advantage of the protected bay and fine timber. Logging came to a halt after a vigorous campaign spearheaded by a local woman, Perrine Moncrieff, who persuaded the government to create the park in 1942.

Despite its small size, Abel Tasman is one of the most popular national parks in the country with hikers. The coastal track follows a succession of beautiful clean beaches and shimmering bays backed by rolling hillsides of rainforest thick with *nikau* palms, vines, perching plants and tree ferns. An alternative inland route passes through magnificent beech forests. An added bonus is that the tracks are easy and accessible: there are no mountainous gradients on the coastal section, and scheduled boat services even hop between the bays to drop off and pick up day-trippers and backpackers.

The three main access points to the park are at Marahau, Totaranui and Wainui Bay. Marahau lies just north of Motueka (*see p98*), while Wainui Bay lies 21km (13 miles) from Takaka (*see* Golden Bay, *pp94–5*) and Totaranui lies 12km (7½ miles) further on (this last section is on a narrow, unsealed road). For day walks, Totaranui and Marahau are the best bets (*see p148* for more details on the track).

For more information contact the Nelson i-SITE Visitor Centre, Millers Acre Centre, 77 Trafalgar Street, Nelson. Tel: (03) 548 2304. www.doc.govt.nz. Open: daily Mon–Fri 8.30am–5pm, Sat & Sun 9am–5pm. For sea kayaking, boat cruises and guided walks and coastal hikes, contact the award-winning Abel Tasman Wilson's Experiences, 265 High Street, Motueka. Tel: (03) 528 2027 or toll-free 0800 223 582. www.abeltasman.co.nz

Blenheim

This busy provincial centre, the largest town in the Marlborough region, is situated at the confluence of the Taylor and Opawa rivers in the flatlands of the Wairau Plain. The region has an enviable sunshine record, which prompted the setting up of the Montana vineyards here in the late 1960s. Blenheim is now the centre of a flourishing wine industry.

This neatly laid-out town is renowned for its gardens such as **Pollard Park** (just off Parker Street), which covers 25 hectares (62 acres) around the spring-fed Fulton Creek. There are rock gardens and herbaceous borders to admire; there is a fitness trail too, as well as a children's playground. Seymour Square, in the town centre, is an attractive mix of lawns, specimen trees and floral displays.

The town's main historical interest lies in the **Marlborough Provincial Museum**, which has an extensive collection of vintage farm machinery, relocated colonial buildings that create an early 20th-century streetscape, and a miniature railway.

Blenheim is 28km (17½ miles) south of Picton, 132km (82 miles) north of Kaikoura. Gardens open during daylight hours.

Marlborough Provincial Museum, Brayshaw Park, New Renwick Rd. Tel: (03) 578 1712. www.marlboroughmuseum.org.nz. Open: daily (except Christmas Day & Good Friday) 10am–4pm. Admission charge.

The mild climate in the Wairau Plain has led to the growth of numerous vineyards around Blenheim

The waters of Golden Bay are good for sailing

Golden Bay

Golden Bay lies at the mouth of the Takaka river valley and is reached by a tortuous mountain road over Takaka Hill from Motueka. Like the Coromandel, Golden Bay became something of an 'alternative lifestyle' centre in the 1970s because of the availability of cheap smallholdings; today it is known mostly for its safe swimming beaches (with good windsurfing) and for the intensive dairy farming in the valley. Golden Bay is also one of the main access points for the coastal track through the Abel Tasman National Park (*see p92*).

The main centre for Golden Bay is the small township of **Takaka**, where you can find the Golden Bay Information Centre and the **Golden Bay Museum & Gallery**. The museum documents Tasman's arrival in the bay and has giant snail shells, Maori and European artefacts and model *waka* and ships, as well as regional arts and crafts in the gallery, which is housed in the historic post office building next to the museum.

Just outside Takaka, **Pupu Springs** (abbreviation of the Maori name, Waikoropupu) are the largest freshwater springs in New Zealand. With 62m (203½ft) horizontal visibility, the fresh water here is renowned for being the second clearest in the world, which makes for gorgeous, colourful views of the dancing sands (where the springs emerge) and the many fish that live here. Water from the upper river valley disappears down into a huge underground cave system and emerges here at the rate of around $21m^3/s$ ($741.6\ ft^3/s$). There are at least 16 springs in the vicinity; the two main springs can be seen from a platform located a short walk from the car park.

North of Takaka is the even smaller community of **Collingwood**, first settled during the 1850s gold boom. Visitors to Collingwood today (with its one general store, hotel, garage and café) will find it hard to believe that at one time there was even a proposal to make it the capital of the country.

Beyond Collingwood is **Farewell Spit**, a 24km (15-mile) long sand bar which acts as a breakwater for Golden Bay. The 20m (65½ft) high sand dunes form an internationally renowned bird sanctuary, with over 90 species having been recorded here. Hundreds of thousands of migratory waders spend the summer here, including large flocks of bar-tailed godwits (up to 20,000) and knots (up to 30,000), and turnstones, long-billed curlews and many others. There are also large numbers of gulls, gannets, cormorants and other sea birds. Access to this area is strictly controlled.

Takaka is 57km (35½ miles) from Motueka on SH60.
Golden Bay i-SITE Information Centre, Willow St. Tel: (03) 525 9136.
Golden Bay Museum & Gallery, Commercial St. Tel: (03) 525 6268. Open: daily: 10am–4pm. Closed: Sun in winter. Free admission.
Pupu Springs are 5km (3 miles) north of town, signposted off SH60. Free admission.
Collingwood is 28km (17 miles) from Takaka on SH60.
Farewell Spit: You can visit only the small area which is at the base of Farewell Spit, unless you go along with licensed operators, such as the following:
Farewell Spit Tours. Tel: (03) 524 8257 or toll-free 0800 808 257. www.farewellspit.co.nz

Havelock

Havelock lies on the road between Picton and Nelson, and stands at the head of Pelorus Sound, the largest of the Marlborough Sounds. The town is the main landing point for the tasty green-lipped mussels which are

Lake Rotoiti in the Nelson Lakes National Park

grown on ropes suspended in Marlborough Sounds and brought here for processing and export. Scallops are another local delicacy, and if you want to catch your own fish there are plenty of small boats for hire at the wharf.
35km (22 miles) west of Picton, 75km (46½ miles) east of Nelson.

Kaikoura

The small seaside town of Kaikoura curves around an attractive bay, with the snowcapped peaks of the Kaikoura Mountains rising up behind it. This former whaling port is now enjoying a huge boom in ecotourism as people flock here to watch the sperm whales, seals and dolphins that abound in the offshore waters and around the rocky coastline of the peninsula.

Kaikoura has always been known for its sea life: the Maori came here for the same reason and christened the spot *kai* (meaning 'food' or 'to eat') *koura* (meaning 'crayfish').

Whaling began here in 1842. The only building still standing from this era is **Fyffe House** (1860), the residence of George Fyffe, one of the original whaling masters. The piles of his weatherboard cottage are giant whale vertebrae; the house has been restored by the Historic Places Trust. Other reminders of whaling days are on show in the **Kaikoura Museum**, which also displays various local mementoes and a 1910 police lock-up (complete with padded cell).

Just outside the town is **Maori Leap Cave**. Discovered in 1958, the 90m (295ft) long sea cave is known for its delicate cave straws, tubular formations that grow at the rate of about 25mm (1in) every hundred years.

Other activities in and around Kaikoura include fishing, diving, swimming, snorkelling with seals and dolphins, or exploring the scenic Kaikoura Peninsula Walkway (*see pp100–101*).

The **Kaikoura Visitor Centre** has an excellent audiovisual theatre which features spectacular multimedia presentations on the whales, dolphins, seals and sea birds. Shows are held on the hour. There is an admission charge.
Kaikoura is 132km (82 miles) south of Blenheim.
Fyffe House, 62 Avoca St.
Tel: (03) 319 5835. Open: summer daily 10am–6pm; winter (except Christmas Day & Good Friday) Thur–Mon 10am–4pm. Admission charge.
Kaikoura Museum, 14 Ludstone Rd.
Tel: (03) 319 7440. Open: Mon–Fri 10am–4.30pm; weekends & public holidays 2–4pm. Closed: Christmas Day & Good Friday. Admission charge.
Maori Leap Cave, 3km (2 miles) south on SH1, behind the Caves Restaurant.
Tel: (03) 319 5023. Conducted tours six times daily all year round.
Admission charge.
Kaikoura i-SITE Visitor Centre, West End Esplanade. Tel: (03) 319 5641. www.kaikoura.co.nz. Open: daily 9am–5pm.

Whale and dolphin watching

A whale near Kaikoura on the South Island's east coast

Marine mammals abound in the waters around New Zealand, but there are few places in such a fortunate position as Kaikoura when it comes to close-up viewing. Kaikoura's abundant marine resources are due to two phenomena. First, nutrient-rich subantarctic waters meet subtropical waters here, resulting in an abundance of microscopic phytoplankton, which form the basis of a complex food chain. Second, the sea bed drops away nearly 1,000m (3,281ft) into the Kaikoura Canyon, a mere 1km (½ mile) from the coast, which means that deep-water feeders such as sperm whales surface in these coastal waters alongside the dolphins and seals.

Although the sperm whales are the main attraction, you may also spot the tiny Hector's dolphin (the world's rarest dolphin), bottlenose and dusky dolphins, orcas and pilot whales, and sea birds including albatross, petrels and shearwaters.

The whale-watching catamarans use hydrophones (underwater microphones) to locate the distinctive clicking of the sperm whale. A tell-tale plume from the whale's blowhole pinpoints the spot where it has surfaced, and where it will remain for 10–12 minutes while it replenishes its oxygen supply before diving again. At this point the whale raises its massive tail flukes above the surface before disappearing from sight.

It is rare to see a sperm whale 'breach' (leap into the air) in the way humpbacks do, and only a small proportion of the resting whale is visible on the surface until it starts to dive. For some visitors, this is frustrating, but for others it is privilege enough to be so close to this once-threatened creature.

Whale Watch Kaikoura operates tours daily (except Christmas Day) at 7.15am, 10am & 12.45pm, with an extra 3.30pm tour in summer. Advance reservations are advisable; allow more than one day in case ocean conditions force cancellations. **Whale Watch Kaikoura Ltd**, *Railway Station Rd, Kaikoura. Tel: (03) 319 6767 or toll-free 0800 655 121. www.whalewatch.co.nz. Admission charge.*

Motueka

Motueka is a busy base for trekkers and day-trippers setting off for the Abel Tasman National Park (*see p92*), and for seasonal fruit workers who arrive in the autumn. Motueka has a range of accommodation, plus shops for stocking up on supplies if you are hiking.
51km (31½ miles) northwest of Nelson, reached via SH6 and then SH60.

Nelson

Nelson is a bright, breezy city humming with activity, particularly arts and crafts, as many potters have been drawn here by the availability of good local clay. You can explore Nelson's numerous galleries and workshops with the *Arts Trail and Gallery Guide* leaflet (available at the Visitor Centre), or by taking an Arts Trail Guided Walk.

A good place to browse (and shop) is at **Craft Habitat**, with its ceramics, stained glass, weaving and jewellery workshops. Crafts are also often on display alongside a fine collection of early colonial oils and watercolours in the historic **Suter Art Gallery**.

Nelson's **Christ Church Cathedral** stands at the end of the main thoroughfare, Trafalgar Street. Colonial architecture is represented by an early cob house, **Broadgreen House** (1855), whose interior has been restored in period style. Another historic homestead, **Isel House**, is surrounded by century-old trees, rhododendrons and azaleas in the superb setting of Isel Park. For an entire village of relocated and replica historic buildings and artefacts of Nelson, visit the **Founders Heritage Park**. With a 3-D maze, windmill, horse-drawn carriages, fire engines and a working train, it is a great place to take children.
Nelson i-SITE Visitor Centre, Millers Acre Centre, 77 Trafalgar St. Tel: (03) 546 9339. www.doc.govt.nz. Open: daily. Craft Habitat, just outside Richmond on SH6. Tel: (03) 544 7481. Open: weekdays 9am–5pm, weekends 10am–5pm.
Suter Art Gallery, Queen's Gardens, 208 Bridge St. Tel: (03) 548 4699. www.thesuter.org.nz. Open: daily (except Christmas Day) 10.30am–4.30pm. Admission charge.
Broadgreen House, 276 Nayland Rd, Stoke. Tel: (03) 547 0403. Open: daily (except Christmas Day & Good Friday) 10.30am–4.30pm. Admission charge.
Isel House, Isel Park, The Ridgeway, Stoke. Open: daily 11am–4pm. Admission charge.
Founders Heritage Park, 87 Atawhai Drive. Tel: (03) 548 2649. Open: daily (except Christmas Day & Good Friday) 10am–4.30pm. Admission charge.

The World of Wearable Art and Collectable Cars

Opened in October 2001, this centre is home to the spectacular World of Wearable Art collection. It has been built up since the Montana Wearable Art awards – an alternative fashion show – started in Nelson in 1987. The WOW gallery showcases garments from

this collection in a theatrical exhibition full of light, sound, movement and humour. The second gallery features an imaginatively displayed array of collectable cars from around the world.
95 Quarantine Rd, Annesbrook, Nelson. Tel: (03) 548 9299. www.worldofwearableart.co.nz. Open: daily (except Christmas Day) summer 10am–6pm; winter 10am–5pm. Admission charge.

Nelson Lakes National Park

The Nelson Lakes National Park covers 102,000 hectares (252,000 acres) of forests, mountains and river valleys, and is perhaps best known for its two beautiful lakes, Rotoiti and Rotoroa, which nestle beneath scenic alpine peaks.

The main gateway to the park is the tiny hamlet of St Arnaud, on the shores of Lake Rotoiti, which is as beautiful in summer as in winter when the ski fields of the Rainbow Valley and Mount Robert beckon.

The lake is fringed by beech forests, and there are opportunities for boating, fishing, short walks and picnics. Water taxis ply the lake for short cruises or drop-offs to hiking tracks.

Lake Rotoroa has fewer facilities – and more sandflies – but is popular with fishermen after rainbow trout.
Nelson Lakes Transport. Tel: (03) 521 1802. Operates daily buses. DOC Visitor Centre, View Rd, St Arnaud. Tel: (03) 521 1806. Open: daily 9.30am–4.30pm (during summer till 8.30pm). St Arnaud lies 119km (74 miles) southwest of Nelson on SH6, then along SH63.

Picton

Lying at the southernmost point of Queen Charlotte Sound, Picton is the terminus for the Cook Strait services and the starting point for exploring the Marlborough Sounds. If you are waiting for a ferry (or a launch to whisk you off to a secluded beach) there are a couple of places to visit.

Next to the ferry terminal are the remnants of the last-surviving convict ship of the British East India Company, the *Edwin Fox*, gradually being restored at the **Edwin Fox Museum**. Built in 1853, the teak-hulled ship carried troops to the Crimean War and convicts to Australia before ending up as a storage hulk in Picton's harbour. Also on the waterfront, the **Picton Museum** is worth a visit for its whaling relics.
Edwin Fox Museum, Dunbar Wharf. Tel: (03) 573 6868. Open: daily summer 9am–5pm; winter 9am–3pm. Admission charge.
Picton Museum, Waterfront. Tel: (03) 573 8283. Open: daily 10am–4pm. Admission charge.

The small port of Picton is the gateway to the extensive Marlborough Sounds

Walkway: Kaikoura Peninsula

*Kaikoura is renowned for its marine life (*see pp96–7*), and this walkway round the peninsula is a great way of getting close to New Zealand fur seals. The walkway also features ancient Maori stepped* pa *(fortified settlements), limestone caves and wonderful views. This route follows the Clifftop Path 3.7km (2¼ miles), returning along the Shoreline Path 4.5km (2¾ miles).*

Allow 2 hours each way, although the walk is easy and you can complete the circuit much faster if necessary.

From Kaikoura, follow the Esplanade south for 5km (3 miles) until you arrive at Point Kean. Park here and take the path marked Clifftop Walk; the well-signposted path is easy to follow.

1 Clifftop walk

A short, steep climb up a zigzag path brings you to the grassy downlands on the cliff top, where the views stretch back inland to the Kaikoura Mountains and down the coast as far as Banks Peninsula. The grassy track is a good vantage point from which to observe the gull colonies below; around 10,000 adult red-billed gulls nest here, along with smaller colonies of black-backed gulls and white-fronted terns. This is a good place to spot waders such as turnstones, oystercatchers and herons on the tidal platforms.
Continue on to Whalers Bay.

2 Whalers Bay

Whalers Bay once provided safe anchorage for whaling boats, and from the cliff top above, the whalers watched and waited, looking for their quarry out to sea. The track used by the whalers to return to their boats descends the cliff face – you can use this as a short cut down to the Shoreline Walk if required.
Follow the signs for South Bay along the cliff top.

3 Maori *pa* sites

Taking advantage of the abundant seafood, the Ngati Toa occupied Kaikoura during the 16th century; they were driven south by the Ngai Tahu in the early 19th century, but during the intervening period they occupied at least 14 different *pa* sites on the peninsula. Some of these fortified settlements are clearly visible on this stretch of the track, the characteristic rounded hill tops edged with terracing.
Descend into South Bay, turning left where the tracks meet to follow the Shoreline Path.

4 Seal colony

Skirting Mudstone Bay you come to Atia Point, which has one of the biggest seal colonies. Hundreds of fur seals can be seen here during the winter months, but even in summer dozens of them bask on the rocks: they are so numerous you might have to scramble around the rocks to bypass them. Do not provoke the seals (especially large bulls or mothers with pups) as they may bite. Other seal colonies can be seen at **East Head** and **Point Kean**.

Continue around the base of the cliffs.

5 Hidden caves and outcrops

The peninsula is relatively young in geological terms, and the limestone base has been pounded by the sea into many weird and wonderful formations – particularly at **Atia Point**, which is best appreciated if you look back at it from the succeeding bays. One of the biggest caves is **Whalers Cave**, partially obscured by trees at the back of Whalers Bay.

Cross Whalers Bay, and continue past Sugar Loaf Point and Rhino Point to return to the car park via Point Kean.

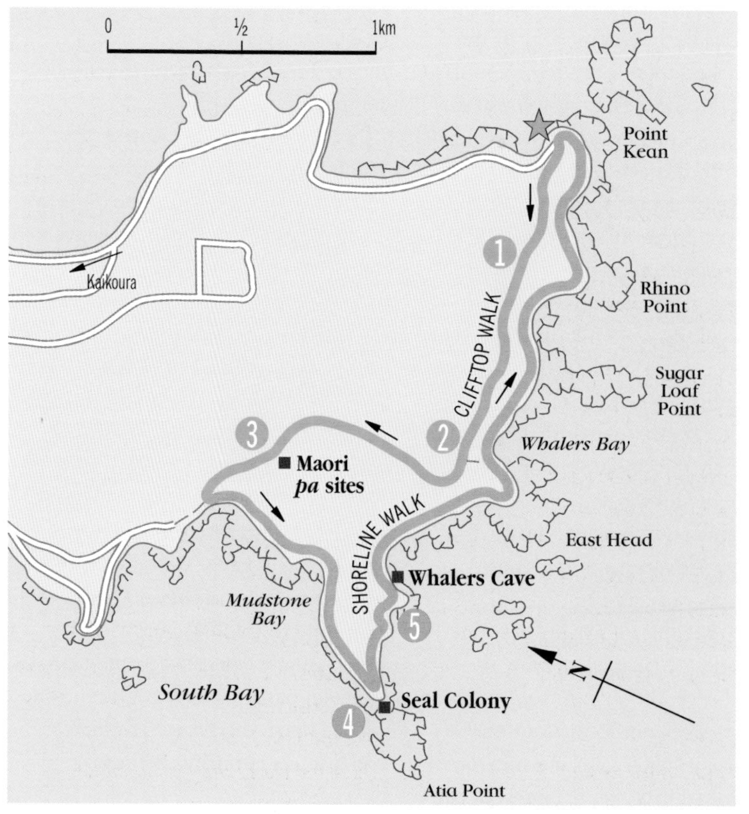

Central South Island

Separated from one another by the Southern Alps, the western and eastern coasts of central South Island are as different as chalk and cheese. Hemmed in by the Alps on one side and the Tasman Sea on the other, the west coast is a rugged, wild strip of land where the one constant factor is the almost incessant rain, though between showers you will be rewarded with magnificent views of jagged Alpine peaks, tumbling waterfalls, tranquil lakes, and the spectacular glaciers descending into the rainforests at Fox and Franz Josef. The east coast is cultivated plains.

In the heady gold-rush days of the 1860s, the west coast was one of the busiest, wealthiest areas in the country. Around Ross and Greymouth you can still try your hand at gold fossicking, or see how the experts do it at the re-created Shantytown. The west coast is also rich in greenstone (nephrite jade) or *pounamu*, which was traded by the Maori from the earliest times. In the coastal town of Hokitika, skilled craftspeople can still be seen working this beautiful mineral.

Further south, the Westland coastline reaches an appropriate end in the pristine rainforests and coastal lagoons of the almost untouched World Heritage Area surrounding Haast.

The east coast, in comparison, is intensively cultivated. Lying between the plains and the Pacific is the city of Christchurch, the second major gateway into New Zealand. To the southeast is Banks Peninsula – a curious outcrop of land formed from the remnants of two sunken volcanoes – with many bays and beaches to explore, and Akaroa, a former French settlement, the most southerly in the world.

Looping across the Canterbury Plains are many shallow, shingle-bed rivers that were almost impossible to navigate until a local engineer invented the jet-boat, now a common feature of outdoor adventure in New Zealand. The Rakaia and Waimakariri rivers are popular for jet-boating.

Finally, there are the Southern Alps. Most visitor facilities here are in the breathtaking Mount Cook/Aoraki National Park and around the shores of the sparkling blue glacial lakes of Pukaki and Tekapo. Here, too, is the mightiest glacier in the Southern Hemisphere, the 27km (16½-mile) long Tasman, where ski-planes land on a regular basis. The more adventurous can ski down the glacier, weather conditions permitting, accompanied by a guide.

Central South Island

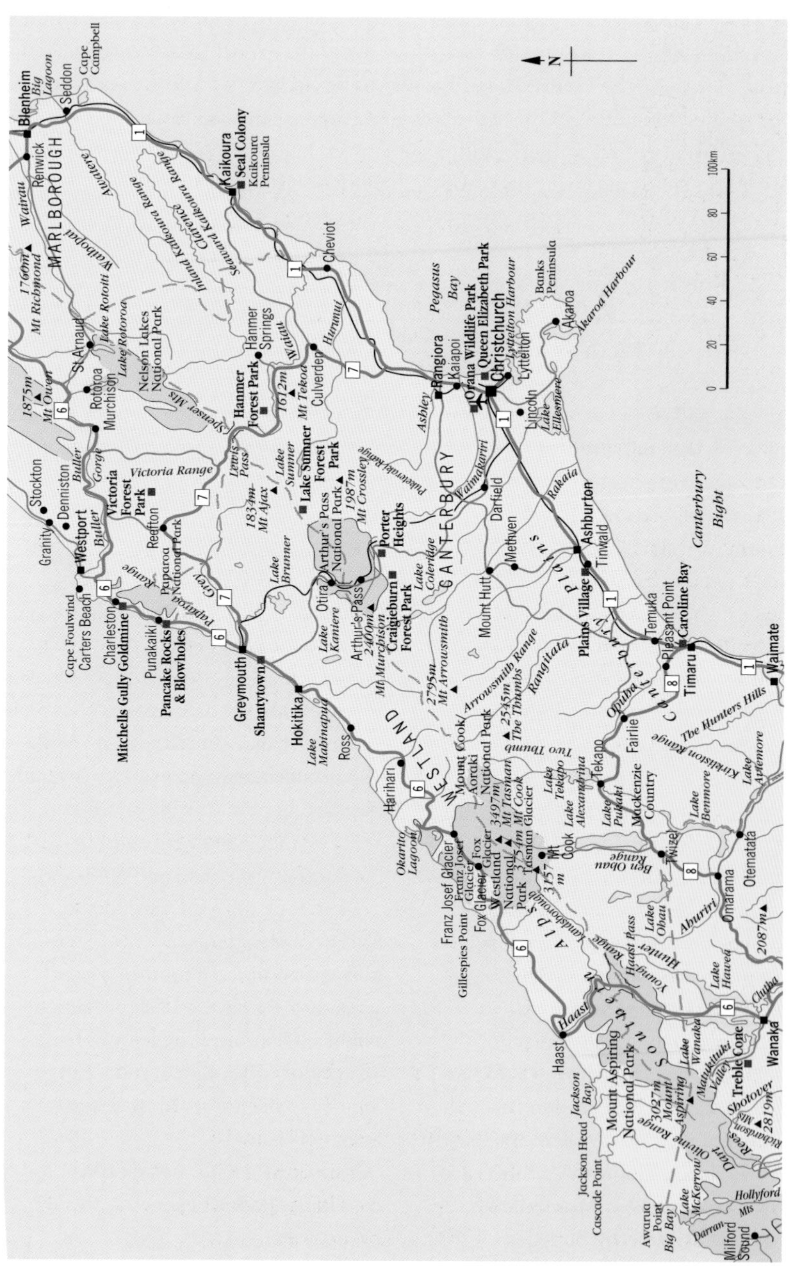

Central South Island

Christchurch

Christchurch is the South Island's largest city and is also one of the liveliest and most attractive in the country. It has long enjoyed the epithet of the 'Garden City', with numerous leafy parks and gardens providing a relaxing backdrop to the well laid-out city centre. An added bonus is the delightful Avon River meandering between the city's neo-Gothic stone buildings. Streetside cafés and trendy wine bars have mushroomed in recent years, adding to the vitality of streetlife, and complementing a vibrant arts scene with numerous festivals and drama and music performances. Christchurch is also said to be the most English city in New Zealand. The first four ships carrying the so-called Canterbury Pilgrims arrived at Lyttelton Harbour in 1850, and the newcomers soon established clubs for the very English pastimes of rowing, archery, lawn tennis and cricket.

Today, Christchurch has something of a reputation for breeding eccentricity and individualism. Creativity, however, is the flip side of the same coin, and the city has produced enormous numbers of talented craftspeople, whom you can see at work in the vast Arts Centre complex.

Christchurch is a city made for walking, as many of the top sights are within easy reach of the central Cathedral Square. However, the historic **Christchurch Tramway** (*tel: (03) 366 7830; www.tram.co.nz*) and the free **Central City Electric Shuttle** (*tel: (03) 379 4620; www.redbus.co.nz*) are also enjoyable ways to sight-see the main central attractions. There are excellent bus services to non-central attractions and areas as well, all departing from the Bus Exchange in Colombo St, a block south of Cathedral Square. For more information, timetables and fares, contact **MetroInfo** (*tel: (03) 366 8855; www.metroinfo.org.nz*).

Outdoor enthusiasts reckon that, after Queenstown, there is no better place in the South Island than Christchurch to live in. Pacific Ocean beaches are close by, the Southern Alps are less than an hour's drive away for rock climbing, mountain biking, river rafting and the like, and in the winter there are 12 ski fields from which to choose. Taking advantage of the extensive Canterbury Plains to the west of the city, Christchurch has also become a major centre for hot-air ballooning.

Finally, Christchurch is the gateway to Banks Peninsula (*see pp120–21*) and the starting point for the famous TranzAlpine Express rail route across the Southern Alps (*see pp124–5*).

Air Force Museum

This museum won a tourism design award in 1991 for the 28 classic aircraft exhibits. There are also plenty of hands-on exhibits, video shows, and a hall devoted to the history of New Zealand military aviation.

Wigram RNZAF Base, Main South Rd. 20 minutes from downtown. Tel: (03) 343 9532.

www.airforcemuseum.co.nz. Open: daily (except Christmas Day) 10am–5pm. Admission charge.

Christchurch

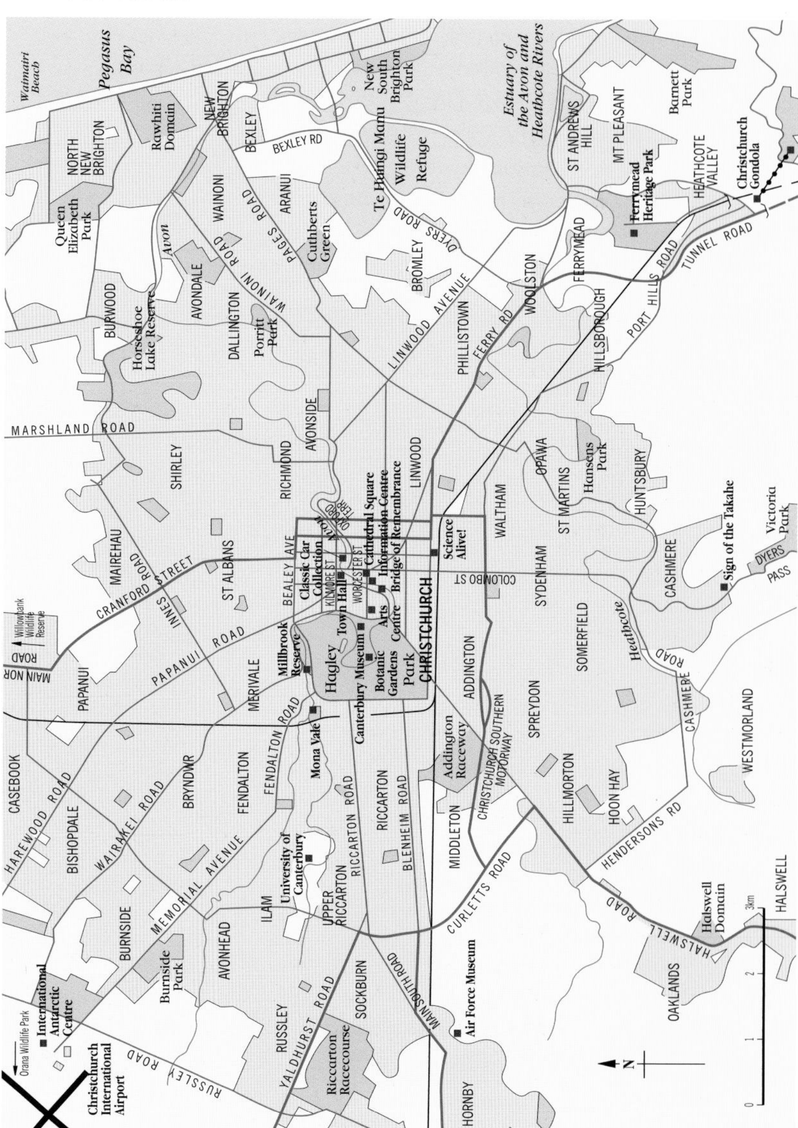

Arts Centre

Housed in a rambling complex of neo-Gothic buildings (once the home of the University of Canterbury), the Arts Centre is a lively mix of galleries, shops, studios and theatres, and cafés, bars and restaurants. You can wander around peering into small workshops or browsing in half a dozen galleries, then drop in on a lunchtime concert, a dance performance, or a foreign film screening. The festive weekend crafts market is also well worth visiting, with more than 100 arts and crafts stalls, live entertainment, and exotic foods from around the world.

Worcester Blvd. Tel: (03) 366 0989. www.artscentre.org.nz. Open: daily (except Christmas Day, Good Friday & ANZAC Day morning) 9.30am–5pm; weekend market 10am–4pm. Free admission and free guided tours 10am–3.30pm.

Avon River

Winding through the heart of the city, with oaks and willows lining its banks, the Avon adds immeasurably to the enchantment of Christchurch. A good

A punt glides along the tranquil River Avon in the heart of Christchurch

way to get to know the city from this different viewpoint is on a sedate punting trip; alternatively, you can hire a canoe or paddle-boat.
Punt trips depart from behind the Christchurch i-SITE Visitor Centre in Cathedral Square. Tel: (03) 379 9629 for bookings. Canoes and paddle-boats may be hired at the Antigua Boat Sheds, 2 Cambridge Terrace. Tel: (03) 366 5885. www.boatsheds.co.nz. Open: daily summer 9.30am–5.30pm; winter 9.30am–4pm.

Botanic Gardens

The 30-hectare (74-acre) Botanic Gardens, set within the 160-hectare (395-acre) Hagley Park and bounded on three sides by the River Avon, are ideal for a relaxing stroll; extensive lawns and bedding displays provide the backdrop to a huge variety of exotic plants. The first trees were planted in 1863, and the collection now encompasses special sections for native plants, heathers, roses, herbs, water plants, primulas, plus a conservatory complex with exotic species.
Rolleston Ave. Tel: (03) 941 7590. Grounds open: daily 7am until one hour before sunset. Free admission. Conservatories open: daily 10.15am–4pm. Information centre open: Mon–Fri 9am–4pm, Sat & Sun 10am–4pm.

Canterbury Museum

Housed within a stunning historic building, the museum includes displays on Antarctica, New Zealand birds, award-winning Maori galleries, an Arts of Asia gallery, a Victorian street, and a colonial costume collection.
Rolleston Ave. Tel: (03) 366 5000. www.canterburymuseum.com. Open: daily (except Christmas Day) summer 9am–5.30pm; winter 9am–5pm. General admission free. Guided tours (donations) four times daily.

Cathedral Square

This spacious, pedestrianised square is a great place to while away a sunny day. This is where you will find the main Visitor Centre, at the Old Post Office, Cathedral Square (*tel: (03) 379 9629*). Atheists and the faithful mount their stepladders to battle it out verbally in front of amused crowds on the cathedral's steps – this is the city's free speech corner, where anything and everything goes. Watch out for the famous Wizard, so adept an orator-performer that he has been classified as a 'living work of art'. A regular crafts market and a clutch of stalls selling ethnic food add to the colour of the city's main focal point.

Christchurch Cathedral

Built over a period of 40 years and completed in 1904, the cathedral is in neo-Gothic style and is worth visiting for the climb (133 steps) to the top of its bell tower, which has good views of the city centre.
Tel: (03) 366 0046. www.christchurchcathedral.co.nz. Guided tours: weekdays 11am & 2pm,

The neo-Gothic cathedral dominates Cathedral Square in Christchurch

Sat 11am, Sun 11.30am.
Cathedral open: Mon–Sat 9am–5pm, Sun 7.30am–5pm. Free admission.
Tower open: daily 8.30am–4pm. Admission charge.

Christchurch Gondola

The gondola scales the city side of the Port Hills to the 500m (1,640ft) Mount Cavendish summit, from where you get spectacular views of Christchurch and Banks Peninsula. Within the complex, the **Heritage Time Tunnel** recounts the history of the area with innovative displays, including a volcanic area which exudes hot air, and a superb mock-up (complete with musty smells) of below-decks in an immigrant ship. There is a shop and a restaurant.
10 Bridle Path Rd, Heathcote.
Tel: (03) 384 0700. www.gondola.co.nz.
Open: daily 10am until late evening. Guided walks from summit station 11am, 1pm (fee). Admission charge.

Ferrymead Heritage Park

The two separate sites of this park (linked by tramway) contain old locomotives and historic vehicles, a replica Edwardian township, a fire-fighting display, horse-and-carriage rides, and other transport-related exhibits.
50 Ferrymead Park Drive.
Tel: (03) 384 1970. www.ferrymead.org.nz.
Open: daily (except Christmas Day) 10am–4.30pm. Admission charge.

International Antarctic Centre

Christchurch has been one of the principal gateways to the frozen south since Scott's famous expeditions, and the International Antarctic Centre (next to the airport) is now the main supply and administration base for the New Zealand, American and Italian Antarctic programmes. The award-winning visitor centre within the complex includes a compelling and dramatic audiovisual show, a re-creation of the current Scott Base, the world's only polar aquarium, the Antarctic Hägglund Ride Snowphone™, an ice cave, and plenty of hands-on exhibits. This is a highly recommended stop.
Orchard Rd, Christchurch Airport.
20 minutes by car from downtown.
Tel: (03) 353 7798 or toll-free 0508 736 4846. www.iceberg.co.nz. Open: daily summer 9am–7pm, winter 9am–5.30pm. Admission charge.

Orana Wildlife Park

This open-range, 80-hectare (197½-acre) zoo is the country's largest wildlife and conservation centre. There are 15 daily animal feeds, and a host of opportunities for close encounters with exotic and endangered animals, from hand-feeding giraffes and patting llamas, to meeting a white rhino and riding with the animal keepers through the African Lion Reserve. You can also see kiwis, *tuatara*, *kea* and other endangered native New Zealand species, or pet farmyard animals. Visitors can walk, join guided tours, or catch the complementary Safari Shuttle around the park.

McLeans Island Rd, Harewood, 20 minutes' drive from downtown. Tel: (03) 359 7109. www.oranawildlifepark.co.nz. Open: daily (except Christmas Day) 10am–5pm – last entry 4.30pm. Admission charge.

Science Alive!

Discovering science and technology through play and hands-on fun and experimentation is the key theme of this extensive display, aimed at all age groups from pre-teens to adults. Special exhibits often have a local flavour.

392 Moorhouse Ave. A 10-minute walk from Cathedral Square. Tel: (03) 365 5199. www.sciencealive.co.nz. Open: daily (except Christmas Day, Boxing Day & New Year's Day) 10am–5pm. Admission charge.

Willowbank Wildlife Reserve

This small, well laid-out park focuses on indigenous wildlife, although it also has monkeys, camels and other introduced species, and a farmyard section containing rare breeds of colonial animals such as *kuni kuni* pigs. An unusual feature is the floodlit, night-time viewing, when you can see kiwis and other nocturnal species in their natural bush setting. There is an award-winning restaurant and guided tours are free to dinner guests (*see p170*). You can also book tickets here for Ko Tane, a Maori cultural experience that includes entertaining performances, dinner, and a village and wildlife tour.

60 Hussey Rd, 15 minutes' drive from downtown. Tel: (03) 359 6226. www.willowbank.co.nz. Open: daily 9.30am–dusk. Admission charge. Heritage New Zealand and Wild New Zealand close at dusk, but the Natural New Zealand area is lit and open till 10pm, with guided tours every hour from 5.30pm.

A ride on the Christchurch Gondola provides spectacular views

Sheep

Sheep farming is an important component in the New Zealand economy

It is an often-quoted fact that there are 10 sheep for every person in New Zealand and, with 40 million sheep compared with 4.2 million people, this figure is not far off the mark.

It was Captain Cook who landed the first sheep in New Zealand, but the two merinos didn't last long, and it wasn't until 1834 that the first sizeable flock arrived. The first major 'runs' (as ranches are called here) were in the North Island, but sheep farming developed even more rapidly in the South Island, where there was less forest to clear.

Fortunes had been made from wool exports, but falling prices in the 1880s jeopardised this lucrative commodity. However, refrigerated shipping was invented just in time, and when the *Dunedin* sailed for Britain in 1882 loaded with sheep carcasses, it marked a new era in the country's export trade. With the subsequent increase in meat exports, the merino was gradually replaced by hardy Romneys, great producers of fat lambs. As the wool of the Romney is far coarser than the fine fleece of the merino, production switched to those industries that require stronger, more resilient wools such as the carpet industry.

The biggest farms today are in the South Island, spread over vast areas of comparatively poor land that supports low densities of sheep. These high-country stations often run up to 12,000 or more sheep, so mustering the flocks and bringing them down before the winter snows arrive is a major part of the farming calendar. Previously, this would have been done on horseback, but modern shepherds are more likely to use rugged, all-terrain motorbikes to get around.

Perched on the back of the bike or running alongside will be the

A sheep farm in Masterton, home to the 'Golden Shears' competition

shepherd's trusty sheepdogs. Descended from border collie stock, there are two main types: first, there is the 'heading' or 'eye' dog, which prowls silently around the sheep, fixing them with its stare and heading them in the right direction; second, there is the big, noisy 'huntaway', which controls the flocks by barking loudly. Finally, there are the all-important sheep-shearers, who usually travel together in gangs from station to station. A good shearer can clip up to 300 sheep a day, although the record is an astonishing 831 sheep in nine hours. The average fleece yields around 4.5kg (10lb) of wool.

Franz Josef and Fox Glaciers

These two vast glaciers lie at the heart of Westland National Park, which stretches from the coastline up to the highest peaks in New Zealand. The glaciers are unusual in that they extend right down through the forest into the temperate coastal zone, a phenomenon found nowhere else in the world.

The 12km (7½-mile) long Franz Josef (named after the Austrian emperor by explorer Julius Haast in 1864) and Fox (named after the country's prime minister, Sir William Fox, in 1871) are the two largest glaciers of the 140 that lie within Westland National Park. Close to the bottom of each glacier are the respective villages of Franz Josef and Fox Glacier; the constant 'thud-thud' of helicopters taking off from helipads attests to the popularity of aerial sightseeing, with helicopter companies and ski-plane operators offering rides to the top of each glacier. A handful of restaurants, motels and shops provide for everyday needs alongside the helicopter booking offices and guided tour companies.

From either village you can drive or walk out to the 'snout' of each glacier. Looming above, the towering blocks of ice (known as seracs) lie dramatically jumbled together, creaking and heaving as blocks split and tumble into the moraine below. The Franz Josef Glacier moves at an exceptionally fast rate of 1.5m to 3.5m (5ft to 11½ft) per day, depending on the snowfall.

A helicopter trip is a great way to experience the glaciers

The Fox Glacier is unusual in that blocks of ice remain buried beneath rock debris downstream of the terminal face, melting to create the milky grey or translucent blue kettle lakes – including the picturesque Lake Matheson (just south of the village along a short forest track) – that lie dotted around the bed of the Fox River. Stunning views of the peaks of Mount Cook and Mount Tasman are reflected in the waters.

Franz Josef is 172km (107 miles) southwest of Hokitika, and 273km (169½ miles) northwest of Wananka. Fox is 25km (15½ miles) further down SH6.

The DOC Westland National Park Visitor Centre in Franz Josef village has general information, walking leaflets for the surrounding forests, and a glacier display. Tel: (03) 752 0796. www.doc.govt.nz. Open: daily 8.30am–4.45pm. Closed: noon–1pm.

Guided walks (do not attempt them on your own), as well as adventure tours, heli-hikes and ice-climbing, are run by the following:

Franz Josef Glacier Guides, Franz Josef village. Tel: (03) 752 0763 or toll-free 0800 484 337. www.franzjosefglacier.com.

Alpine Guides Fox Glacier, Fox Glacier village. Tel: (03) 751 0825 or toll-free 0800 111 600. www.foxguides.co.nz.

For ski-plane flightseeing, contact Mount Cook Ski Planes, Franz Josef village. Tel: (03) 752 0714 or toll-free 0800 368 000. www.mtcookskiplanes.com.

Helicopter tours with glacier landings are available through the following, all of which have offices on the main streets of both Franz Josef and Fox Glacier villages:

Fox Glacier, named after a former New Zealand prime minister

Glacier Southern Lakes Helicopters. Tel: (03) 752 0755 or toll-free 0800 800 732. www.heli-flights.co.nz or www.glacierhelicopters.co.nz.

Fox and Franz Josef Heliservices. Tel: (03) 752 0793 or toll-free 0800 800 793. www.scenic-flights.co.nz.

The Helicopter Line. Tel: (03) 752 0767 or toll-free 0800 807 767. www.helicopter.co.nz

Greymouth

This former gold and coal centre, today the main commercial centre and largest town on the west coast, is known locally simply as 'Grey'; the tag can seem particularly appropriate on a typically rainy west-coast day.

Shantytown, just outside Greymouth, is a replica 1880s town set in native bushland on the site of a former goldfield. The township features an old bank, a bootshop, printing works, a blacksmiths', a fire station, a 'Chinese den' and a fascinating colonial hospital. Other attractions include a steam-train ride through the bush to an old wooden railway station, gold panning, stagecoach and a working replica sawmill.
Greymouth is 105km (65 miles) south of Westport on SH6, 256km (159 miles) from Christchurch.
Shantytown, Paroa, is 10km (6 miles) from Greymouth, signposted off SH6. Tel: (03) 762 6634 or toll-free 0800 742 689. www.shantytown.co.nz. Open: daily (except Christmas Day) 8.30am–5pm. Admission charge.

The Southern Alps aglow at sunrise

Haast

Haast lies at the southernmost end of the Westland coastline, and has always been a staging post for the Haast Pass across the Southern Alps into Otago. The Haast area is a birdwatchers' paradise, and has won recognition for its magnificent rainforests, coastal lagoons and wetlands (the most extensive in the country).

The region was designated the South West New Zealand World Heritage Area by UNESCO in 1991, and the excellent Visitor Centre was opened on the banks of the Haast River in 1993. The centre has first-rate displays on early Maori settlers, the abundant local wildlife, swamp forests, and the unique sand-dune forests nearby. The staff also provides information on local walks, jet-boating on the Haast River, fishing (the coastal lagoons are particularly renowned for their whitebait), hiking and helicopter rides.
120km (74½ miles) southwest of Fox Glacier, 345km (214½ miles) southwest of Greymouth.
Haast Visitor Centre, corner of SH6 & Jackson Bay Rd, Haast. Tel: (03) 750 0809. www.doc.govt.nz. Open: daily 9am–6pm (peak); 9am–4.30pm (off-peak).

Hanmer Springs

These thermal springs, first discovered by Maori hunters who named them Waitapu or 'Sacred Waters', were rediscovered by a local farmer in 1859.

By the turn of the 20th century, the springs were the focus of a popular sanatorium. Today, the springs are incorporated into an award-winning, modern, open-air resort complex, the **Hanmer Springs Thermal Pools & Spa**, located in the centre of this tranquil little alpine village. If you want some action and adventure before soaking away your aches and pains in the pools, the area offers an enormous number of activities from golf to rafting, fishing, bungee-jumping, climbing and horse-trekking, and plenty of walking trails (details available from the Visitor Centre).

Hanmer Springs is 136km (84½ miles) north of Christchurch.

Thermal Pools, Amuri Ave. Tel: (03) 315 7511. Open: daily 10am–9pm. Admission charge.

Hurunui i-SITE Visitor Centre: 42 Amuri Ave West, Hanmer Springs. Tel: (03) 315 7128 or toll-free 0800 442 663. www.hurunui.com

Hokitika

The next major town south of Greymouth is Hokitika, first settled by Maori in search of greenstone and later by Europeans in the gold rush of the 1860s. Today, life centres around farming, fishing and tourism, although some gold-mining is still carried out.

Hokitika is an attractive town which has become a focus for local craftspeople and is also well known as a centre for greenstone carving. There are several workshops in town where you can watch these massive blocks being shaped and fashioned into intricate designs for pendants, sculptures and so on; this is a fascinating process, and it costs nothing to wander about, watching the greenstone carvers at work. There are numerous other outlets in town for pottery, textiles, wood carvings, and hand-crafted jewellery made from gold nuggets found in the area.

The history of the area is narrated in the **West Coast Historical Museum**, where a well-constructed audiovisual show covers both greenstone and gold discoveries in the region, among the other displays.

Not for the squeamish, the annual **Wildfoods Festival** in March (*www.wildfoods.co.nz*) offers a huge array of stalls selling unique food (from magpie pies and cows' udders to gorse flower wine) alongside loads of musical entertainment. The festival has been so successful in recent years that the organisers have had to cap ticket sales at 18,000. Tickets can be bought from the Visitor Centre.

Hokitika is 46km (28½ miles) south of Greymouth on SH6.

West Coast Historical Museum, Carnegie Building, Tancred St. Tel: (03) 755 6898. Open: daily summer 9.30am–5pm; winter weekdays 9.30am–5pm, weekends 10am–2pm. Admission charge.

Westland i-SITE Visitor Centre, Carnegie Building, Tancred St, Hokitika. Tel: (03) 755 6166. Open: summer daily 8.30am–6pm; winter weekdays 8.30am–5pm, weekends 10am–2pm.

Inside Mount Cook/Aoraki National Park

Mount Cook/Aoraki National Park

Covering just over 70,000 hectares (173,000 acres), Mount Cook/Aoraki National Park runs in a narrow strip down the eastern side of the Southern Alps. Within this relatively small area are located 22 of New Zealand's 27 highest peaks, including, of course, the best known, Mount Cook itself. This is an area of great natural beauty, where alpine scrub and forests are interspersed with glacial lakes that reflect the snowcapped crests soaring above. The park also includes the impressive 28km (17½-mile) long Tasman Glacier, the largest glacier in the Southern Hemisphere outside of Antarctica.

Known as Aoraki by the Maori, Mount Cook was renamed by Captain Stokes who sighted it from his survey ship in 1851. Rev. Green, an Irishman, was the first to attempt to climb the peak in 1882, but storms prevented him from reaching the summit; eventually three New Zealanders (Fyfe, Graham and Clarke) conquered Mount Cook in 1894. Sir Edmund Hillary trained here before becoming the first man, with Sherpa Tenzing, to climb Mount Everest in 1953.

This is one of the finest regions for mountaineering in the world, with well-equipped high-level mountain huts for climbers' use. Walkers are restricted to the valley floor, but there are still some superb short walks near the base (*see pp122–3*).

The central focus of the national park is Mount Cook village, where there is a youth hostel, a campsite, self-contained chalets and the famous Hermitage Hotel. The Visitor Centre can provide climbers with details on hut fees, routes and weather conditions.

More than 300 species of plants are to be found within the park, including the famed Mount Cook lily (*Ranunculus lyallii*), the largest buttercup in the world. Of the 40 species of birds, the most noticeable is the *kea*, known for pilfering hikers' belongings. Hunting of the Himalayan thar and European chamois (species of goat – both of which destroy vegetation) is encouraged.

Skiing is possible from July to October, but the only way up to the available slopes is by ski-plane or helicopter. The most spectacular run is the descent of the Tasman Glacier, suitable only for experienced and advanced snowboarders or skiers.

Aerial sightseeing is another popular option and provides opportunities for some breathtaking photographs of the peaks and glaciers.

333km (207 miles) west of Christchurch. DoC Mount Cook/Aoraki Visitor Centre, 1 Larch Grove, Mount Cook.
Tel: (03) 435 1186. www.doc.govt.nz.
Open: daily 9.30am–4.30pm.
The following companies offer a variety of flight options, including those covering all the major mountains and glaciers in both Mount Cook and Westland National Parks:
Air Safaris runs flights from Lake Tekapo, Franz Josef village and Glentanner Park (near Mount Cook).
Tel: (03) 680 6880. www.airsafaris.co.nz.
Mount Cook Ski Planes flies from Mount Cook Airport and Franz Josef village.
Tel: (03) 430 8034 or toll-free 0800 800 702. www.mtcookskiplanes.com.
The Helicopter Line offers helicopter rides from Glentanner Park.
Tel: (03) 435 1801 or toll-free 0800 650 651. www.helicopter.co.nz

Paparoa National Park

The coastal road between Westport and Greymouth is at its most spectacular as it passes the fringes of Paparoa National Park, located about halfway between the two towns. Created in 1987, the national park covers around 30,000 hectares (74,130 acres).

On the coastal strip, steep limestone cliffs plunge down to the sea, creating a subtropical microclimate where tree ferns and *nikau* palms thrive. Inland, the park is a virtually untouched wilderness with unusual limestone karst formations, large caves and waterfalls.

The undisturbed nature of Paparoa means that it is a good area for bird-watching (*tui*, fantails, grey warblers, New Zealand pigeons and bellbirds are commonly spotted).

At the heart of the park is the Paparoa Range, a rugged series of peaks and pinnacles covered in almost impenetrable bush and often shrouded in clouds. The best-known walking route through the park is the Inland Pack Track, but there are also several short walks which start from Punakaiki. For details on the local DOC Visitor Centre and how to reach the park, *see* Punakaiki, *p118*.

Punakaiki

Punakaiki is best known for its extraordinary Pancake Rocks, reached by a short, 15-minute walk from the main road, suitable even for wheelchairs. The stratified coastal limestone here has been weathered into a dramatic formation that looks just like a stack of giant pancakes; in rough conditions the sea forces itself up through fissures in the 'pancakes' to form spectacular blowholes.

The DOC Visitor Centre at Punakaiki provides details on short walks in the area which lead back into the rainforests of Paparoa National Park (*see p117*).

Punakaiki is 57km (35½ miles) south of Westport, 47km (29 miles) north of Greymouth on SH6.

The DOC Visitor Centre is on the main road. Tel: (03) 731 1895. Open: daily 9.30am–4.30pm.

Ross

Early prospectors descended on Ross in their thousands at the turn of the last century to fossick in the creeks running down from Mount Greenland. The Ross Historic Goldfields lie just off the highway through town. At the entrance of the old Bank of New South Wales building (1870) is the Information & Heritage Centre. Just across from the centre is the **Miner's Cottage**, dating back to 1885.

The Jones Flat Walkway leads from the information centre up to the old workings, which include miles of intertwined water races and dams that are used to bring water to the sluicing claims.

Ross is 30km (18½ miles) southwest of Hokitika.

Ross Information & Heritage Centre, Aylmer St. Tel: (03) 755 4033. www.ross.org.nz. Open: daily 9am–4pm (until late in summer).

Tekapo

This small settlement straddles the road leading from Mount Cook/Aoraki National Park back down to the coast, and is located right where the Tekapo River drains out of the 20km (12½-mile) long Lake Tekapo, next to the first of the hydroelectric stations linked to the Waitaki river system. The milky turquoise lake and its stunning natural surroundings offer a fabulous venue for a wide variety of activities, including fishing, hunting, mountaineering, hiking, horse trekking and scenic flights, all based in Tekapo village (*www.tekapotourism.co.nz*).

On the edge of Tekapo is the famous **Church of the Good Shepherd**, a sublime stone-clad chapel erected as a memorial to pioneer farmers in the area.

105km (65 miles) west of Timaru.

Timaru

This large coastal port city, lying roughly midway between Christchurch and Dunedin, is famous for its annual carnival, which takes place on sandy Caroline Bay at Christmas.

164km (102 miles) south of Christchurch, 202km (125½ miles) north of Dunedin.

Twizel

This town, established as the centre for the upper Waitaki Valley hydroelectric development, lies just half an hour's drive from Mount Cook village, making it a convenient base for exploring the national park and the surrounding Waitaki River and Mackenzie Basin. The road from Twizel to Mount Cook runs alongside lovely Lake Pukaki, one of the four Mackenzie Basin lakes.

Just outside town is the **Black Stilt Visitor Hide**, a DOC centre for a breeding programme aimed at saving this endangered species. Once common throughout New Zealand, the habitat of the black stilt (or *kaki*) is now confined to the Mackenzie Basin. One-hour guided tours include close-up views of captive stilts and explanations of the breeding programme and rearing aviaries.

Twizel is 162km (100 miles) west of Timaru.

Black Stilt Visitor Hide, 3km (2 miles) south of town on SH8. Regular tours are run in spring and summer. Admission charge. Tours must be booked in advance at the Twizel Information Centre, 61 Mackenzie Drive, Twizel. Tel: (03) 435 3124.

Westport

Gold-mining, and later coal-mining, formed the basis of Westport's prosperity. If you are passing through, there are some good exhibits and interactive displays on coal-mining in the aptly named **Coaltown Museum**.

Nearby **Cape Foulwind** is one of six breeding colonies on the west coast for the New Zealand fur seal. Walkways lead to a series of wooden platforms on the cliff tops, from where you can get a clear view of the seals below without disturbing them.

Westport is 105km (65 miles) north of Greymouth.

Coaltown Museum, Queen St South, signposted from the town centre. Tel: (03) 789 8204. Open: daily 8.30am–5.30pm, winter 9am–4.30pm. Admission charge.

Cape Foulwind is 12km ($7^1/_2$ miles) west of town on SH65A.

The Pancake Rocks at Punakaiki are one of the most striking features of Paparoa National Park

Tour: Banks Peninsula

Banks Peninsula is the site of the only attempt at a settlement by the French in New Zealand, and its offshore waters are home to one of the highest concentrations of the world's smallest and rarest marine dolphins, New Zealand's Hector's dolphin.

Allow a full day for this 185km (115-mile) round trip from Christchurch.

Leave Christchurch on SH75, following signs for Akaroa. Turning away from the sea and past Little River, the road climbs up and over the crater rim, and descends into Barry's Bay.

1 Barry's Bay

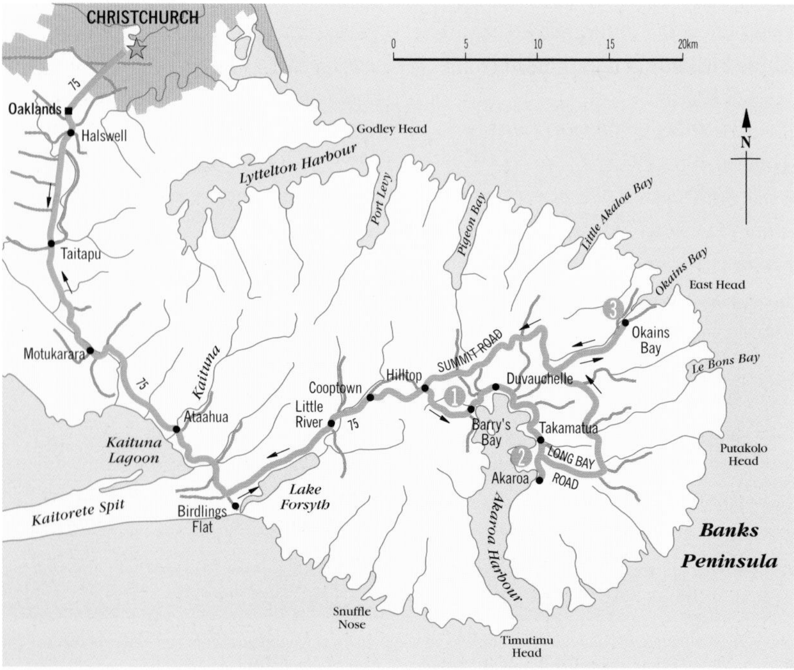

Banks Peninsula was one of the first areas in New Zealand to produce cheese (commercial shipments were sent to Australia as early as the 1850s). This tradition continues today at the **Barry's Bay Cheese Factory**, where you can watch cheese being made through the gallery window.

Barry's Bay Cheese Factory: Barry's Bay. Tel: (03) 304 5809. Open: weekdays 8am–5pm, weekends 9.30am–5pm, viewing only on alternate days between October and April.

Continue around the bay to Akaroa. Akaroa can also be reached on the Akaroa Shuttle (tel: toll-free 0800 500 929; www.akaroashuttle.co.nz); there are twice-daily departures in each direction.

2 Akaroa

In 1838, Jean Langlois, captain of a whaling ship, negotiated to buy Banks Peninsula from the local Maori. He assembled a group of 63 colonists on his return to France, but by the time they arrived back in New Zealand the Maori had already ceded sovereignty to the British. The settlers still chose to remain, founding Akaroa. Today, this is a delightful township, with considerable emphasis placed on the French connection in the shops, bars and restaurants.

One French colonist's home, the Langlois-Eteveneaux Cottage, now houses the small **Akaroa Museum**, with exhibits on Maori life on the peninsula and whaling. Further along the seafront, two plaques mark the landing site of the original settlers on 16 August 1840.

Nearby is a jetty from which you can take harbour cruises, with a reasonable chance of seeing some of the hundreds of Hector's dolphins that inhabit the harbour.

Akaroa Museum: 71 Rue Lavaud. Tel: (03) 304 1013. Open: daily summer 10.30am–4.30pm; winter 10.30am–4pm. Admission charge.

Turning back towards Barry's Bay, take Long Bay Rd, and follow the signs for Okains Bay, 19km (12 miles) from Akaroa.

3 Okains Bay

This lovely bay is a popular picnic spot, and the beach and lagoon provide safe, sheltered swimming.

In such a remote location it comes as a surprise to find a fascinating collection of artefacts in the **Maori and Colonial Museum**, located at the entrance to the village. This started as a private collection and has since grown to include a working blacksmith's shop, horse-drawn carriages, and an old 'slab cottage', built from large, adzed slabs of *totara* wood. The Maori collection is extraordinary and many rare objects are on display, including war weapons, flax cloaks, adzes, and an unusual and valuable 'god stick' dating back to 1400. There is also a war canoe (1867), and one of the only fully carved meeting-houses in the South Island.

Maori and Colonial Museum: Okains Bay. Tel: (03) 304 8611. Open: daily 10am–5pm. Admission charge. Return to Christchurch along the panoramic Summit Rd, rejoining SH75 at the Hilltop junction.

Walk: Hooker Valley

The Hooker Valley Walk is one of the loveliest walks in Mount Cook/Aoraki National Park, with wonderful panoramas of the surrounding ranges and of Mount Cook itself. It runs along a gentle gradient, crossing the Hooker River twice on swingbridges, meandering through alpine pasturelands, and finishing at the lovely terminal lake below the Hooker Glacier. Most people return from here (a 3- or 4-hour round trip), but if you haven't yet had your fill of views you can continue for a while longer up to the Hooker Hut (allow another 2 hours).

From the Hermitage, follow the Kea Point Track across the Hooker Flats, crossing the road and then joining the Hooker Valley Track.

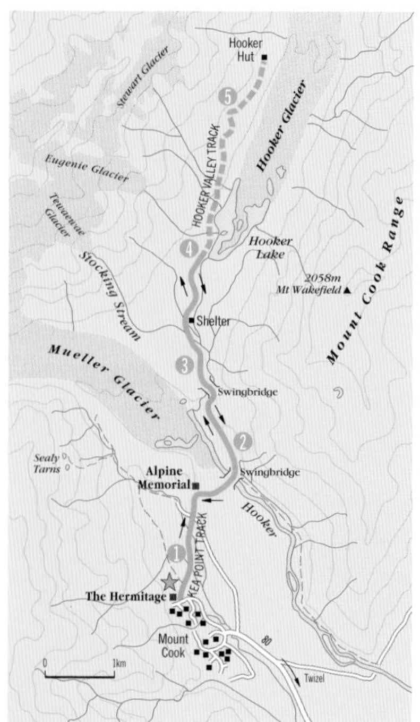

1 Campsite to Hooker River

The path zigzags between tussock mounds past the site of the original Hermitage (1884–1913) before reaching the Alpine Memorial, which you can climb up to for good views of the Hooker Valley ahead. From the memorial, the track loops up and around low, hummocky hills of moraine (glacial debris), before arriving alongside the Hooker River. It should take you about an hour to complete this round trip. *Cross the first swingbridge.*

2 Hooker Valley

Leading away to the left is the grey, debris-ridden expanse of the Mueller Glacier, with the mighty hanging glaciers and icefalls of Mount Sefton towering above it. The other peaks in the Main Divide of the Southern Alps curve round on the north side of the Hooker Valley, with Mount Cook now visible at the head of the valley. The track continues beneath a series of small bluffs at the foot of Mount Wakefield before arriving at the second swingbridge. This is a two-hour round trip.

Cross the Hooker River again on the second swingbridge.

3 Alpine pastures

The great ice faces of Mount Cook's southern flank dominate the view as the track leaves the Hooker River and crosses alpine pastureland to reach an open shelter at Stocking Stream, where there is an orientation table. Grasses and alpine plants cover the flatlands, with dense bushes clinging to the older moraine ridges above. In spring and summer these alpine meadows are a glorious profusion of buttercups (including the famous Mount Cook lily), giving way to daisies, and, in the autumn, gentians.

Continue on past the Stocking Stream shelter.

4 Hooker Lake and Glacier

A gentle climb alongside the river brings you to the terminal lake (the Hooker Lake) at the foot of the Hooker Glacier. Ice floes that have formed on the lake's waters create a photogenic foreground to the towering bulk of Mount Cook to the west.

Return the way you came or, if you can spare another 2 hours for the round trip, continue up to the Hooker Hut.

5 Hooker Lake to Hooker Hut

The route follows the edge of the lake and then branches off diagonally upwards across the terminal moraine, marked by a series of cairns. The track crosses two side-streams on top of the moraine wall before zigzagging down to the hut in its sheltered basin. From here there are terrific views of Mount Cook, with the Noeline and Mona glaciers spilling down into the Hooker Valley. The Hooker Hut is the starting point for the Copland Pass, which crosses the Alps, but you should not proceed beyond here unless you are properly equipped.

Mount Cook dotted with clouds

Tour: The TranzAlpine

This 233km (145-mile) journey from Christchurch to Greymouth is one of the classics of rail travel, connecting the two coastlines via the mountain passes of the Southern Alps on a narrow-gauge, single-track line which winds its way through tunnels and along impressive viaducts spanning deep canyons.

1 The Canterbury Plains

Leaving Christchurch station behind, the train crosses the rolling Canterbury Plains and passes through several small towns before halting at Springfield, the last stop before the climb into the mountains. The Southern Alps, dominated here by Mount Hutt (2,188m/7,178ft high), loom ahead.

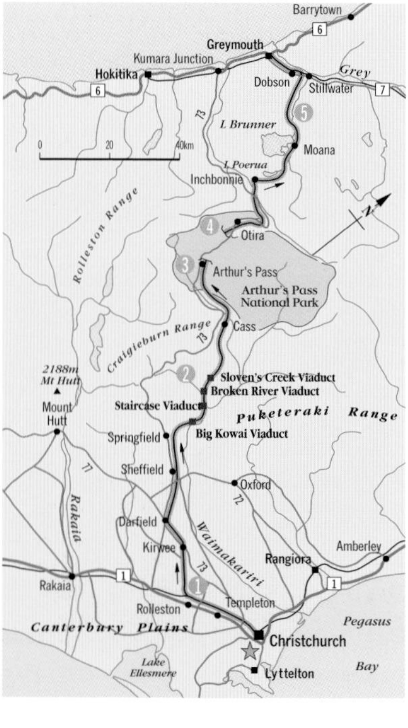

2 Springfield to Arthur's Pass

This is undoubtedly one of the most spectacular sections of the journey – try to get a seat on the right-hand side of the observation car if possible. The train soon crosses Big Kowai Viaduct, the first of five high viaducts that span rushing mountain torrents, and then enters the first of 16 tunnels chiselled through the rock. As you emerge from the sixth tunnel you will see the Waimakariri River way below, a raging blue-green snake twisting through the canyon. Next is Staircase Viaduct, the highest and most impressive on the line – at a height of 73m ($239\frac{1}{2}$ft) it could easily accommodate Christchurch Cathedral. All the tunnels on this part of the route are relatively short (the longest, Tunnel 10, is just 600m/1,969ft long), although in the days of steam trains even these were long enough to nearly suffocate the footplate crews. *Once past Broken River Viaduct (with spectacular views back down the Waimakariri River), the train clings to the northwest side of Broken River Gorge. Six tunnels are then passed in quick succession, before Sloven's Creek Viaduct is crossed and the broad, open valleys of the uplands are entered.*

3 Arthur's Pass

This small township is the starting point for hikes into the surrounding Arthur's Pass National Park, and at 737m (2,418ft) above sea level it is the highest railway station in New Zealand. Arthur's Pass was once the change-over point from steam to electric locomotives, as the next section is the steepest on the route.

4 Arthur's Pass to Otira

After a brief halt at Arthur's Pass, the TranzAlpine enters the 8.5km (5-mile) long Otira Tunnel for the 400m (1,312ft) descent to Otira; when it first opened in 1918 the tunnel was the longest in the British Empire, and seventh-longest in the world. The TranzAlpine cruises through in both directions with its diesel-electric locomotive, but coal trains making the long haul up from Greymouth to Arthur's Pass need up to four electric locomotives to overcome the gradient.

5 Otira to Greymouth

On the left after leaving Otira station you will see the escape track for

A scenic panorama on the TranzAlpine route

runaway trains coming down from Arthur's Pass; this has been used at least twice, in 1957 and 1962, with locomotives failing to hold on the 1-in-33 grade track. The contrast with the east-coast landscapes is immediately apparent, the rainforests of Westland spreading out across the hillsides.

Skirting the edges of Lake Poerua and Lake Brunner, the TranzAlpine meets up with the west-coast railway and follows the Grey River into Greymouth itself.

The TranzAlpine departs from Christchurch at 8.15am daily, arriving in Greymouth at 12.45pm, leaving Greymouth an hour later to return to Christchurch by 6.05pm. There is a full on-board buffet and bar service. Bookings can be made with any Tranz Scenic accredited travel agent or through Tranz Scenic central reservations (*tel: (04) 495 0775 or toll-free 0800 872 467; www.tranzscenic.co.nz*).

The Deep South

Known to the Maori as Muruhiku *(the 'tail' of New Zealand), the Deep South encompasses a rich diversity of landscapes and attractions, ranging from the splendours of Milford Sound in Fiordland National Park to the impressive architecture of Dunedin, the historic gold-mining towns of Arrowsmith, and the rare wildlife of the Otago Peninsula and Stewart Island.*

Almost the entire southwestern corner of the South Island is occupied by the massive Fiordland National Park, with its spectacular glaciated landscapes, inland lakes and deep fiords.

The lakeside resort of Te Anau is one of the main access points to Fiordland, as is the busy resort of Queenstown on the shore of Lake Wakatipu. Outdoor adventures – from guided hiking to tranquil lake or fiord cruises – are well catered for, with Queenstown providing more thrills and spills than almost any other location in New Zealand.

Adjoining Fiordland is Southland, with the regional capital, Invercargill, serving as a springboard for Stewart Island (Rakiura), New Zealand's 140th and newest national park.

The Otago region has strong Scottish connections, a heritage evident in the well-preserved architecture of the regional capital, Dunedin. On the city's doorstep is the Otago Peninsula, where royal albatrosses and rare penguins can be seen at remarkably close quarters.

Alexandra

Built on the back of the Otago gold rushes, Alexandra later turned to fruit farming. It is a thriving service centre for the surrounding agricultural community. Tourism is also alive and kicking, with adventure activities such as jet-boating and kayaking in the nearby Roxburgh Gorge, and mountain biking and 4WD tours in the rugged terrain around the town. Visitors can also see the local wineries and the country's first freshwater crayfish farm.
93km ($57^1/_2$ miles) southeast of Queenstown.

Arrowtown

This picturesque gold-mining town is usually full of people taking snapshots of its old stone-miners' cottages and, in the autumn, of the glorious foliage on the trees lining Buckingham Street and the banks of the Arrow River. Ironically, the complete treelessness of the area forced the 1860s gold-miners to build in stone, and caused the later arrivals to plant non-indigenous broadleaved trees such as the sycamore and oak, which give Arrowtown its unique appeal today.

The story of those early pioneering days is recounted in the **Lakes District Museum**, where you can also pick up the leaflet *Historic Arrowtown* which will guide you around over 40 historic buildings in the township – many are private houses, viewable only from the street.

Arrowtown is 21km (13 miles) northeast of Queenstown. Regular tours from the Mall in Queenstown on the Double Decker Bus. Tel: (03) 441 4421. www.doubledeckerbus.co.nz. Lakes District Museum, 49 Buckingham St. Tel: (03) 442 1824. www.museumqueenstown.com. Open: daily 9am–5pm. Admission charge.

Dunedin

Sprawling in a horseshoe shape around the head of the deep-water inlet of Otago Harbour, Dunedin is an attractive, solidly built city that was originally founded by Scottish settlers. It grew prosperous on the back of the 1860s gold rush in Central Otago and was the wealthiest city in New Zealand at the turn of the last century. The legacy of those days is visible in the numerous well-preserved Victorian and Edwardian buildings that dot the city, such as the University of Otago (1869), the Railway Station (1906), the Municipal Chambers (1880) and the Otago Boys' High School (1885).

Dunedin retains a distinctive Scottish heritage. It has the country's only whisky distillery. Scottish Week is celebrated with bagpipe-playing and highland flings in March, and you can even arrange a haggis ceremony or buy a kilt here.

The South Island's second-largest city is also a thriving university town and cultural centre, and makes the world-famous Cadbury chocolate. The city is a convenient base for visiting the wonderful Otago Peninsula (*see pp133–4*) right on its doorstep.

Cadbury World

The secrets and history of chocolate and chocolate making are all here. Exhibits are followed by a 45-minute tour of the factory and a visit to the store. In early July you can catch the annual Cadbury Chocolate Festival.

280 Cumberland St. Tel: (03) 467 7967 or toll-free 0800 223 287. www.cadburyworld.co.nz. Open: daily 9am–3.15pm, extended hours in summer. Admission charge. Bookings advised.

Rolling hills in Otago

The Octagon

Dominated by a statue of the Scottish bard Robbie Burns, the Octagon is the focal centre of the city and has a clutch of lively cafés and restaurants along its eastern side. On the western side you will find the visitor centre and the Anglican St Paul's Cathedral, built from Oamaru stone in 1919.

Olveston

Built at the start of the 20th century, Olveston is a gracious Jacobean stone mansion with a wealth of decorative detail, furnishings, treasured artefacts and paintings collected by the Theomin family who lived here.
42 Royal Terrace. Tel: (03) 477 3320 or toll-free 0800 100 880. www.olveston.co.nz. Open: daily (except Christmas Day) 9.30am–5pm; 6 one-hour guided tours daily. Admission charge.

Otago Museum

Founded in 1868 and renowned for its Maori and Pacific Island artefacts, the museum also has a good natural history section. Discovery World has numerous hands-on science exhibits for children.
419 Great King St. Tel: (03) 474 7474. www.otagomuseum.govt.nz. Open: daily (except Christmas Day) 10am–5pm; guided tours 11.30am & 3.30pm. Free admission to museum; admission charge to Discovery World.

Otago Settlers Museum

Just a short distance west of the railway station is the Otago Settlers Museum.

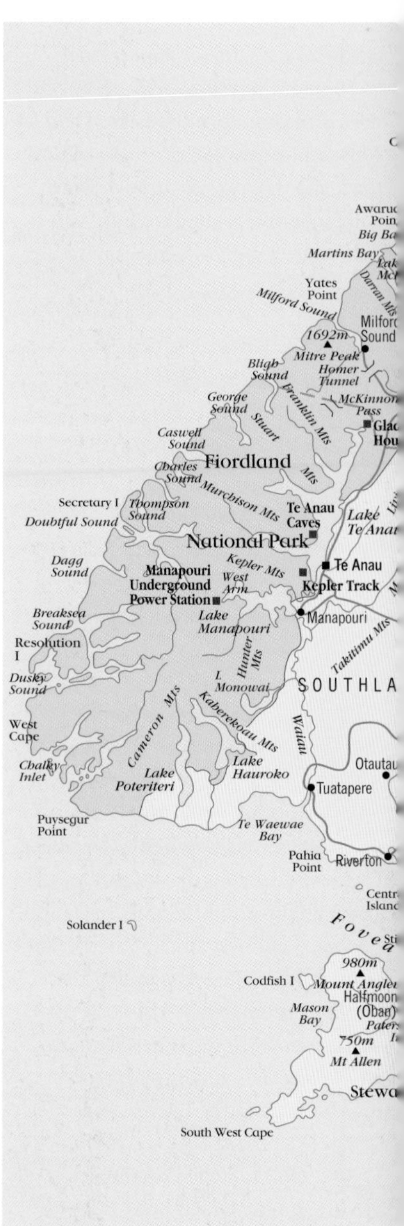

The Deep South

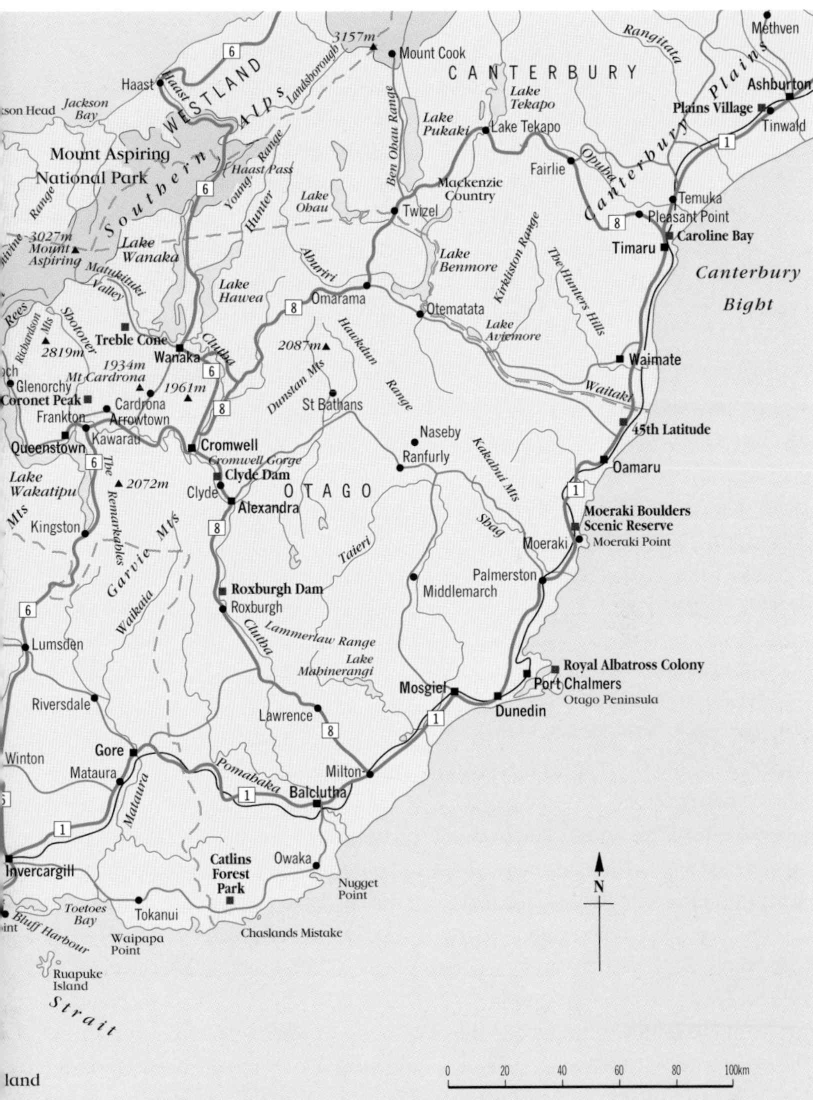

This museum houses New Zealand's leading collection of colonial memorabilia, priceless archives, manuscripts and photographs.
31 Queens Gardens. Tel: (03) 477 5052. www.otago.settlers.museum. Open: daily (except Christmas Day & Good Friday) 10am–5pm. Admission charge.

Speights Brewery Heritage Tour

This 90-minute tour introduces you to the story of beer in New Zealand, and includes tasting a selection of the finest of 'The Pride of the South' beers.
*200 Rattray Rd, Dunedin.
Tel: (03) 477 7697. www.speights.co.nz. Tours: daily (except Christmas Day), Mon–Thur 10am, noon, 2pm & 7pm; Fri–Sun 10am, noon, 2pm & 4pm. Booking essential.*

Fiordland National Park

Spread over 1.2 million sq km (748,000sq miles) in the most remote corner of the South Island is Fiordland, New Zealand's largest national park, and also one of the world's largest. The park's serrated coastline is punctuated by beautiful fiords which reach back into the bush-clad hills and mountains. In the hinterland, deep, branching lakes – also carved out by glaciers – add further allure to this stunning region. The impenetrability of Fiordland's rainforests and rugged mountains has kept intruders at bay for centuries, and much of the region remains an unspoilt wilderness where rare species – such as the blue duck and the *takahe* – have managed to retain a foothold. The high annual rainfall creates hundreds of cascading waterfalls, often leading to dramatic landslips as it washes away whole hillsides of vegetation.

An alpine stream flowing through Fiordland National Park

The most northerly of the 14 fiords along the coast is **Milford Sound**, dominated by the majestic Mitre Peak. The hanging valleys that flank the fiord drain Milford's phenomenal annual rainfall (at an average of 6,526mm (257in) per annum, the country's highest) into a series of spectacular waterfalls, while the fiord's sheer walls (rising 1,200m (3,937ft) vertically from the sea) dwarf even the biggest visiting cruise liners as they make their way down the sound.

Milford is the most accessible and heavily visited of the fiords. You can reach it by coach tour, drive there from

Te Anau (*see pp140–41*), or fly in by helicopter or light aeroplane. Another option is to walk in along the famous Milford Track.

The main gateway to Fiordland is the lakeside township of **Te Anau**, which has a wide range of accommodation and activities on offer. The 53km (33-mile) long Lake Te Anau is the largest in the South Island, and cruises across to the **Te Anau Glow-worm Caves** are popular; accessible only by boat, these feature underground waterfalls and a glow-worm grotto.

To the south of Te Anau lies beautiful **Lake Manapouri**, once threatened by a hydroelectric scheme. The huge public outcry that greeted this plan led to the idea being vetoed; although a power plant was still built, it was sited underground to placate the protesters. Tours of the giant **Manapouri Underground Power Station** at West Arm (200m/656ft underground and reached via a 2km/1 1/3-mile long spiral access tunnel) can be combined with a trip onwards over the mountains across Wilmot Pass to **Doubtful Sound.** This fiord is home to fur seals, dusky and bottlenose dolphins, and the Fiordland crested penguin.

Te Anau lies 167km (104 miles) from Queenstown. The main agency for tours and activities is the Fiordland i-SITE Visitor Centre, Lakefront Drive, Te Anau. Tel: (03) 249 7924. Open: daily summer 8.30am–6pm; winter 8.30am–4.30pm. Real Journeys, Lakefront Drive, operates cruises and tours to the Glow-worm Caves, Manapouri Power Station and Doubtful Sound. Tel: (03) 249 7416 or toll-free 0800 656 501. www.realjourneys.co.nz. Glow-worm Caves tours are two-and-a-half hours long and run daily at 2pm & 7pm, with an additional 5.45pm tour Oct–Apr and 8.15pm tour Nov–Mar. Doubtful Sound cruises are all-day or overnight, run daily, and include a guided tour of Manapouri Power Station in Oct–Apr.

Invercargill

This is the southernmost city in New Zealand, and the main gateway to Stewart Island (*see pp136–7*). If you are passing through, the **Southland Museum and Art Gallery** (housed inside a giant pyramid) is a must: the exhibits span hundreds of years of cultural and natural history, including the subantarctic islands, with stunning photography and audio-visual effects.

Invercargill is also the starting point (or the finish, depending on which way you're travelling) of the excellent **Southern Scenic Route**, which traverses the remote southeastern coastline up to Balclutha. This 172km

Rugged peaks and deep glacial valleys are characteristic features of Fiordland

(107-mile) route encompasses the untouched coastal forests of the **Catlins** (home to many rare birds) as well as the fossilised remains of 180-million-year-old trees at Curio Bay and colonies of seals, yellow-eyed penguins, gannets and sooty shearwaters.
Invercargill is 225km (140 miles) southwest of Dunedin.
Southland Museum and Art Gallery, Queens Park. Tel: (03) 219 9069. www.southlandmuseum.com.
Open: weekdays 9am–5pm, weekends 10am–5pm. Closed: Christmas Day. Admission charge.

A church in Oamaru, noted for its pure Oamaru stone

Moeraki

Just outside this small fishing port is the **Moeraki Boulders Scenic Reserve**, a small area of beach on which lie several spherical boulders. These geological curiosities were formed in the surrounding mudstone some 60 million years ago when North Otago was covered by the ocean; there are around 50 boulders along this section of coast, the largest more than 2m (6½ft) in diameter. A boardwalk runs around the low cliffs and along the beach.
38km (23½ miles) south of Oamaru, 78km (48½ miles) north of Dunedin. The Reserve is signposted off the main road (SH1), with open access.

Oamaru

Oamaru is the main coastal town in North Otago and best known for its exceptionally pure, creamy white limestone, used to good effect in fine public buildings in the 19th century, including, on the tree-lined Thames Street, the National Bank, the Bank of New South Wales (now an art gallery) and the first Post Office (now a restaurant).

The Old Harbour area is gradually being restored as a typical Victorian waterfront village, with some huge old warehouses and grain and wool stores being converted for use by craft-workers and others. Oamaru is noted for its extensive **Public Gardens** set up in 1876, including a wallaby park, fountains, statues and floral displays.

Just outside Oamaru is a blue penguin colony; from two viewing platforms you can see the penguins return to their nesting sites each night. The yellow-eyed penguin colony is on Bushy Beach.

Oamaru is 250km (155 miles) south of Christchurch, 116km (72 miles) north of Dunedin. Heritage tours can be booked through the Oamaru i-SITE Visitor Centre, 1 Thames St. Tel: (03) 434 1656.
Oamaru Public Gardens, Severn St. Tel: (03) 434 8060.
Details on viewing times and access regulations to both penguin colonies are available from the Oamaru Blue Penguin Colony, Waterfront Rd, Oamaru (tel: (03) 433 1165; www.penguins.co.nz) or Penguin Express, 12 Main St (tel: (03) 434 7744; www.coastline-tours.co.nz).

Otago Peninsula

Jutting out from Dunedin and protecting its harbour from the Pacific Ocean is the Otago Peninsula, remarkable for the variety of wildlife concentrated here, close to the city centre. New Zealand fur seals are numerous around the coastline, and colonies of yellow-eyed and blue penguins nest on several beaches. The peninsula's scenic inlets are also home to large numbers of wading and water fowl, and, to cap it all, **Taiaroa Head** boasts the only royal albatross nesting site in the world which exists this close to civilisation.

The peninsula also has its man-made attractions, prime among which is **Larnach Castle** in its spectacular setting overlooking the sea and the peninsula. The castle is the legacy of William Larnach, whose family had a colourful history. (Larnach committed suicide in 1898 after a series of financial disasters.) Built between 1871 and 1887, the castle has a huge ballroom, a skilful Georgian hanging staircase, several fine Italian marble fireplaces, and elaborately decorated ceilings. The castle is surrounded by 14 hectares (34½ acres) of attractive gardens.

Another popular spot is **Glenfalloch Woodland Garden** on the seashore, with 12 hectares (29½ acres) of rhododendrons, azaleas, magnolias, fuchsias and roses, a good café, and a working potter's studio. Further along the coast road, the **New Zealand Marine Studies Centre and Westpac Aquarium** (the largest marine research centre in the country) has a public aquarium in its basement which houses some unusual and fascinating species that can be found around the rocky coastlines of the peninsula, and a touch tank where you can handle invertebrates and other animals. For more details on wildlife and other attractions in the area, *see pp138–9.*
Larnach Castle, Camp Rd, Dunedin. 15km (9 miles) from central Dunedin.

The Moeraki Boulders look like giant marbles on the seashore

Tel: (03) 476 1616. www.larnachcastle.co.nz. Open: daily (except Christmas Day) 9am–5pm. Admission charge.
Glenfalloch Woodland Garden, 430 Portobello Rd, Dunedin.
Tel: (03) 476 1006. Open: daily dawn–dusk. Free admission (donations welcome).
New Zealand Marine Studies Centre, Hatchery Rd, Portobello, Dunedin.
Tel: (03) 479 5826. www.marine.ac.nz. Open: daily noon–4.30pm; guided tours at 10.30am. Admission charge.

Queenstown

The wonderful natural setting of Queenstown on the shores of Lake Wakatipu, with the dramatic Remarkables mountain range rising up behind it, would be a tremendous draw in itself even if the town had no other assets – but it does, by the bucketload. Queenstown is New Zealand's premier tourist resort, offering a remarkable range of activities for visitors to choose from: sensational helicopter adventures, white-water surfing, flightseeing in an old DC3 and jet-boating, tandem parachute or parapente jumps – and A J Hackett's famous bungee-jumping enterprise (*see pp146–7*).

The ultimate Queenstown thrill is the 'Awesome Foursome', an adrenaline-pumping day that combines a helicopter ride with jet-boating, white-water rafting and a bungee jump. Less hair-raising activities include sedate lake cruises, back-country tours, or horse-trekking; in winter, the nearby Coronet Peak and Remarkables ski fields (among the best in the country) are very busy.

Efficient, computerised booking offices line Queenstown's main street. Relax in one of the town's 100 or so restaurants, bars and eateries, many of which have live music. The resort's excellent range of shops stays open until 9pm, seven days a week. More than 40 hotels and motels, and 26 guesthouses and hostels cater for the annual influx of over half a million visitors.

For details of activities, see pp146–51.

Central Otago Wine Trail

Less than an hour's drive from Queenstown along State Highway 6 are the world's most southerly vineyards, and the start of the Central Otago Wine Trail. There are 24 wineries in this fertile countryside, including **Gibbston Valley** (Pinot Noir), **Black Ridge Wines** (Riesling) and **Rippon Vineyard**.

Gibbston Valley, Main Cromwell-Queenstown Highway.
Tel: (03) 442 6910.
www.gvwines.co.nz. Open: daily 10am–5pm, hourly tours 10am–4pm.
Black Ridge Wines, Conroys Rd, Alexandra. Tel: (03) 449 2059.
www.blackridge.co.nz. Open: daily 10am–5pm.
Rippon Vineyard, 246 Mt Aspiring Rd, Lake Wanaka. Tel: (03) 443 8084.
www.rippon.co.nz. Open: Dec–Apr 11am–5pm; July–Nov 1.30–4.30pm.

Closed: May & June (unless by appointment).
The Queenstown Wine Trail departs daily at 12.30pm from the centre of town and allows you a full afternoon for wine tasting. Tel: (03) 442 3799.
www.queenstownwinetrail.co.nz

Kiwi Birdlife Park

The park has a nocturnal kiwi house, as well as aviaries, ponds, a live conservation show, an early Maori hunting village, and a native bush trail, where you can see other native birds too.
Brecon St. Tel: (03) 442 8059. www.kiwibird.co.nz. Open: daily summer 9am–7pm; winter 9am–6pm (hours may vary according to demand). Admission charge.

Skyline Gondola and Luge

A good way to orientate yourself when you first arrive here is to take the Skyline Gondola, which rises 790m (2,592ft) above sea level from central Queenstown and offers stunning views of the lake, the mountains and the town. The Skyline Restaurant serves up wonderful NZ fare as well as magnificent views, or you can enjoy the spectacular outlook in the more casual Skyline Café. For a spectacle of traditional Maori songs and dances, you can book tickets to the evening Kiwi Haka (performances at 5.30pm, 6.30pm or 7.30pm). If you want a more adrenaline-pumping experience, you can hurtle back down to the base of the mountain on the Skyline Luge (*9.30am–30 minutes before dusk*).
Brecon St. Tel: (03) 441 0101. www.skyline.co.nz. Open: daily 9am–midnight. Admission charge.

TSS *Earnslaw* and Walter Peak Farm

The vintage TSS *Earnslaw* is the last of the coal-burning steamers that once plied the lake to supply outlying sheep stations; lovingly restored, the venerable steamer now cruises for pleasure only.

In the afternoons the steamer calls in at Walter Peak, a high-country farm on the other side of the lake, where refreshments are served, and where you can see sheepdog and sheep-shearing demonstrations.
TSS Earnslaw *is operated by Real Journeys, Lakefront Drive, Te Anau. Tel: (03) 249 7416 or toll-free 0800 656 501.*

The TSS *Earnslaw* is a vintage steamer which still plies the waters of Lake Wakatipu daily

www.realjourneys.co.nz. Cruises depart six times daily Oct–Apr, three times daily the rest of the year, except late May–early June, when the boat is out of service. Barbecue lunch options available on several cruises. Walter Peak is also accessible by the Real Journeys launch, which runs all year from Lakefront Drive.

Rakiura/Stewart Island

This triangular-shaped island is a naturalists' paradise, now New Zealand's newest national park. The park has 157,000 hectares (388,000 acres) of protected native bush and rainforest, 750km (466 miles) of indented coastline with hundreds of hidden beaches and sandy bays, and a mere 20km (12½ miles) of roads!

There is just one township, Halfmoon Bay (Oban), and a permanent population of only 400 people.

The island has a rich Maori history, and the harvesting of *titi* (fledgling chicks of the sooty shearwater, also sold in fish shops as mutton birds) continues on the tiny islands around its coastline as it has done for centuries.

Cook sailed around the southern tip in March 1770, but mistakenly thought it was a peninsula. Twenty years later, Captain Chase on board the *Pegasus* brought a sealing gang to these shores and attempted to set up a shipyard on an inlet on the southeast coast (which still bears the name Port Pegasus). The island was named after the vessel's first officer, William Stewart, who charted the inlet.

Today, commercial fishing – principally for *paua* (puff oysters), crayfish and blue cod – is the lifeblood of most islanders, with tourism playing an important part as hikers, hunters, divers and fishermen seek out Stewart Island's wild places. Hikers should arrive well equipped: the North West Circuit (around the top half of the island) takes ten days, while the Rakiura Track (closer to Oban) takes at least three days.

Native birds include the kiwi, *kaka, tui,* bellbird, robin, tomtit, fantail, and the long-tailed and shining cuckoo. One of the great attractions of the island is the chance to see kiwis in their natural habitat – unusually, the Stewart Island brown kiwi forages during the daytime (they are particularly numerous at Mason Bay on the North West Circuit). Launch trips also depart from Oban to watch kiwis foraging for sand-hoppers on Ocean Beach during the evenings.

Stewart Island can be reached on a 20-minute flight (three times daily) with Stewart Island Flights from Invercargill (tel: (03) 218 9129; www.stewartislandflights.co.nz).
There is also a 60-minute catamaran service, the Foveaux Express, from Bluff (tel: (03) 212 7660; www.foveauxexpress.co.nz).
Kiwi-watching trips are operated by Bravo Adventure Cruises, Stewart Island (tel: (03) 219 1144; book well in advance), Ruggedy Range Wilderness Experience, 170 Horseshoe Bay Road,

Stewart Island (tel: (03) 219 1066; www.ruggedyrange.com), and others. For further information, contact the Stewart Island Visitor Terminal, Main Wharf, Halfmoon Bay. Tel: (03) 219 1134 or toll-free 0800 000 511. www.stewartisland.co.nz

Te Anau

See p131.

Wanaka

This more laid-back version of Queenstown is set in similarly stunning scenery on the edge of Lake Wanaka, with the peaks of **Mount Aspiring National Park** rising up in the background. Wanaka's waterfront is at its most majestic in the autumn, when poplars and willows in shades of gold and red frame the alpine views.

Though Wanaka is certainly less commercialised than Queenstown, outdoor adventure is the town's main business, and plenty of thrills are on offer: paragliding, rafting, mountain-biking, jet-boating, four-wheel-drive tours, and cruising on the lake by hovercraft. For something unusual, take a ride in a vintage Tiger Moth biplane.

Wanaka is a major fishing centre, and both coarse fishing on the lake and fly fishing on nearby rivers are available. Hikers are also well catered for as numerous tracks run through Mount Aspiring National Park; shorter walks in the vicinity include the Diamond Lake Track (2½ hours) and Mount Roy Track (5–6 hours return). In the winter, skiers head for the renowned Cardrona and Treble Cone ski fields.

For a gentler form of entertainment, don't miss **Stuart Landsborough's Puzzling World and Great Maze**; built in 1973, it started a trend that led to the creation of numerous mazes throughout New Zealand. The split-level maze has over 1.5km (1 mile) of passageways, whilst the Tilted Towers complex will confuse you even further. Next to the tearooms is the Puzzle Centre, housing a huge collection of mind-bending puzzles and the Illusions Gallery.

Wanaka is 120km (74½ miles) north of Queenstown (recommended route via Cromwell; extra care is necessary if using Crown Range Road during the winter months).

Details on activities are available from the Wanaka i-SITE Visitor Centre, 100 Ardmore St, Lake Front. Tel: (03) 443 1233. www.lakewanaka.co.nz. Hiking information is available from the DOC information centre in the Visitor Centre building. Tel: (03) 443 7660.

Stuart Landsborough's Puzzling World and Great Maze, Main Highway, 2km (1 mile) outside town on SH8A to Cromwell. Tel: (03) 443 7489. www.puzzlingworld.co.nz. Open: daily summer 8.30am to last admission at 5.30pm; winter 8.30am to last admission at 5pm (Christmas Day 10am–3pm). Admission charge.

Tour: Otago Peninsula

This tour around the peninsula is a wildlife extravaganza of sea birds and marine life, with a historic castle thrown in for good measure. Ideally, you should plan to arrive at the Royal Albatross Colony between noon and 2pm; book your tour before leaving Dunedin, and also make sure you are booked into the Penguin Place Yellow-Eyed Penguin Conservation Reserve for the 4pm tour.

Allow a full day.

From the Octagon, head down Princes St and take a left turn down Andersons Bay Rd. After 5km (3 miles), turn left down Silverton Rd and follow the signs to Larnach Castle (see p133) along the ridgetop road. After visiting Larnach return to Highcliff Rd. You should then turn left, continuing down to Hoopers Inlet, and eventually following Sheppard Rd to Papanui Inlet.

1 Hoopers and Papanui Inlets

Both of these lovely inlets are home to a variety of wading and water birds. The innermost part of Hoopers Inlet is a wildlife sanctuary – a plaque shows the birds that can be seen here.

Take Weir Rd to Portobello Bay and continue along the coast road. Stop at Southlight Wildlife for the key to the reserve. Continue on to Taiaroa Head.

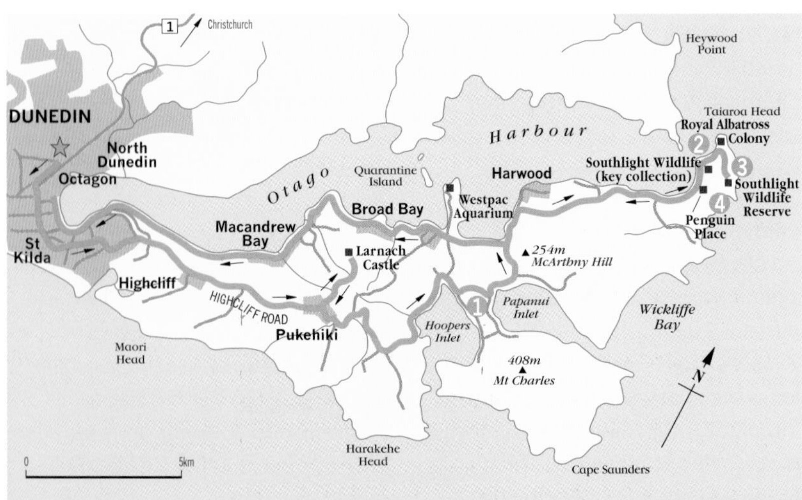

2 Royal Albatross Colony

This reserve is one of the most special wildlife zones in New Zealand, and the only mainland albatross colony in the world. The area has been protected since 1937, and public viewing started in 1972. The Albatross Centre has displays and an audiovisual presentation on these magnificent birds, and from here you are led by trained guides up to the hide overlooking the nesting sites on the hill top.

Winging in from Antarctic waters, the albatross build their nests in late September and, once all the eggs have been laid (usually by 24 November), the colony is open to the public. The tasks of incubation and guarding the new-born chicks are shared by both parents, with hatching taking place between January and February. The fluffy albatross chicks remain at Taiaroa until they are ready to set off in late September.

Taiaroa Head Dunedin.
Tel: (03) 478 0499 or toll-free 0800 528 767. www.albatross.org.nz. Centre open: daily (except Christmas Day), summer 9am–dusk; winter 10am–dusk; no tours Tue mornings. Tour reservations essential. Admission charge.

Continue past the car park, through the gate and along the cliff-top road to Southlight Wildlife Reserve.

3 Southlight Wildlife Reserve

Yellow-eyed penguins come ashore in the late afternoons to nest above the beach here, but you won't get as close to them as you will in the Penguin Place Reserve. There are plenty of fur seals to photograph at close quarters, and, at the end of the beach, a spotted shag colony.

932 Harrington Point. Tel: (03) 478 0287. Open: daily dawn–dusk. Admission charge.

Return along the coast road to Penguin Place. If you have time, you could also detour back to the Westpac Aquarium (see p133).

4 Penguin Place

This is by far the better of the two penguin reserves. Following a brief introductory talk at the farm headquarters, you are ferried over the hill to the penguin beach where a series of crafty tunnels and hides allows you to pop up very close to the many nesting sites in this colony.

Yellow-eyed Penguin Reserve: Harrington Point. Tel: (03) 478 0286. www.penguinplace.co.nz. Open: daily 9am–dusk. Tours depart every 30 minutes from 10.15am–90 minutes before sunset in summer, every 30 minutes from 3.15–4.45pm in winter. Admission charge.

Return to Dunedin around the shoreline.

A royal albatross at Taiaroa Head on the tip of the peninsula

Tour: Milford Sound

This tour starts and finishes in Te Anau, following the Milford Road, with several interesting stop-offs before arriving at Milford itself, where you have a choice of cruise options on the Sound. If you are based in Queenstown it is better to do the trip by coach or cruise excursion so that someone else drives the six hours involved.

Allow a full day to complete the tour at a leisurely pace.

From Te Anau, follow signs for Milford Sound.

1 Lake Te Anau

The road skirts Lake Te Anau, with views across to the Murchison Mountains, before arriving at Te Anau Downs and then heading away from the lake up towards the Livingstone and Humboldt mountains.

At the 40km (25 mile) mark you pass the entrance to Fiordland National Park; after 58km (36 miles) you arrive at the Mirror Lakes.

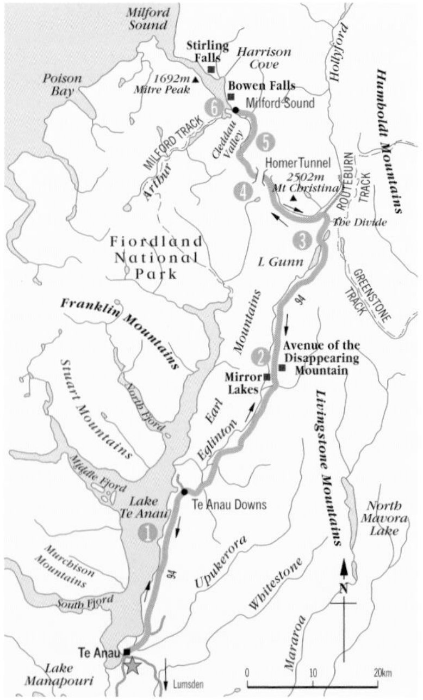

2 Mirror Lakes

A boardwalk from the road leads around the edge of two small, sheltered lakes which mirror the mountains opposite – hundreds of tourists stop to capture this scene on film. Shortly afterwards, you drive along the Avenue of the Disappearing Mountain, so-called because the peak at the end of the road seems to diminish in perspective the closer you get to it.

At 76km (47 miles) the road skirts Lake Gunn.

3 Lake Gunn

Lake Gunn sometimes also has a mirror image of the mountains, although less reliably so than the Mirror Lakes. This large lake is named after an early explorer, George Gunn. From the road a loop track leads through red beech forest to the lakeside (a pleasant half-hour's ramble). Shortly afterwards you pass The Divide, the lowest east-west pass 534m (1,752ft) across the Southern Alps and the departure point for the Routeburn and Greenstone tracks.

Continue on to the Homer Tunnel 101km (63 miles).

4 Homer Tunnel

The tunnel was started in 1935 when just five men set to the mountain with picks and shovels. Not surprisingly, it wasn't completed until 1952, and at the cost of five lives. Hewn out of solid rock, the tunnel is narrow and unlined, dropping along a gradient of one in 11 over its 1.2km (1/2-mile) length. You can't help but drive through with extreme caution.

5 Cleddau Valley

As the road emerges from the Homer Tunnel it spirals down the Cleddau Valley, with dozens of waterfalls tumbling over the sheer sides of the valley. Further down, the Cleddau River plunges beneath a natural rock bridge to create another spectacular waterfall.

At the 120km (74 1/2-mile) point you arrive at Milford Sound, from where cruises depart down the Sound to the Tasman Sea. A visitor centre with facilities is available.

6 Milford Sound

The rainfall is practically incessant in Milford Sound (averaging over 6,526mm (257in) per year with more than 200 rainy days), giving it an almost permanent misty, moody atmosphere and contributing to the dozens of spectacular but temporary waterfalls that pour down the sheer rock faces into the sea. Most cruises take a similar route down the 16km (10-mile) long sound, first passing by Mitre Peak (1,692m/5,551ft) and then nosing in for a spray-filled view of the Bowen Falls before approaching a fur seal colony and heading up to the Tasman Sea. On the return journey, your captain will point out hanging glacial valleys and other features, and will try to seek out schools of dolphins. The boat passes the wind-lashed Stirling Falls, Harrison Cove, and, once again, the Bowen Falls before docking back at the visitor centre jetty.

Return to Te Anau along the same route.

Dramatic scenery in Milford Sound

The Routeburn Track

Weather and hazards

The Routeburn is a well-used and clearly marked path, with tracks, huts and bridges maintained efficiently by park staff. Most people walk the track during the summer months (mid-November to March), though autumn (April to mid-May) can also be excellent, with fewer people on the trail. Remember that advance booking is essential. Mountain flowers are at their best from November to January. Rainfall can be high during midsummer, so the best views are often to be had from February to April.

The main hazard is the southerly or northwesterly storms which come in from the Tasman Sea any time of year. Be prepared for adverse conditions with waterproofs and warm clothing.

Guided walks

Guided walking is a comfortable option that allows anybody of average fitness to enjoy this wonderful area, even if they have had no previous hiking experience. Routeburn Walk Ltd has its own private mountain lodges with comfortable accommodation and hot showers. All meals are prepared by the guides and the lodge managers, which means that during the day you have only to carry a light day pack with your clothing and other requirements. The knowledgeable guides will ensure a safe journey and allow you to make the most of this superb walk.

Emergency shelters on the track

For full details on costs and bookings, contact: Routeburn Walk, PO Box 259, Queenstown. Tel: (03) 442 8200 or toll-free 0800 659 255. www.ultimatehikes.co.nz

Independent walking

If you'd rather make your own way, public transport is available from both ends of the track; hut wardens are in residence from November to May. *Maps and information can be obtained from the DOC Great Walks Booking Desk at the Fiordland National Park Visitor Centre, Lakefront Drive, Te Anau. Tel: (03) 249 7924. www.doc.govt.nz. Open: summer daily 8.30am–6pm; winter weekdays 8.30am–4.30pm.*

Impressive scenery along the Routeburn Track

Walk: The Routeburn Track

This is one of New Zealand's great walks, a relatively easy, well-marked track passing from Fiordland National Park over the Harris Saddle and into Mount Aspiring National Park. It is a popular route, with spectacular alpine panoramas along much of its 39km (24-mile) length. The track can be walked independently in either direction, or on a guided hike from west to east, as described here. For practical details, see pp142–3.

Allow three days, two nights.

Your trek begins with a coach ride from Queenstown, through Te Anau and along the Milford Highway to The Divide, from where you start walking.

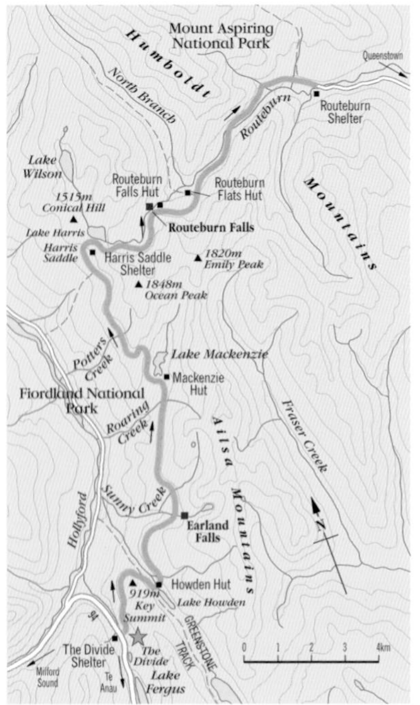

Day One: The Divide to Lake Mackenzie

The track climbs gently through magnificent silver-beech forests, where the gnarled trunks of larger trees are cloaked in moss, lichen and epiphytes. Emerging above the tree line, detour briefly (30 minutes) up to Key Summit (919m/3,015ft), a small, rocky knoll surrounded by a swampland of bogs and tarns, with extensive views of the peaks and valleys of Fiordland. From here it is a quick descent to Lake Howden, where you break for lunch. The afternoon's walk is a steady, gentle climb from Lake Howden to Lake Mackenzie, passing the dramatic Earland Falls on the way. The track goes almost directly underneath these 100m (328ft) high falls; the surrounding rocks and ferns are drenched in spray. Further along, you get occasional glimpses of the snow-capped peaks and glaciers of the Darren Range. A last, rocky descent through silver-beech forest comes out at the Mackenzie Hut, where you stop for the night.

Day Two: Lake Mackenzie to Routeburn Falls

After breakfast you set off alongside Lake Mackenzie, which on a calm day will reward you with a breathtaking image of Emily Peak (1,820m/5,971ft) reflected in its emerald depths. The track zigzags steeply up above the tree line before levelling out and hugging the Hollyford Face for the next two to three hours; from here there are magnificent views across the valley to the Darren Range. A brief ascent brings you to Harris Saddle (1,217m/3,993ft), where you pass from Fiordland National Park into Mount Aspiring National Park.

From the shelter at Harris Saddle it is well worth making the extra effort to climb Conical Hill (1,515m/4,970ft). From its summit there are awe-inspiring views of the Routeburn Valley leading down to Lake McKerrow, Martins Bay and the Tasman Sea.

Beyond Harris Saddle the track skirts Lake Harris, emerging into the fragile tussock and swampland of the Harris Basin. The track then follows the Routeburn River down to the Routeburn Falls, well known as a haunt for mischievous *kea*. Your hut for the night is within earshot of the falls.

Day Three: Routeburn Falls to Routeburn Shelter

The track descends through silver-, mountain- and then red-beech forest. At the Routeburn Flats, the river winds placidly across the grass-covered plains, with Mount Somnus (2,294m/7,526ft) dominating the view. After you have crossed the Routeburn on a suspension bridge, a gentle downhill amble along the river's forested banks leads you to the Routeburn Shelter, from where you will be transported back to Queenstown.

Spectacular alpine scenery in Fiordland National Park

Getting away from it all

*Many people come to New Zealand specifically for its wide-open spaces and unspoilt natural environment, and since New Zealanders themselves are equally keen on the great outdoors there is no shortage of opportunities to get away from it all. The activities listed here form just a sample of the options available (*see also pp160–63*), but they can be enjoyed by anyone and are, in their own way, typically Kiwi ways to escape – whether only for a few seconds on a bungee jump or several days on a rafting or walking trip.*

Ballooning

The Canterbury Plains is the biggest centre for hot-air ballooning in New Zealand, thanks largely to the ideal conditions provided by the rolling countryside; balloons drift quietly high above the sheep and farmlands. The scenery is spectacular: the Southern Alps rear up to the west, and to the east the Pacific coastline stretches off into the distance. Most balloon flights start at dawn (to take advantage of calm conditions), but the trauma of having to get up so early is soon forgotten in the excitement of clambering into the basket and lifting off. After the initial roar of the gas burners you can settle back to enjoy your hour-long flight. Champagne is always served on landing (a tradition with balloonists worldwide), followed by a hearty breakfast.

Aoraki Balloon Safaris, Methven. Tel: (03) 302 8172 or toll-free 0800 256 837. www.nzballooning.co.nz.
Sunrise Balloon Adventures, Queenstown. Tel: (03) 442 0781 or toll-free 0800 468 247. www.ballooningnz.com.
Up, Up, and Away, Merivale, Christchurch. Tel: (03) 381 4600. www.ballooning.co.nz.
Most ballooning companies operate daily, weather permitting, all year round. Bookings are essential.

Bungee-jumping

Jumping off high places with nothing but a piece of elastic tied to your ankles is perhaps one of the oddest adventure sports ever invented, but at least 70,000 people a year are now taking the plunge.

The attraction lies partly in conquering your inner fears sufficiently to throw yourself off, partly in the exhilaration of the 'drop', and partly in the relief that floods through you as the bungee cord drags you back up again, and you bounce gently in mid-air before being hoisted aboard a raft on the river below.

Bungee-jumping was invented by a New Zealander, A J Hackett, and started

Bungee-jumping in Queenstown

as a commercial operation in Queenstown in 1988 with the Kawarau Bridge jump (43m/141ft). You can also try the Nevis Highwire (the highest at 134m/439½ft), The Ledge (an urban jump of 400m (1,312ft) over Queenstown), the gorgeously scenic jump at Skippers Canyon Suspension Bridge (71m/233ft), or jumps in Auckland, Lake Taupo and several other locations throughout the country. It is surprising how many people come back for more, and there is no age limit either – over-65s go free, and the oldest person ever to have jumped was 89. The whole organisation is highly professional (the sport has an excellent safety record), and motorised cameras and videos capture your jump on film so that you can astound your friends later.

A J Hackett Bungy, corner of Camp and Shotover St, Queenstown. Tel: (03) 442 4007 or toll-free 0800 286 495. www.ajhackett.com/nz.
It is essential for you to book ahead.

Jet-boating

Jet-boats were invented by the Kiwi engineer and farmer Bill Hamilton to operate on the shallow and otherwise unnavigable rivers of the South Island. Unlike normal boats, the propeller on the jet-boat is on the inside of the hull, driving water out through a nozzle at the rear with tremendous force.

The nozzle also steers the boat, giving it incredible manoeuvrability: jet-boats can execute high-speed, 360-degree turns almost on their own axis. High-speed 'jet-spins', 'flick turns' and other manoeuvres provide thrills and excitement for passengers on rivers such as the Shotover and Kawarau, but the real benefit of jet-boats is that they can venture far into the wilderness up shallow river systems as they can operate in just 10cm (4in) of water.

If you can, take a jet-boat safari up through the beautiful **Dart River Valley** or somewhere similarly remote; you will find jet-boats for hire at many riverside localities throughout the country.

Dart River Safaris, Mull St, Glenorchy. Tel: (03) 442 9992 or toll-free 0800 327 8538. www.dartriver.co.nz.
Huka Jet, Wairakei Park, Taupo. Tel: (07) 374 8572. www.hukajet.co.nz.
Shotover Jet, Gorge Road, Arthurs Point, Queenstown. Tel: (03) 442 8570 or toll-free 0800 746 868. www.shotoverjet.com.
Most jet-boat companies operate daily (except Christmas Day) and year round. Bookings are essential.

Walking

There is no better way to experience New Zealand's wild and beautiful backcountry than by spending a few days walking on one of the many long-distance tracks that traverse the country. Forests, mountains, lakes, beaches, volcanoes – each track has its own special characteristics, most taking two to five days to complete. Tramping, as it's called in New Zealand, is one of the most popular (and certainly one of the best-value) activities for getting away from it all.

The network encompasses more than 100 hiking tracks, although most visitors opt for one of the four main tracks listed below. The best season for walking runs from October to March.

Abel Tasman

Rated the easiest walk of its length in New Zealand, this is a good choice if you have never hiked before and want to give it a go. The track is well marked and well graded and passes beach after beach along a seashore backed by native forests. This is considered to be one of the most beautiful coastal walks in the world, through an area renowned for its mild, sunny weather. Not surprisingly, it is the most popular track in the country; boats also ferry walkers between the beaches.

50km (31 miles), three to four days. Marahau to Totaranui or Wainui, or vice versa. Daily bus connections to/from Nelson. Easy.

A variety of ferns greets walkers in the woods

Kepler

This is the newest and certainly the best-planned hiking track in New Zealand, and was designed to take the pressure off other Fiordland walks; as a result, the Kepler has become a classic in its own right. The track follows a circular route, passing through stunning alpine landscapes of lakes, mountains and beech forests. Steep gradients make this tougher than the Routeburn or Milford.

67km (41½ miles), four days. Start and finish near Te Anau. Difficult.

Milford

This is New Zealand's best-known track, and for this reason is the only one that requires pre-booked hut accommodation.

Although highly regulated (you can walk only in one direction, and must complete it in the time allotted, so there are no allowances made for taking breaks in bad weather), the walk is still worth doing for its spectacular views of alpine meadows, forests and waterfalls – including **Sutherland Falls**, the highest in the country at 580m (1,903ft). Although the track can be rough in places, it is within the capabilities of the averagely fit.
53km (33 miles), three to six days. Lake Te Anau to Milford Sound. Medium. Book well in advance during the peak summer months with the DOC Great Walks Booking Desk in the Fiordland National Park Visitor Centre, Lakefront Drive, Te Anau. Tel: (03) 249 7924. www.doc.govt.nz. Open: summer daily 8.30am–6pm; winter weekdays 8.30am–4.30pm.

Routeburn

A walk from Lake Wakatipu to Upper Hollyford Valley, or vice versa.
See pp142–5.
39km (24 miles), three to four days. Medium.

Other major tracks

The most frequently used tracks in the North Island are the Tongariro Crossing in Tongariro National Park, the shoreline track around Lake Waikaremoana, and the Coromandel State Forest Park Walk.

Popular tracks in the South Island include the Heaphy and Wangapeka in the North-West Nelson Forest Park (which comes within the Kahurangi National Park), the Travers-Sabine Circuit in the Nelson Lakes National Park, and the Rees-Dart, Hollyford and Greenstone-Caples Tracks in Fiordland. The Rakiura Track on Stewart Island is also classified as one of the 'great walks'.

Independent walking

Your first stop for information should be the Department of Conservation (DOC) information centres. The DOC maintains thousands of kilometres of tracks and over 900 huts. The department also publishes a number of useful brochures, including *New Zealand's Walkways* (available free on-line), plus individual brochures on most tramping tracks.
DOC Information Centre Auckland, Ground Floor, Ferry Building, Quay St. Tel: (09) 379 6476. www.doc.govt.nz. Open: Mon–Fri 9.30am–5pm; Sat 10am–3pm (Oct–Apr). Closed: Sun & public holidays.

Guided walks

If you are not used to carrying a large backpack for several days, a guided walk allows you to experience some tracks by staying in privately owned, comfortable huts en route and carrying just a day pack.

Such walks are more costly than going it alone, but may suit inexperienced or more elderly walkers.
Ultimate Hikes offers a range of guided walks, from day hikes to week-long treks,

in the South Island. Tel: (03) 442 8200 or toll-free 0800 659 255 (for the Milford Track); (03) 442 8200 or toll-free 0800 659 255 (for the Routeburn and Greenstone Tracks). www.ultimatehikes.co.nz.
For listings of nationwide hiking companies endorsed by Tourism New Zealand, visit www.newzealand.com

White-water rafting

Given the number of rivers and rapids in New Zealand, it is hardly surprising that rafting is one of the most popular outdoor adventures for visitors. There are more than 50 rafting companies in the country, which between them offer a wide range of trips to suit everyone from beginners to more experienced rafters looking for wild and wet adventures.

The season usually runs from late October to March, although many trips now operate year round, with rafters simply donning thicker wetsuits.

Queenstown is the main focus of rafting in the South Island, with half-day trips available on the nearby Shotover and Kawarau rivers, and two-day expeditions to the beautiful Landsborough River which flows through deep gorges from its source in Mount Cook National Park. The Buller, Clarence, Waimakariri, Rakaia and Rangitata are other well-known rafting rivers in the South Island. The most challenging white-water rafting in the South Island is on the Karamea, a grade 5 river which runs down from the Tasman Mountains in Nelson; you need to go by helicopter to get to the start-point.

In the North Island most rafting takes place on the Mohaka, Rangataiki, Rangitikei and Motu rivers. The Wairoa is also popular, although its grade 5 ride is only possible on 26 days of the year as the river is controlled by hydroelectric schemes. The ultimate rafting sensation in the Rotorua area is the upper Kaituna River (grade 5+), which drops 7m (23ft) over Hinemoa's Steps – the world's highest commercially rafted waterfall.

Buller Adventure Tours
Half-day tours on the Buller River, with spectacular scenery in Buller Gorge.
Buller Gorge Rd, Westport.
Tel: (03) 789 7286 or toll-free 0800 697 286. www.adventuretours.co.nz

Queenstown Rafting
Winners of the 1999 award for best Activity Adventure Operator. You can choose from half-day trips to three-day adventure packages and heli-rafting on the Kawarau, Shotover and Landsborough rivers.
35 Shotover St, Queenstown.
Tel: (03) 442 9792 or toll-free 0800 723 8464. www.rafting.co.nz

River Rats
One of the largest North Island rafting companies, they offer a wide choice of rivers, including the Kaituna.
Te Ngae, Rotorua. Tel: (07) 345 6543 or toll-free 0800 333 900.
www.riverrats.co.nz

The Shotover Jet, Queenstown

Shopping

New Zealand is not renowned for bargain shopping. While there are locally produced goods of excellent quality, these can be fairly pricey: a recent survey showed that thousands of tourists were leaving the country with money still in their wallets because the things they wanted to buy were too expensive. So, be warned that you may have to dig deep for that coveted item. The best buys are sheepskin, crafts and greenstone. For shop opening times, see p185.

What to buy

Arts and crafts

Craftspeople seem to thrive in New Zealand, and if you like hand-crafted items you will be spoilt for choice. Many souvenir shops stock handicrafts, but you can find better bargains by buying directly from studios. In major craft centres such as Nelson, Golden Bay and the Coromandel you can pick up 'Craft Trail' leaflets listing the locations, opening times, as well as specialities of local studios.

Pottery and wood-carvings are perhaps the most widely available products, although you can also find glassware, hand-weaving, metalwork, patchwork, wooden toys, jewellery, bone-carvings, decorative boxes and much more. Traditional and contemporary Maori woodcarvings are also widely available.

Jewellery and other souvenirs made from iridescent *paua* (abalone) shell are also worth looking at. In comparison to elsewhere in the world, greenstone or jade is excellent value, particularly smaller items such as finely carved *tiki* good-luck charms. Larger sculpted pieces, which may take many months to work, can run into thousands of dollars.

TAXES AND SHIPPING

All goods and services are subject to the 12.5 per cent Goods and Services Tax (GST), which is always included in the price displayed. Apart from this unitary tax there are no other local taxes. Visitors cannot reclaim this tax, though if a supplier agrees to export a major item to a visitor's home address, GST will not be charged on either the goods or freight. With some items – sheepskins or fragile crafts such as ceramics – shipping is often more convenient anyway.

In major centres such as Wellington, Auckland, Christchurch, Queenstown and Rotorua, there are duty-free outlets in the downtown areas. Take your airline ticket and passport with you when purchasing goods; the shop then arranges for them to be waiting for you at the airport on the day of your departure.

Clothing and sheepskin

Rugged outdoor clothing (such as jackets and bushwacker hats) is worth looking at, particularly classic designs made with deerskin, sheepskin, leather or suede. Hand-knitted sweaters and other woollen items are expensive but worth splashing out on.

One of the best-known labels for leisurewear is Canterbury of New Zealand, whose colourful, all-cotton rugby shirts are a good buy; other good-quality brands include Jackson Bay, T&Ski and MacKenzie Country Knitwear.

Sheepskin is turned into everything from bedroom slippers to car seat covers and floor rugs; the leading manufacturer is Bowron. Lambskin, luxuriously soft since it has only been shorn once, is particularly popular.

Other specialities

Wines, cheeses, pre-packed Bluff oysters and honey scented with native flowers are further options if you want to take home a taste of New Zealand. CDs and cassettes of Maori songs make appealing souvenirs, and are usually sold at Maori concerts as well as record and souvenir shops.

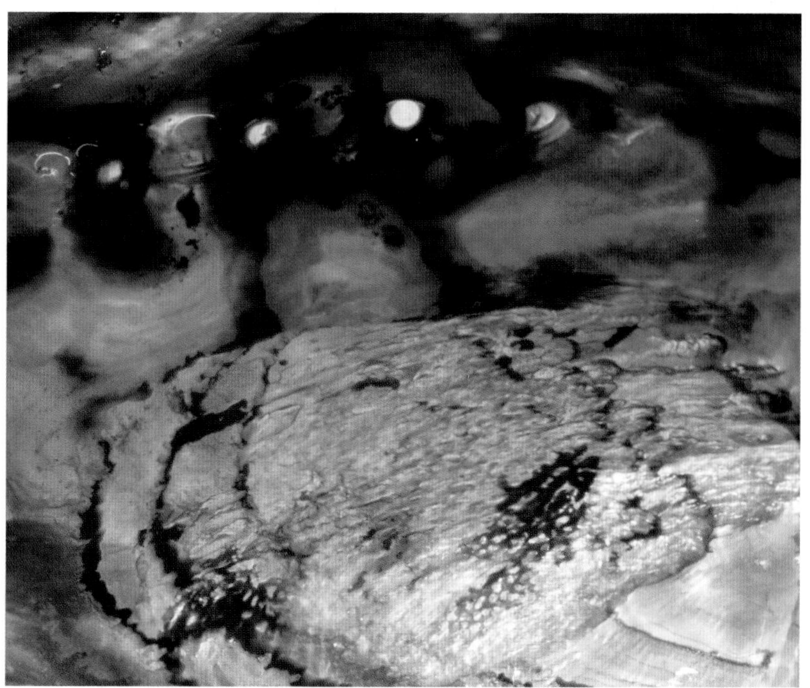

Items made from *paua* shell are good souvenirs

Where to buy
NORTH ISLAND
Auckland

Auckland Museum
Excellent-quality Maori arts and crafts, as well as jewellery and other well-designed souvenirs. Good selection of Maori CDs and tapes.
The Domain. Tel: (09) 309 2580. www.aucklandmuseum.co.nz. Open: daily 10am–5pm.

Karangahape Road (or K Rd)
Straight up the hill from Queen Street, K Rd has an edgy collection of alternative shops and galleries. Southwest of here lies Ponsonby with its historic shopfronts and elegant boutiques.

Parnell
Probably the best up-market shopping area in Auckland, with dozens of high-quality craft shops, art galleries, antique shops and fashion boutiques that spread out into the streets surrounding the quaint shopping arcade known as Parnell Village.
Parnell St and environs.

Queen Street
Auckland's main shopping street, with a mix of department stores, fashion outlets, souvenir shops and jewellers. The side streets on the east side (such as High Street and Vulcan Lane) are worth a look, with interesting bookshops, boutiques and cafés.

Victoria Park Market
A good selection of off-beat arts and crafts, as well as T-shirts and reasonably priced leather and sheepskin goods.
Victoria St West and corner of Wellesley St. Tel: (09) 309 6911. www.victoria-park-market.co.nz. Open: daily 9am–6pm.

Rotorua

As one of the country's premier tourist destinations, Rotorua has numerous souvenir and duty-free shops.

Agrodome
Like Rainbow Springs (*below*), the Agrodome is geared towards a huge throughput of package tourists, and all the usual sheepskin, woollen and leather goods can be purchased here.
Western Rd, Ngongotaha. Tel: (07) 357 1050 or toll-free 0800 339 400. www.agrodome.co.nz. Open: daily 8.30am–5pm.

New Zealand Maori Arts and Crafts Institute
Authentic hand-crafted Maori carvings and woven work from workshops where the traditional styles are taught.
Hemo Rd, Whakarewarewa. Tel: (07) 348 9047. www.nzmaori.co.nz. Open: daily summer 8am–6pm; winter 8am–5pm.

Rainbow Springs
The recently rebuilt international shopping complex here claims to be the largest souvenir shop in New Zealand, and stocks a huge range of items including knitwear, sheepskin, leather goods, bone- and woodcarvings, and opal and *paua* (abalone shell) jewellery.
Fairy Springs Rd, Auckland Highway (SH5). Tel: (07) 350 0440 or toll-free 0800 724 626. Open: daily summer 8am–11pm; winter 8am–5pm.

SOUTH ISLAND

Christchurch

There is a good selection of shops in central downtown Christchurch, including pedestrianised malls.

Arts Centre

The Arts Centre, with its numerous small workshops and galleries, is one of the best places in the South Island for crafts; there is even more choice at the centre's weekend markets.

Arts Centre, Worcester Blvd. Tel: (03) 366 0989. www.artscentre.org.nz. Open: daily (except Christmas Day, Good Friday & Anzac Day morning) 9.30am–5pm. Weekend market open: 10am–4pm.

New Regent Street

One block north of the square (leading off from Gloucester Street) is New Regent Street, a quaint row of pastel-painted shops which formed the first 'shopping mall' in the country when it opened in 1931. You can find crystals, antiquarian books and herbal remedies.

Hokitika

Jade Factory

Exquisite jade carvings, sculptures and jewellery.

41 Weld St. Tel: (03) 755 8007. www.jadefactory.com. Open: daily 9am–7pm (till 6pm in winter). Also stores in Auckland, Rotorua, Christchurch & Queenstown.

Westland Greenstone Ltd

One of the largest processors of greenstone, with a wide range of individual and indigenous designs in jade and *paua* jewellery.

34 Tancred St. Tel: (03) 755 8713. Open: daily 8am–5pm.

Queenstown

Queenstown has an excellent range of shops, and is the only place in New Zealand where major stores and boutiques stay open until 10pm, seven days a week. Jewellery, leatherwork, sheepskin shops, and a huge range of fashion and outdoor clothing stores all lie within a few minutes' walk of each other in the pedestrianised streets parallel to the Mall in the downtown area.

Wellington

The main shopping street is Lambton Quay, with many covered arcades and some small, speciality shops on its north side. Further on, three streets – Willis, Manners and Cuba – all have a similar mix of shops. A good place to look for crafts, posters, clothes and so on is Wakefield Market (corner of Jervois Quay & Taranaki St), which is open Fridays, weekends and public holidays. A good area for craft souvenirs, jewellery, antiques and art galleries is Tinakori Road.

Shopping in Christchurch

Entertainment

New Zealand is a farming country, so every town holds an annual agricultural show – known as A&P, for agricultural and pastoral – that is well worth a look. However, there is much else besides to occupy you when you have had your fill of sightseeing.

Classical music, dance and theatre

The main classical orchestras are the New Zealand Symphony Orchestra (based in Wellington) and the Auckland Philharmonic Orchestra, which give regular concerts from their home bases and in regional centres. The Royal New Zealand Ballet (based in Wellington) also tours extensively, often with visiting soloists. Despite the fact that New Zealand boasts such talented opera stars as Dames Kiri Te Kanawa and Malvina Major, grand opera is staged regionally in only the four main centres. Dame Kiri does, however, sometimes perform at outdoor concerts and other events.

Theatre has proliferated in New Zealand, with many professional and semi-professional theatre groups staging productions in the major centres.

Other entertainment

The most internationally renowned pop group to have come out of New Zealand was Split Enz, now disbanded (although Neil Finn went on to become lead singer and songwriter for Crowded House). Auckland, Wellington, Christchurch and Queenstown are best for live music. Most towns and cities have cinemas, with new films shown soon after their international release.

Maori concerts

Although most Maori concerts are performed principally for the tourist trade, they still present a genuine example of the culture. They are also highly professional, with many of the concert groups touring overseas. A typical performance will start with a *wero* (challenge), followed by a *powhiri* (welcome) and a *hongi* (a greeting that involves the touching of noses), all of which are explained. These introductions will then be followed by songs and dances, such as the *haka* or *poi* (*see pp22–3*). Many concerts are followed by a *hangi* feast.

Daytime concerts are held at the Auckland Domain (*see p33*) and at the Whakarewarewa Thermal Village in

Rotorua (*see pp65–6*). Several large hotels in Rotorua put on concerts, but by far the best way to experience authentic Maori culture is to go to a concert and *hangi* held on a *marae*. The following Maori groups run excellent programmes: **Rotoiti Tours** *Rakeiao Marae, Lake Rotoiti, Rotorua. Tel: (07) 348 8969. www.worldofmaori.co.nz. Courtesy coach pick-up provided.*
Tamaki Maori Village *1220 Hinemaru St, Rotorua. Tel: (07) 349 2999. www.maoriculture.co.nz.*
Te Puia *Whakarewarewa Thermal Valley, Hemo Road, Rotorua. Tel: (07) 348 9047. www.tepuia.com*

Events

New Zealand stages a huge range of events and cultural activities each year, from gumboot-throwing competitions to arts festivals. The best source of information is the Events Calendar at *www.newzealand.com*. Some of the regular annual events include:

January
Annual Yachting Regatta, Auckland.
Summer City Mardi Gras, Wellington.
February
6th: Treaty of Waitangi Celebrations.
1st weekend: Speight Coast to Coast Race.
2nd Sat: NZ International Festival of the Arts, Wellington (biennial – even years).
Last weekend: Devonport Wine and Food Festival, Auckland.
Late Feb: Kapa Haka Fest, Orakei Marai, Auckland.
March
2nd weekend: Wildfoods Festival, Hokitika.
Mid-Mar: New Zealand Cheese Festival, Auckland.
Waiheke Jazz Festival, Auckland.
April
Easter weekend: Silverstone Race to the Sky, Cardrona Valley, Queenstown.
May
1st fortnight: TV2 International Laugh Festival, Wellington.
June
Auckland Winter Festival.
International Car Rally, Auckland.
July
Wellington International Film Festival.
Canterbury Winter Carnival.
August
2nd weekend: Jazz and Blues Festival, Bay of Islands.
Mid-Aug: Queenstown Winter Festival.
September
The Great NZ Craft Show, Christchurch.
Annual Citrus Festival, Te Puke.
Russell Oyster Festival.
October
1st weekend: Kaikoura Seafest.
World Festival of Golf, Canterbury.
Mid-Oct: Wellington International Jazz Festival.
November
Cup Carnival Week, Christchurch.
Rhododendron Festival, Taranaki.
3rd week: Ellersie Flower Show, Botanic Gardens, Manurewa, Auckland.
December
Summertime Festival, Christchurch.

Children

New Zealand is in many ways a family-oriented country, and children will be made to feel welcome almost everywhere. There are no problems with language, strange food or culture shock, and no dangerous animals or poisonous insects! Adequate protection from the sun is absolutely essential as New Zealand has high levels of damaging ultraviolet rays. Supplies of baby foods, nappies and other essentials are widely available, and the water is clean and safe to drink everywhere.

There are plenty of parks and playgrounds where children can run wild, and as well as enjoying purpose-built attractions such as funfairs (the biggest are Splash Planet in Hastings and Rainbow's End in Auckland), they will be enthralled by natural wonders such as volcanoes, glaciers and bubbling, smelly mud pools.

Adventure sports

Older children will enjoy adventure sports such as sea kayaking and river rafting, and some companies offer family discounts. Jet-boating is perfectly safe for kids of any age, and, if you can afford it, a helicopter ride will no doubt prove to be a highlight of the trip. The youngest person ever to bungee jump off the Kawaru Bridge near Queenstown was only seven!

Unless you have considerable experience, hiking with children is not advisable, although you could certainly walk short sections of the Abel Tasman Coastal Track, where there are regular boat shuttles to and from various beaches. There are plenty of short bush walks and nature trails all over the country.

Boat trips

Scenic cruises are very popular. There is a huge choice of such cruises, from old sailing ships in the Bay of Islands to catamarans on the Marlborough Sounds and old steamships on Lakes Taupo, Rotorua and Wakatipu. Many single-day yacht charters from Auckland include stops for swimming, snorkelling and beach picnics.

Museums and science centres

New Zealand has some exceptionally well-designed museum exhibits that make the past come alive in an entertaining way. The Heritage Time Tunnel (*see p108*) at the top of the Gondola in Christchurch, for instance, has volcanoes that blast hot air and a below-decks scene in an immigrant ship that even smells realistic; the

National Maritime Museum (*see pp35–7*) in Auckland also has a convincing mock-up of a ship's interior. Other top spots for children include: Kelly Tarlton's Antarctic Encounter and Underwater World, Auckland (*see p34*); the Sky Tower, Auckland; the International Antarctic Centre, Christchurch (*see p108*); and there is plenty to see at the Air Force Museum, Christchurch (*see p104*) and at the Museum of Transport and Technology, Auckland (*see p35*). But by far the best and most innovative of such centres in New Zealand is Capital Discovery Place, Wellington (*see p84*). The Museum of New Zealand/Te Papa Tongarewa, Wellington (*see p86*), another hugely popular venue, is the country's first national museum and covers every aspect of New Zealand's life – past, present and future.

Swimming

There are opportunities for swimming in the ocean, rivers and lakes almost everywhere in the New Zealand countryside, as well as in swimming pools in most major towns and cities. Swimming outdoors is, however, only practicable from late October to early March – except in the north.

Not all the country's beaches are safe for swimming, and you should always check locally for hazardous conditions. Surf life-savers operate patrols at popular beaches during the summer. If children spend too long near lakeshores in the summer months, they may develop 'duck itch', an unpleasant but harmless irritation caused by a parasite that is carried by ducks.

Wildlife

There are numerous opportunities for getting close to wildlife, particularly on the east coast of the South Island where seal and penguin colonies can be reached after just a short walk. Whale watching (Kaikoura) or swimming with dolphins (Bay of Islands and Whakatane) will provide memorable experiences.

Most wildlife centres have nocturnal houses where you can spot kiwis. If native bird aviaries don't appeal, there are always bigger, more exotic animals in places such as Auckland Zoo, Wellington Zoo and the Orana Wildlife Park (Christchurch), which also have children's farms.

Explore the beaches of Abel Tasman

Sport and leisure

New Zealand is a nation of sports and fitness fanatics, with more than 35 per cent of the population belonging to a sports club of some kind. National teams and individual competitors are followed with considerable pride, and television coverage of sport is extensive. The country has no less than five museums devoted entirely to sport!

Competitive sports

Rugby football is the most popular sport in the country, with more than 119,000 registered players and many more supporters. The national team, the All Blacks, is held in high esteem (the team members are probably better known to most New Zealanders than elected politicians) and its progress in international matches is followed avidly.

During the winter, netball (a sport in which New Zealand has been world champion several times), soccer and hockey are also played. During the summer months, cricket takes over from rugby as the focus of national aspirations abroad. Tennis, squash, basketball and lawn bowls are also very popular.

New Zealanders are also passionate about horse-racing; over 70 tracks around the country feature 'the gallops' by day and 'the trots' by night.

Cycling

With its scenic attractions and uncrowded roads, New Zealand is ideal for cycling – but be warned, distances between destinations can be considerable, and, of course, the country is also fairly mountainous. If you are heading into the hills or off the beaten track, a mountain bike is essential for the unmetalled side roads. There are, as yet, very few dedicated off-road routes. Several local cycle-touring guidebooks are available if you want to go it alone, and mountain bikes can be hired in many resort areas.

Numerous companies all over New Zealand offer guided group tours, from easy day outings and heli-biking trips to two-week-long mountain adventures with meals, accommodation and back-up vehicles. A full list of officially endorsed companies may be found at *www.newzealand.com*, and includes the following:

Active New Zealand
Queenstown. Tours nationwide.
Tel: (03) 450 0414.
www.activenewzealand.com

Adventure South
Christchurch. Tours in the South Island's mountains and national parks. Tel: (03) 942 1222. www.advsouth.co.nz

Back of Beyond
Mt Somers, near Ashburton. Tours in the central South Island. Tel: (03) 303 0940. www.mountainbiking.net.nz

Cycle Safari
29 Finlayson Rd, Hamilton. Cross-water tours in the Rotorua Lakes District and Lake Waikaremoana. Tel: (07) 825 2076. www.cyclesafari.co.nz

Fat Tyre Adventures
Queenstown. Tours in Queenstown area. Tel: toll-free 0800 328 897. www.fat-tyre.co.nz

Fishing

Unpolluted rivers and miles of clean, accessible coastline make New Zealand a fishermen's mecca. Licences for inland fisheries are available from fishing-tackle and sports shops for daily, weekly or monthly periods; sea fishing requires no licence. A special tourist licence, valid for the whole of the country for one month, is also available.

Lake Taupo is a great spot for fishing

The introduction of trout and other species such as salmon and perch has given New Zealand some of the best dry-fly fishing in the world, and reputable and experienced fishing guides can be hired locally. Lake Taupo is the main centre for trout fishing, but numerous rivers and lakes on both islands are also stocked. Quinnat salmon is caught in the rivers on the east coast of the South Island between January and March.

New Zealand is also well known for its big-game fishing, particularly around the east coast of the North Island where marlin, broadbill, shark, yellowfin tuna and other pelagic species abound. The main season runs from January to May.

NZ Professional Fishing Guides Association *provides a full list of accredited fly fishing guides throughout the country. 295 Gladstone Rd, Gisborne. Tel: (06) 867 7874. www.nzpfga.com*

Golf

Golfers will find no shortage of places to play – with over 400 golf courses, New Zealand has more per head of population than anywhere else in the world. Many of the courses are set in beautiful scenery and may even include hazards such as boiling mud pools or sheep! Golf is a year-round activity and visitors are welcome at most clubs.

New Zealand Golf Association
Exchange Place, 5–7 Willeston St, PO Box 11 842, Wellington. Tel: (04) 385 4330. www.nzga.co.nz

Horse-riding

There are numerous opportunities for horse-riding, with half-day, full-day or longer treks available for all abilities. Most stables will supply all gear if necessary. Many country lodges and farmsteads offer their guests horse-riding.

New Zealand Equestrian Federation
Level 4, 3–9 Church St, PO Box 6146, Wellington. Tel: (04) 499 8994. www.nzequestrian.org.nz

Hunting

Whereas it might be frowned upon elsewhere, recreational hunting is considered an important method of controlling the damage to native forests caused by New Zealand's large mammals. A permit is required to hunt in national parks. Some of the world's best deer-stalking is found in New Zealand, with autumn (March to May) being the optimum season. Chamois, thar, goats, pigs, opossums, rabbits, hares and wallabies can also be hunted.

Fish and Game New Zealand *provides information and permits for freshwater fishing and gamebird hunting.*
2 Jarden Mile, Ngauranga, PO Box 13–141, Wellington. Tel: (04) 499 4767. www.fishandgame.org.nz

The **Department of Conservation** *provides hunting permits (and fishing licences for trout fishing in the Taupo region), which can be obtained at local DOC offices. For a full list of offices contact the Auckland Area Office, North Head Historic Reserve, 18 Takarunga Rd, Devonport. Tel: (09) 445 9142. www.doc.govt.nz*

Skiing

New Zealand is proud of its skiing facilities. Because of the low prices of lift passes, lessons, ski hire and so on, one in every ten New Zealanders can ski. And since the cost of reaching virgin, high-altitude runs by helicopter is very reasonable, heli-skiing is also very popular. There are 25 ski fields, mostly along the Southern Alps.

The biggest winter resort is Queenstown: the nearby Coronet Peak and Remarkables ski fields have a wide variety of runs, all with fabulous views. The Cardrona and Treble Cone ski fields near Wanaka offer terrains suitable for all skiers, beginners or advanced.

Mount Hutt, inland from Christchurch, has the longest season in the country (late May–early November); other nearby fields include Porter Heights, Mount Dobson, Ohau, and the country's newest ski area, Mount Lyford.

On the North Island, the main ski fields are Whakapapa and Turoa, both on the volcanic slopes of Mt Ruapehu, in Tongariro National Park. See *www.newzealand.com*, Tourism New Zealand's official website, for more details.

Watersports

With its numerous lakes and rivers, and over 10,000km (6,214 miles) of coastline, New Zealand has tremendous opportunities for virtually every kind of watersport. Apart from jet-boating and rafting (*see p147 & pp150–51*), canoeing and kayaking are also popular, particularly sea kayaking in the sheltered waters of the Bay of Islands, the Marlborough Sounds and along the coast of Abel Tasman National Park. One of the most popular canoeing rivers is the Whanganui, which has both rapids and long stretches of calm water. Rentals and/or organised tours are available in all these locations.

Surfing is possible all year round. In the North Island, the most frequented beaches are in the Auckland area, Raglan (west of Hamilton), around New Plymouth, Gisborne, and Mount Manganui in the Bay of Plenty. In the South Island, the beaches near Dunedin, Kaikoura and Westport are popular.

Scuba diving takes place mostly off the North Island where the sea is warmer, especially the Poor Knights Marine Reserve off Whangarei, which supports a wide variety of marine life. Other good spots include the Bay of Islands Maritime Park (where the wreck of the Greenpeace ship *Rainbow Warrior* was resunk after it was destroyed by the French secret service in Auckland Harbour), Marlborough Sounds, the Hauraki Gulf, Stewart Island and even Fiordland.

See *www.newzealand.com* for information and company listings.

Yachting

Yachting seems to be in the lifeblood of most New Zealanders. Charter boats of all kinds are available to visitors. The classic sailing areas include the Hauraki Gulf, Bay of Islands, Marlborough Sounds and Coromandel Peninsula.

The prestigious America's Cup, the oldest sporting trophy in the world, was won in 1995 by Team New Zealand, who went on to become the only non-USA syndicate to successfully defend their title in 2000.

Yachting New Zealand
85 Westhaven Drive, Westhaven Marina.
Tel: (09) 361 1471.
www.yachtingnz.org.nz

Lakes and harbours present numerous opportunities for messing about in boats

Food and drink

It has become something of a cliché to say that New Zealand has witnessed a 'culinary revolution' in recent years; nonetheless, this is true. You might still find plenty of stodgy food, meat pies and overdone steaks, but there are also hundreds of restaurants, wine bars and hotels where you can eat the best local produce cooked with imagination and flair.

Natural ingredients

The raw ingredients have always been here, and it was only a matter of time before Kiwi chefs developed their own distinctive cuisine. The rich pasturelands and mild climate produce excellent beef and lamb, and deer are now also farmed extensively (local venison appears on menus as 'cervena', and has a much milder, less gamey taste than wild venison). Dairy products such as butter, cheese, milk, yoghurt and cream have always been of top quality.

New Zealanders are particularly partial to what the Maori call *kai-moana* (meaning 'food from the sea'), and some of the best eating fish include blue cod, snapper, orange roughy, John Dory, *tarakihi* and *hapuka* (grouper). Shellfish are plentiful, and include rock lobsters (known as crayfish), scallops, Bluff oysters and green-lipped mussels. Whitebait is a much-prized delicacy, particularly on the west coast, usually served in fritters or sandwiches. You will also find salmon on the menu, but never trout, as it is illegal to buy or sell it.

Fresh fruit and vegetables grow in abundance, and apart from the usual standards such as apples, apricots, cherries, grapes, peaches, pears, nectarines, raspberries and strawberries, you should also try boysenberries, feijoas and tamarillos – not forgetting, of course, the ubiquitous kiwifruit.

For the sweet-toothed, New Zealand has excellent ice creams, flans and pastries, as well as the national dessert of pavlova, a rich concoction of meringue, whipped cream and fresh fruit.

Eating places

Almost every town and village has at least one tea shop serving refreshments and snacks. If you are in the middle of nowhere, the worst you can expect are plain meat pies and dry, lifeless sandwiches, but elsewhere, pies, scones, pastries and sandwiches are often fresh, home-made and quite delicious.

Take-aways all over the country churn out fish and chips, pies and the like, often highly variable in quality. Pub food follows more or less the same format, although in cities and tourist areas some pubs have evolved into far more trendy places where you can get a decent meal in civilised surroundings.

Restaurants are either fully licensed (selling wines and spirits), licensed (wine and beer only) or BYO (bring your own alcohol, in which case a small corkage charge is added to the bill); some are both licensed and BYO. Wine bars and licensed cafés have also proliferated in recent years, and you will find plenty of places where you can enjoy a meal and a drink outdoors at pavement tables, Mediterranean-style.

Ethnic cuisine has had its impact and, although Chinese take-aways are by far the most frequented, there are also Greek, Italian, Mexican, Thai and Indian restaurants.

Vegetarian food is widely available and usually very good.

The kiwifruit is just one of numerous succulent fruits which thrive in New Zealand soil

New Zealand wines are now exported worldwide

Maori feasts

You should try a Maori *hangi* at least once. This is a feast of meat, seafood and vegetables (including the delicious *kumara*, or sweet potato, a Maori staple) steamed on heated stones in an 'earthen oven' (the *hangi*). The best *hangi* are those that follow an authentic Maori concert, although some hotels offer their own versions.

Beer and wines

Beer is practically the national drink, and the New Zealand lager, Steinlager, has won many international awards. Lion and DB are the two main brands served in pubs, but recently there has been a proliferation of 'boutique' or 'micro' breweries that produce excellent beers in small quantities.

In recent years, New Zealand wines have begun gaining international renown. The first vines were planted by the British Resident, James Busby, in his back garden at Waitangi in the 1840s, but it has only been during the last decade that the New Zealand wine industry has come of age.

White wines

New Zealand's relatively cool climate is well adapted to vine-growing, with the long autumn giving the grapes a chance to ripen slowly, concentrating their flavour to the full.

These conditions are ideally suited to Sauvignon Blanc, the slightly tart, 'grassy' grape which originates in France's Loire Valley. Nearly 60 per cent of Sauvignon comes from the Marlborough region.

The Chardonnay grape has also done very well here, producing a subtle, full-bodied wine. Gisborne is one of the prime Chardonnay areas, and the local wine-growers have many medals to their credit. Other successful white varieties are Gewürztraminer, dry Riesling and Müller-Thurgau.

WINE TRAILS

In the major wine-growing areas, local tourist offices provide 'Wine Trail' brochures detailing the locations and opening hours of vineyards you can visit to taste and buy wines.

Red wines

Although New Zealand is well known for its white wines, progress has been slower with the reds. However, Cabernet Sauvignon seems to have found a natural home in the Hawke's Bay area. Pinot Noir, a notoriously fickle variety, is also doing well in the Martinborough district north of Wellington and in Central Otago.

Vines near Napier on North Island

Where to eat

For a comprehensive list of restaurants, cafés and bars, along with customer reviews, visit *www.dineout.co.nz.* See *www.menus.co.nz* for the most highly recommended eating spots in Auckland and Wellington.

In the following list of selected restaurants, the star ratings indicate the approximate cost of a meal for one person, not including drinks:

★	up to NZ$20
★★	NZ$20–30
★★★	Over NZ$30

NORTH ISLAND

Auckland

Kermadec ★★★
Fine seafood restaurant with Polynesian décor serving excellent fish and traditional fare.
1st floor, Quay St.
Tel: (09) 309 0412.
www.kermadec.co.nz

The Occidental ★★
Belgian bar serving good mussels and an excellent range of beers and wine.
8 Vulcan Lane.
Tel: (09) 300 6226.

Tony's on Lorne St ★★/★★★
Popular steakhouse and seafood restaurant with a wide selection of perfectly cooked cuts. Also lunches and other meals available.
32 Lorne St.
Tel: (09) 373 2138.
www.tonyslornestreet.com

Paihia

The Sugar Boat ★★★
Stylish cocktail bar and restaurant on board a historic sugar lighter. Particularly popular for fish and seafood dishes. Licensed.
Waitangi Bridge.
Tel: (09) 402 7018.
www.sugarboat.co.nz

Tides ★★
Homely bistro specialising in venison, mussels, fresh fish and lamb dishes. Licensed.
Williams Rd.
Tel: (09) 402 7557.

Rotorua

Cableway Restaurant & Bar at Skyline Skyrides ★★★
Incredible views, excellent lunch and dinner buffets with a particularly extensive seafood selection and tasty desserts. Freshly prepared, innovative New Zealand and fusion dishes.
185 Fairy Springs Rd.
Tel: (07) 347 0027.

Capers Epicurean ★/★★
Award-winning café with an excellent and extensive menu for breakfast, lunch and dinner (from kumara wraps to salad and lasagne), great coffee, and a children's play and video area.
1181 Eruera St.
Tel: (07) 348 8818.
www.capers.co.nz

Mitas Restaurant ★★
The best of 'East meets West'. Award-winning, authentic Indonesian cuisine. Licensed.
1114 Tutanekai St.
Tel: (07) 349 6482.

Mr India ★★
A family-owned chain across the lower North Island. Delicious *tandoori* cuisine, coupled with good service.
1161 Amohau St.
Tel: (07) 349 4940.

Pig & Whistle City Bar ★★
Serves generous portions of food and brews its

own ales. Also offers live entertainment on Friday and Saturday evenings.
Corner of Haupapa & Tutanekai sts.
Tel: (07) 347 3025.
www.pigandwhistle.co.nz

Relish ★★/★★★
Fashionable, modern café serving imaginative fusion food at reasonable rates.
1149 Tutanekai Street.
Tel: (07) 343 9195.

Sirocco Bar Café ★/★★
Cosy eating-house with a trendy, Mediterranean-style atmosphere. Serves a variety of bar snacks (*nachos*, sandwiches, soups) and main-course pasta, seafood and salads. Delicious desserts and good coffee. Licensed. Good value.
1280 Eruera St.
Tel: (07) 347 3388.

Taupo

The Bach ★★★
Award-winning restaurant with good food, gorgeous views of Lake Taupo, and an impressive and extensive wine list. Licensed.
2 Pataka Rd.
Tel: (07) 378 7856.
www.thebach.co.nz

Huka Vineyard Restaurant ★★★
Set among two acres of Pinot Noir grapes, lovely food and good wine, indoor or outdoor dining with fabulous views of the Lake Taupo area. Licensed.
56 Huka Falls Rd.
Tel: (07) 377 2326.

Lotus Thai ★★
Popular Thai restaurant serving great curries and stir-fries in generous portions.
137 Tongariro St.
Tel: (07) 376 9497.

Villino ★★★
Sophisticated downtown eatery serving eclectic mix of European and Pacific dishes.
45 Horomatangi St.
Tel: (07) 377 4478.
www.villino.co.nz

Wellington

The Backbencher Pub ★★/★★★
Light, airy pub opposite Parliament with a jovial atmosphere (plenty of political cartoons and so on). A fun theme pub with a good range of tasty dishes.
34 Molesworth St.
Tel: (04) 472 3065.

Floriditas ★★/★★★
Smart, stylish place serving quality bistro fare at very reasonable rates.
161 Cuba St.
Tel: (04) 381 2212.

Logan Brown ★★★
Well-established restaurant set in a 1920s bank chamber offering international fare.
192 Cuba St.
Tel: (04) 801 5114
www.loganbrown.co.nz

SOUTH ISLAND

Christchurch

Canterbury Tales ★★★
Located in the city's top hotel, this elegant, multi award-winning restaurant (with tapestries depicting Chaucerian scenes on the walls) has an extensive menu and is deservedly popular. Bookings essential.
Crowne Plaza Christchurch, corner of Durham & Kilmore sts.
Tel: (03) 365 7799.

Dux de Lux ★★
Popular restaurant and micro-brewery serving great vegetarian and seafood dishes with indoor and outdoor seating. Has its own

range of house-brewed beers.
Corner of Hereford & Montreal sts.
Tel: (03) 366 6919.

Mainstreet Vegetarian Café & Bar ★/★★
Rated as one of the best vegetarian restaurants in New Zealand, with tasty and imaginative food at reasonable prices. Licensed and BYO.
840 Colombo St.
Tel: (03) 365 0421.

Retour ★★★
Intimate dining in a historic band rotunda. The beautiful riverside setting is matched by an excellent European-style menu. Licensed.
Band Rotunda, Cambridge Tce.
Tel: (03) 365 2888.
www.retour.co.nz

Willowbank ★★/★★★
This excellent licensed restaurant is part of a wildlife reserve (*see p109*), so you can enjoy views of the gardens and wildlife while you sample traditional New Zealand dishes and desserts. Guided tours are free to diners, and offer the chance to see kiwis and other nocturnal species in their natural (floodlit) bush habitat.
Willowbank Wildlife Reserve, Hussey Rd.
Tel: (03) 359 6226.
www.willowbank.co.nz

Dunedin

Bell Pepper Blues ★★★
Fine dining venue producing gourmet dishes, good bread and sumptuous desserts, all presented and served excellently.
474 Princes St.
Tel: (03) 474 0973.

High Tide ★★★
Licensed waterfront restaurant with lovely harbour views, good seafood and meat dishes.
29 Kitchener St.
Tel: (03) 477 9784.
www.hightide.co.nz

Rhubarb ★/★★
Popular licensed café serving great deli food and snacks, excellent coffee and a good range of wines, which you can purchase from the attached wine shop.
299 Highgate, Roslyn.
Tel: (03) 477 2555.

Queenstown

Boardwalk ★★★
Swish seafood restaurant serving freshly caught food in imaginative ways. Great views and quite a dressy crowd.
1st floor, Steamer Wharf.
Tel: (03) 442 5630.

The Cow ★/★★
Very cosy and popular pizza and spaghetti house in an old stone building, with a roaring fire. Book in advance or expect a long wait.
Cow Lane.
Tel: (03) 442 8588.
Open: noon–late hours.

Fishbone Bar & Grill ★★/★★★
Good seafood and fish dishes in an unpretentious, café-style setting. Oysters, mussels, calamari, crayfish, fish fillets, and so on, are served in generous portions, so go with a hearty appetite if you want more than one course.
7 Beach St.
Tel: (03) 442 6768.
www.fishbonequeenstown.co.nz

Speights Ale House ★★
Good pub food, generous portions at a reasonable

price in a relaxed atmosphere.
Corner of Stanley & Ballarat sts.
Tel: (03) 441 3065.
Other Ale Houses in Auckland, Wellington, Napier, Christchurch, Timaru and Dunedin.

Tatler ★★★
Centrally located, cosmopolitan place well known for its traditional New Zealand dishes, lively atmosphere and live jazz.
5 The Mall.
Tel: (03) 442 8372.

A rural restaurant near Arrowtown, South Island

Hotels and accommodation

New Zealand has a huge range of accommodation to suit every budget, ranging from campsites in national parks to stylish country retreats and smart city business hotels. There is rarely a problem, even in the most remote location, of finding a clean, comfortable room, although during the peak summer season (mid-December to January) you may need to telephone ahead to make reservations in popular tourist centres such as Rotorua and Queenstown.

Advance reservations are also necessary for up-market country lodges and places with very limited accommodation options, such as the Mount Cook National Park.

One of the more useful publications, covering numerous options all over the country, is the *AA New Zealand Accommodation Guide,* which has over 3,000 listings of hotels, motels, holiday parks, camping grounds and backpackers. It is available in shops for around $10, or you can access the information on the Automobile Association's comprehensive website, *www.aatravel.co.nz.* A classification system for accommodation, developed jointly by the tourism board and the New Zealand AA, has been introduced under the 'Qualmark' logo, by which hotels and all other lodgings are graded with a one- to five-star rating.

Luxury hotels

International chain hotels such as Sheraton, Regent and Hyatt are found in the major cities and resorts, alongside locally owned hotel chains such as the Pacific Park Group and Scenic Circle Hotels. Many of the prime tourist hotels in the country that were once part of the government-owned Tourist Hotel Corporation are now operated by Southern Pacific Hotels. The cost of a room in an international-standard hotel ranges from around NZ$250 to over NZ$1,000 a night for deluxe suites.

Retreats and sporting lodges

Wilderness hideaways are something of a New Zealand speciality, and if your budget allows it, you should certainly try to stay in one of these exclusive, highly individual retreats for a few days. Exceptionally high standards of accommodation, coupled with good food, plenty of atmosphere and first-class facilities, are the hallmarks of this type of lodge. Many concentrate on hunting and fishing, with professional guides on tap (the world-renowned

Huka Lodge and Tongariro Lodge, both near Lake Taupo, are sports-oriented), while others are remarkable for their beautiful natural surroundings – such as the Puka Park Lodge in the Coromandel and Moose Lodge on Lake Rotoiti. Around two dozen lodges are described in *Lodges of New Zealand*, the New Zealand Lodges Association catalogue, copies of which can be downloaded or requested online at *www.lodgesofnz.co.nz*

Motor inns, motels and other hotels

Although there is quite a lot of overlap between these categories, motor inns usually have more facilities than motels, with a house bar, swimming pool and licensed restaurant. They include chains such as Flag Hotels, Best Western, Quality Inns and Manor Motor Inns. Expect to pay NZ$80–200 per night.

Motels are located everywhere and provide one of the best options for mid-market, independent travellers. The clean, comfortable units usually have one or more bedrooms, a lounge and a reasonably well-equipped kitchen. Some also have swimming pools, spa pools, in-house video channels, laundry rooms and other facilities. You can often find motel rooms from NZ$70 in the off season. Many motels are affiliated to booking chains, as at Jason's, Flag Hotels and Best Western.

New Zealand also has numerous independent hotels, often older buildings in town or city centres. Budget rooms in these hotels are invariably one of the cheapest options (apart from hostels or backpacker accommodation), costing from around NZ$40–50. However, standards vary widely and at these prices your room is unlikely to have a private bathroom. Some historic hotels (such as the Brian Boru in Thames) have been renovated to higher standards and still represent good value for money.

Accommodation throughout the country is covered in the free accommodation guide *Jason's Motels and Motor Lodges*, which can be ordered online at *www.jasons.com*, or picked up from listed properties.

Guesthouses and bed and breakfast accommodation

Staying in a private guesthouse or B&B is a good way to meet people and find out about the locality. Again, standards vary widely: a room in a basic guesthouse costs from NZ$50 per person, while one in a more comfortable B&B establishment where breakfast (usually huge!) is included will set you back around NZ$80–100 per person. The New Zealand *Bed & Breakfast Book* and its associated website, *www.bnb.co.nz*, are good sources.

Farmstays and homestays

The difference between farmstays and B&Bs is that at the former you usually get the chance to take part in day-to-day activities and learn about the Kiwi way of life; you will be staying in a real family home and will usually share home-cooked meals with your hosts.

On farmstays, you can help out with activities such as shearing and milking, and a range of other outdoor activities (bush-walking, fishing, cycling and so on) is usually available. Homestays are an urban version of the farmstay.

An up-market variation on farmstays is high-country sheep stations; these have purpose-built facilities where you can stay in complete luxury and take part in almost anything you want, from hunting expeditions to heli-skiing. Some (such as the Mount Hutt Station Resort) even have international-standard restaurants and conference facilities!

You can arrange farmstay accommodation for just one night or for a whole holiday, and your room may either be in the family home or in a separate unit or farm cottage. Rates start as low as NZ$30–40 for shared, self-catering units, reaching around NZ$80–120 for full board and rooms with private facilities. There are several agencies which specialise in bookings:

Rural Holidays New Zealand Ltd
PO Box 2155, Christchurch.
Tel: (03) 355 6218.
www.ruralholidays.co.nz

New Zealand Farm Holidays Ltd
PO Box 74, Kumeu, Auckland.
Tel: (09) 412 9649 or toll-free 0800 803 276. www.nzfarmholidays.co.nz

Hostels and backpacker accommodation

Hostels are as common in New Zealand as motels, providing clean, basic accommodation almost everywhere tourists are likely to go – and a few more places besides. While there are numerous 'official' hostels (run by the YHA, YMCA and YWCA), there are also hundreds more private hostels – usually called 'backpackers'.

Gone are the days of segregated dormitories and lights out by 10pm: hostels now have private rooms as well as a more liberal attitude. Communal facilities usually include kitchens, lounge areas, laundries and so on, and although you may sometimes have to provide your own bedding this can often be hired for a small charge. Nightly costs are around NZ$15–25 for a dormitory bed.

Numerous guides and information booklets are available from information centres and hostels, including the *BBH Backpacker Accommodation Guide*, which lists over 350 hostels and can also be ordered online for free at *www.bbh.co.nz*. The website also provides hostel listings and customer reviews, as does *www.thebackpacker.net*

Camping and motorcamps

There are well-equipped campsites all over the country. Some also have cabins and/or 'tourist flats' attached. Campsite costs start at around NZ$10–14 per adult for non-powered tent sites.

The Holiday Accommodation Parks of New Zealand (HAPNZ) directory, *Holiday Accommodation Parks*, gives details of 300 sites operated by its members, who have to meet certain minimum standards. The printed directory is available from visitor centres, HAPNZ parks, or directly from HAPNZ, *PO Box 394, Paraparaumu. Tel: (04) 298 3283. www.holidayparks.co.nz*

The *AA New Zealand Accommodation Guide* offers detailed listings of motor camps and caravan parks (*see p172*).

The Department of Conservation (DOC) maintains a network of huts and campsites in national parks and other wilderness areas. Facilities range from the basic minimum to fully serviced campsites with hot showers, laundry facilities and lighting. Costs are minimal (typically NZ$3–10), and the informal sites are free. A full list of locations and facilities is available at any DOC Visitor Centre, or from the DOC Information Centre in Auckland, *Ground Floor, Ferry Building, Quay Street. Tel: (09) 379 6476. www.doc.govt.nz*

A camper van will give you the flexibility of your own home on wheels

On business

Since the mid-1980s, the New Zealand economy has undergone a programme of wide-ranging reforms designed to create an open, more competitive business environment. Economic growth in the 1980s remained sluggish as the reforms were pushed through by successive governments but by 1994 had risen to 7 per cent per annum. In 1997 there was again a recession following a drought and downturn in tourism. Since 1998, however, the economy has been revived.

Business and investment environment

Foreign investors are welcomed in New Zealand, particularly in sectors contributing to foreign exchange earnings such as tourism and the export of locally manufactured processed goods. Businesses are now subject to much less regulation than they used to be, and the transfer of funds in and out of the country is not restricted. The sale of major national assets to foreign investors has been encouraged; there are no ceilings on the level of non-resident ownership of privatised state enterprises.

Incentives are sometimes available to foreign investors, and investment is widely promoted through bodies such as Tourism New Zealand and New Zealand Trade and Enterprise. Foreign investment is monitored and controlled by the Overseas Investment Office (OIO), but consent is not required for investments below a value threshold of NZ$100 million – unless they are related to broadcasting, commercial fishing or rural land. Stock exchanges operate in Auckland, Wellington, Christchurch and Dunedin.

Business etiquette

New Zealand has a fast-growing entrepreneurial sector with a highly positive outlook on the economic future. You will generally find the people are helpful and efficient.

Business hours

Offices and businesses operate Monday to Friday, 8.30am–5pm. Trading banks are open Monday to Friday, 9.30am–4.30pm.

Communications

(*See* Telephones *on pp188–9* and Post *on pp185–6.*) Internet cafés are found in all cities and large towns, and conference calls and satellite links can easily be arranged. Luxury hotel chains are equipped with modern business facilities.

Conferences

The largest conference centres have single-room capacities of around 3,000 or more, and include the North Shore Events Centre in Auckland (4,765), the SKYCITY Auckland Convention Centre (3,491), the TelstraClear Pacific Events Centre in Auckland (3,000), the Auckland Showgrounds (3,000), the Mystery Creek Events Centre in Hamilton (8,000), the Energy Events Centre in Rotorua (4,000) and Arena Manawatu in Palmerston North (3,000). The largest South Island venues are the Christchurch Convention Centre (2,584) and the Dunedin Centre (2,700). Hotels such as the Carlton, Sheraton and Hyatt in Auckland have facilities for over 1,000 people. Professional Conference Organisers (PCOs) are available to help plan and manage conventions.

Wellington is New Zealand's business capital

Further details can be had from **Conventions and Incentives New Zealand**, *PO Box 331202, Takapuna, Auckland. Tel: (09) 486 4128; fax: (09) 486 4126. www.conventionsnz.co.nz*

Secretarial services

A full range of secretarial and business services is available in the main cities. Hotels catering specifically for executive travellers, such as the Regent in Auckland, have business centres with all the usual facilities.

Further information

Ministry of Foreign Affairs and Trade
195 Lambton Quay, Wellington, New Zealand. Tel: (04) 439 8000. www.mfat.govt.nz

New Zealand Trade and Enterprise is the economic development agency of the New Zealand government.
Level 11, ANZ Centre, 23–29 Albert St, Auckland. Tel: (09) 366 4768. www.nzte.govt.nz

Overseas Investment Office administers the New Zealand government's foreign investment policies.
160 Lambton Quay, Private Box 5501, Wellington. Tel: (04) 462 4490. www.oio.linz.govt.nz

Tourism New Zealand is the country's tourism board providing information for would-be investors and business people, as well as for visitors.
Level 16, 80 The Terrace, Wellington. Tel: (04) 917 5400. www.newzealand.com

Practical guide

Arriving

By air

Auckland is the main international gateway for passengers arriving in New Zealand, although increasing numbers of airlines are also flying into Christchurch in the South Island. Wellington only handles flights to and from Australia. Air New Zealand, the national carrier, has flights to Australia, Japan, Singapore, Malaysia, Hong Kong, Taiwan, the USA and Europe, either directly or via the Pacific Islands. Around 20 international airlines operate scheduled services to New Zealand, with a further 10 operating on a code-share basis.

Auckland's international terminal has all the usual visitor facilities and information centres for accommodation reservations, sightseeing and onward travel arrangements. Special elevators and toilet facilities are available for the disabled. Auckland airport (AKL) lies 22km (13½ miles) from the city centre, and taxis are fairly expensive (between NZ$50–55). Cheaper options are the **Airbus** (*www.airbus.co.nz*), which calls in at most major hotels and backpackers in Auckland City every 20 minutes and costs NZ$15 one way, or the **Super Shuttle** (*www.supershuttle.co.nz*), a door-to-door service that can be booked in advance or at the Visitor Information Desk at the airport, and costs NZ$26 one way. Christchurch (10km/6 miles northwest) and Wellington (8km/5 miles southeast) airports have similar facilities.

An airport departure tax of NZ$25 is payable by all passengers leaving on international flights.

By sea

There are no regular passenger services, but some round-the-world cruises call in at New Zealand. Arriving by yacht is a distinct possibility, since many cruising yachts take on casual crews at various points in the South Pacific before visiting New Zealand.

Customs

There are no exchange controls or restrictions on the import or export of currency. Aside from personal effects, visitors are allowed to bring in 200 cigarettes, 250g tobacco or 50 cigars, three bottles of spirits and 4.5 litres of wine or beer (full details at *www.customs.govt.nz*).

New Zealand has remained largely free of most plant and animal diseases, and there are strict controls on the import of foodstuffs and plant and animal material. If you are carrying walking boots, these may be confiscated, but returned to you cleaned!

If you are planning to go fishing, you may bring your own rods, but lures or flies containing feathers will need to be fumigated. Hunters should check firearms regulations with their nearest embassy before departure (*see p181*), but in general, hunting rifles may be brought in. A firearms permit is compulsory, obtainable from the police after a declaration to customs officers upon arrival.

The import of narcotics is prohibited, and sniffer dogs are used regularly in arrival halls.

Documents

No vaccination certificates are necessary. Passports must be valid for at least three months beyond your intended departure date. Visitors may be granted entry for up to three months, although this can be extended for up to a year for genuine tourists. Visitors must hold fully paid onward or return tickets, and sufficient funds to keep themselves while in the country. Everybody has to complete an arrival card. Visas are normally only required for visitors intending to work or study, or if you are being sponsored during your visit by a friend, relative or business organisation.

Camping

Camping may be permitted on any suitable public open space (apart from those designated 'No Camping') or on private property subject to the owners' permission. For details on campsites, *see pp174–5.*

Children

See pp158–9.

Climate

The seasons in New Zealand are the reverse of those in the Northern Hemisphere: summer runs from December to February, autumn from March to May, winter from June to August, and spring from September to November. However, seasonal variations are not extreme, and a mild winter can often lead to spring growths appearing at the end of July; conversely, autumn weather often carries over well into June in northerly latitudes.

Because the sun is in the northern sky, temperatures are highest in the far north (where summers are subtropical) and lowest in the far south (where winters are closer to subantarctic, but only for short periods). Average daily sunshine figures are seven to eight hours in summer, and four to five hours in winter. Most places get around 2,000 hours of sunshine a year, with the north of the North Island and the north of the South Island slightly above average, with around 2,350 hours or more.

Rainfall is spread fairly evenly throughout the year, averaging 600 to 1,200mm (23½ to 47in). The prevailing winds are westerly, and the backbone of mountains, which runs right through the country, ensures that the western side therefore receives a much higher rainfall than eastern areas; this is particularly marked in the South Island, where the altitude of the Southern Alps means that rain falls on the western coast almost constantly. The highest rainfall is in Fiordland, and although it doesn't rain every day here it does tend to bucket it down. Snow falls on the mountains and hills (particularly in the South Island) during winter.

Auckland and the far north have the hottest and most humid summers, while those around Marlborough and Nelson are comfortably hot and dry. The coldest winters and hottest summers are found in central Otago. Wellington is exposed to southerly winds off Cook Strait (which keep the temperature down all year), as well as occasional gales.

Although seasonal variations aren't dramatic, the weather is highly changeable and may alter several times during the course of the day in any one place, so be prepared for both rain and sun almost all year round. When the sun does shine (even behind cloud cover), it can burn very quickly (*see p28*).

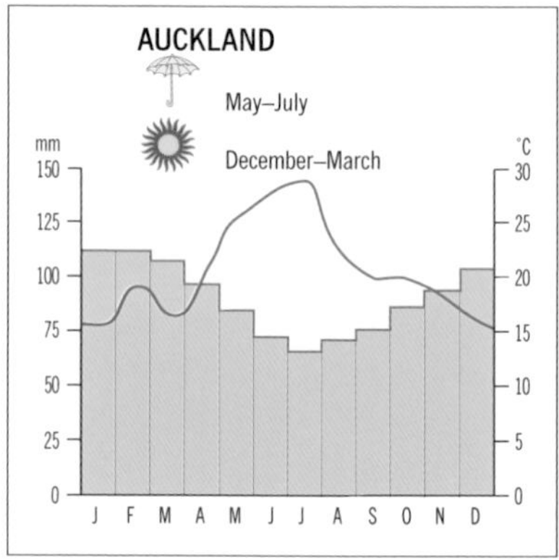

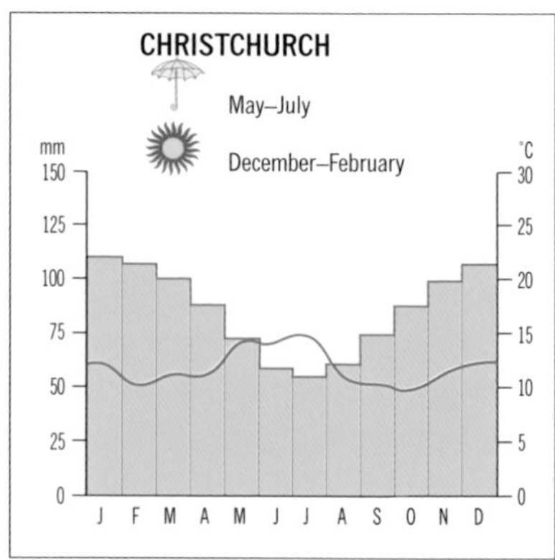

WEATHER CONVERSION CHART

25.4mm = 1 inch

°F = 1.8 × °C + 32

Conversion tables

Clothes and shoe sizes in New Zealand follow the standard sizes used in the UK (*see opposite*).

Crime

Although New Zealand doesn't have a high level of serious crime, there has been a noticeable increase in recent years in assault, rape and petty theft.

Take the same precautions you would anywhere else: avoid dark city backstreets at night; don't leave valuables on view in parked cars; don't leave your car unlocked; make use of hotel safes; and, finally, make sure you are fully insured for loss or damage.

Electricity

The electricity supply is 230–240 volts/ 50 hertz. Hotels and motels provide 110-volt AC sockets for shavers only (rated at 20 watts). For all other equipment you need an adaptor for flat, three- or two-pin plugs (readily available in major hardware stores), but check that it can operate on 230–240 volts first.

Embassies and consulates

New Zealand embassies overseas

Australia *Commonwealth Avenue, Canberra, ACT 2600. Consulate: Tel: (612) 6270 4211.*

Canada *Metropolitan House, Suite 727, 99 Bank Street, Ottawa, Ontario KIP 6G3. Tel: (613) 238 5991.*

UK *New Zealand House, 80 Haymarket, London SW1Y 4TQ. Tel: (020) 7930 8422.*

USA *37 Observatory Circle NW, Washington, DC 20008. Tel: (202) 328 4800.* There are also consulates across the USA.

For a full listing of NZ embassies and consulates in other countries, visit *www.nzembassy.com*

Foreign representation in New Zealand

American Embassy *29 Fitzherbert Terrace, Wellington. Tel: (04) 473 6411.*

Australian High Commission *72 Hobson St, Thorndon, Wellington. Tel: (04) 498 7103. www.australia.org.nz*

British High Commission *44 Hill St, Thorndon, Wellington. Tel: (04) 924 2888. www.britain.org.nz*

Canadian High Commission *Level 11, 125 The Terrace, Wellington. Tel: (04) 473 9577.*

Irish Consulate *6th Floor, 18 Shortland St, Auckland. Tel: (09) 977 2252.*

Emergency telephone numbers

Dial *111* and ask for police, fire or ambulance.

CONVERSION TABLE

FROM	TO	MULTIPLY BY
Inches	Centimetres	2.54
Feet	Metres	0.3048
Yards	Metres	0.9144
Miles	Kilometres	1.6090
Acres	Hectares	0.4047
Gallons	Litres	4.5460
Ounces	Grams	28.35
Pounds	Grams	453.6
Pounds	Kilograms	0.4536
Tons	Tonnes	1.0160

To convert back, for example from centimetres to inches, divide by the number in the third column.

MEN'S SUITS

UK	36	38	40	42	44	46	48
Rest of Europe	46	48	50	52	54	56	58
USA	36	38	40	42	44	46	48

DRESS SIZES

UK	8	10	12	14	16	18
France	36	38	40	42	44	46
Italy	38	40	42	44	46	48
Rest of Europe	34	36	38	40	42	44
USA	6	8	10	12	14	16

MEN'S SHIRTS

UK	14	14.5	15	15.5	16	16.5	17
Rest of Europe	36	37	38	39/40	41	42	43
USA	14	14.5	15	15.5	16	16.5	17

MEN'S SHOES

UK	7	7.5	8.5	9.5	10.5	11
Rest of Europe	41	42	43	44	45	46
USA	8	8.5	9.5	10.5	11.5	12

WOMEN'S SHOES

UK	4.5	5	5.5	6	6.5	7
Rest of Europe	38	38	39	39	40	41
USA	6	6.5	7	7.5	8	8.5

Getting around

By air

The major towns, cities and tourist destinations in New Zealand are served by flights on Air New Zealand, Qantas and Origin Pacific Airways. The three main airlines offer travel passes for overseas visitors (with discounts on normal tickets), either for a set number of sectors or for a limited period of time (usually one month).

Air New Zealand
Auckland Travelcentre, corner of Customs & Queen sts, Auckland. Tel: (09) 336 2424 or toll-free 0800 737 000. www.airnewzealand.co.nz

Qantas Airways
Administration and Travel Centre, 191 Queen St, Auckland. Tel: (09) 357 8700 or toll-free 0800 808 767. www.qantas.co.nz

Origin Pacific Airways
Trent Drive, Nelson Airport, Nelson. Tel: (03) 547 2020 or toll-free 0800 302 302. www.originpacific.co.nz

By rail

See p187.

By car

All the big international agencies have rental depots in the major cities and tourist areas. You need a current national or international driving licence; the minimum age for rentals is 21 years. Insurance is compulsory, and is usually included in hire charges.

Hire charges can be fairly expensive (standard high-season charges are NZ$70–100 per day). If you plan to tour the whole of New Zealand by car you could negotiate discounts with the companies direct.

Camper vans are another alternative for small groups or families, giving a great deal of flexibility on accommodation. Rates start from around NZ$50 per day in low season for a two-berth van, and from NZ$300 per day for a six berth in high season.

The following major car hire agencies have branches at Auckland International Airport and around the country:

Avis *17/19 Nelson Street, Auckland. Tel: (09) 379 2650. www.avis.com*

Budget *163 Beach Road, Auckland. Tel: (09) 976 2270. www.budget.co.nz*

Hertz *154 Victoria Street West, Auckland. Tel: (09) 367 6350. www.hertz.co.nz*

National Car Rental *134 Victoria Street, Christchurch. Tel: (03) 366 5574 or toll-free 0800 800 115. www.nationalcar.co.nz*

Camper van rental agencies include:

Backpacker Campervans
Tel: (09) 275 0200, or toll-free 0800 422 267. www.backpackercampervans.com

Britz *Tel: (09) 275 9090 or toll-free 0800 831 900. www.britz.co.nz*

Kea Campers *36 Hillside Road, Glenfield, Auckland. Tel: (09) 441 7833 or toll-free 0800 520 052. www.keacampers.co.nz*

Maui Motorhomes *Tel: (09) 275 3013 or toll-free 0800 651 080. www.maui-rentals.com or www.maui.co.nz*

Thomas Cook Holidays *Signature* has flexible packages for UK-based travellers which include car rental, rail pass and accommodation options – or fully inclusive tours, at good rates (contact a branch of Thomas Cook).

Driving

New Zealand has an excellent, well-signposted road network and (apart from urban areas) traffic is light. Drive on the left. Speed limits: 100kph (62mph) on motorways and the open road, 50kph (31mph) in built-up areas; other limits may be indicated. In backcountry areas and forests, the roads – known as gravel or unmetalled roads – are often unsealed.

Restrictions may apply in some areas if you have a rental car, although these are usually ignored (there's not much point in hiring a car here if you can't take it to some of the most unspoilt wilderness areas!).

Take extra care driving on unsealed roads, and watch out for the large grading machines. Heavy rains may also cause a 'washout' or road slump, which leaves holes on the edge of the road.

Breakdowns

Many rental companies will include free breakdown services as part of the package.

In the South Island in particular, it is always a good idea to fill up with petrol as the next service station may be some distance away. If you do run out (or even think you are about to run out), rural cafés and shops usually have emergency petrol for sale in small quantities.

Hitch-hiking

Hitch-hiking is perfectly acceptable (and legal) in New Zealand, and although it is far safer here than in many other countries you should still exercise common sense and reasonable care in accepting lifts. Women should not hitch-hike alone.

Health

New Zealand is a clean, healthy country and tap water is safe to drink everywhere. However, the parasite giardia has been found in some lakes, rivers and streams, and can cause diarrhoea if it gets into your system. The probability of catching giardia is remote, but if you are camping it is best either to boil water for three minutes and then add iodine solution or chlorine bleach, or use a giardia-rated water filter.

Public and private health-care facilities operate to high standards, and in case of illness, your hotel or motel will be able to arrange a local doctor. Otherwise, see 'Doctors and Medical Services' at the front of telephone directories.

If you have an accident you will be covered by the Accident Compensation Scheme and entitled to make a claim to the Accident Compensation Corporation, irrespective of blame. Allowable benefits include some medical and hospital expenses and compensation for permanent disability – but not for loss of earnings outside the country. The existence of this scheme means that it is not possible to sue for damages in the courts for accidental injury or death.

Like every other part of the world, AIDS is present and you should take all necessary precautions.

Insurance

A comprehensive personal travel-insurance policy is highly advisable. Make sure your policy covers personal accidents, as not all costs will be covered by the Accident Compensation Scheme (*see pp183–4*). Cover for loss of personal possessions and travel delay is also recommended.

Note that most policies automatically exclude adventure sports such as white-water rafting and skiing, so if you are planning to take part in these activities, you might want to arrange for an extension to the cover. You should contact a specialist travel insurance company who will normally provide cover for most sporting activities considered 'dangerous', except bungee jumping.

Lost property

Always inform the police as soon as possible if you lose any valuables. If you need to make an insurance claim for valuable items, remember you will need to obtain a copy of your statement from the police. Lost credit cards or traveller's cheques should always be reported within 24 hours to the issuing company.

Media

Television and radio

There are four main television channels: Television One for current affairs and sport; Television Two for light entertainment; and TV3 and Channel 4 feature a variety of programmes. All channels carry commercials. Sky TV is also available (including CNN News) in hotels and motels. VHF channels broadcast in many areas with various topic channels.

There are many FM radio stations; also two non-commercial stations: the AM National Programme (mainly news, documentaries, drama and the like); and the FM Concert Programme (classical music).

Tourist FM Radio (in English on 88.2MHz) provides visitors with 24-hour information on history and culture, local activities and attractions.

Newspapers and magazines

There is no national daily newspaper as such, although the *New Zealand Herald* (published in Auckland) has the highest daily circulation, closely followed by the *Dominion Post* (published in Wellington). In addition, there is a handful of regional morning and evening dailies, plus two national Sunday newspapers. Tourist newspapers are also produced in resort areas.

International magazines are widely available. The best local magazine is Auckland's *Metro*, published monthly. The fortnightly *Te Maori News* is mostly written in English. One of the best current affairs magazines is the monthly *North and South.*

Money matters

The New Zealand dollar (NZ$) is divided into 100 cents, with notes in denominations of $5, $10, $20, $50 and $100; and coins of 5, 10, 20, 50 cents, $1 and $2.

Banks are open Monday to Friday, 9.30am–4.30pm, except public holidays. Bureaux de change, which can be found in most major resorts, are open longer hours and often at weekends. Automated teller machines (ATMs) are widespread and can be used with PINs to obtain cash.

Traveller's cheques are not available in the local currency, but if you take cheques in Sterling or Australian dollars, these can be changed in banks, hotels, large stores in cities, and in tourist areas. All international credit cards (American Express, Diners Club, JCB, VISA and MasterCard) are widely accepted.

Opening hours

Shops are usually open Monday to Friday, 9am–5.30pm, with late-night shopping until 8.30 or 9pm one or two nights a week (usually Thursday or Friday). Some shops close at 12.30–1pm on Saturdays (4.30pm in larger centres), while others stay open all day. Many tourist shops and some travel agents are open longer hours. Many supermarkets, grocery stores and some retail chains are also open on Sunday. Local food shops (known as dairies) are usually open seven days a week, 7am–10pm. Petrol (gas) stations are also open longer hours (many are open 24 hours), except in rural areas, and stock food and other sundries.

Pharmacies

Known by the English term 'chemists', pharmacies are open during normal shopping hours and most cities also have urgent dispensaries that open outside these hours (listed under 'Hospitals' in the front of telephone directories). Pharmacies also stock a wide range of other products such as sunblock, cosmetics and film.

Places of worship

The major Christian denominations are Anglican, Presbyterian, Methodist, Baptist and Roman Catholic, each with places of worship in most towns and cities. There are also synagogues and mosques in the larger cities. Your hotel reception will be able to advise on the times of services.

Police

Dial *111* for the police, fire and ambulance.

Post

Post shops are open Monday to Friday, 9am–5.30pm, and stamps can also be bought in grocery shops, bookshops and stationers. The two main types of postal service are standard post (across town and in two to three working days nationwide), and fast post (international mail, plus next-day delivery between major towns and cities within the country). A poste restante service is available at many branches.

Public and school holidays

Most businesses and all banks are closed on public holidays; all shops are closed on Christmas Day and Good Friday except for a few convenience stores and petrol stations.

1 & 2 January New Year
6 February Waitangi Day
March/April Good Friday and Easter Monday
25 April Anzac Day
1st Monday in June Queen's Birthday
4th Monday in October Labour Day
25 December Christmas Day
26 December Boxing Day

There are also regional holidays on the founding days of each province.

During school holidays you are strongly advised to book ahead for accommodation in the more popular holiday resorts.

Summer mid-December to the beginning of February
Autumn middle two weeks of April
Winter first two weeks of July
Spring two weeks in late September/ early October.

Public transport

Coaches

InterCity Coachlines, Newmans Coach Lines and Magic Bus services connect most towns and cities in the country. All the operators offer coach passes, either with discounts on various sectors or for periods ranging from seven to 35 days.

Several companies offer backpackers' 'alternative' coach services that stop off at places of interest. You can hop off some of these services and rejoin the next one that comes along if you want to stay somewhere longer. One of the companies offering these services is Kiwi Experience, which has five different routes all over the country.

InterCity Coachlines *PO Box 26 601, Epsom. Tel: (09) 623 1503. www.intercitycoach.co.nz*
Kiwi Experience *195–197 Parnell Rd, Parnell. Tel: (09) 366 9830. www.kiwiexperience.com*
Johnston's Coachlines *64 Westney Rd, Mangere, Auckland. Tel: (09) 375 4703. www.johnstons.co.nz*
Magic Bus *120 Albert St, Auckland. Tel: (09) 358 5600. www.magicbus.co.nz*
Newmans Coach Lines *PO Box 26601, Epsom. Tel: (09) 623 1503. www.newmanscoach.co.nz*

Ferries

The main form of transport between the North and South Islands is run by Interislander, which operates three ferries between Wellington and Picton several times daily, with a crossing time of just over three hours. The ferry offers a roll-on, roll-off service for cars, and although passenger bookings are rarely necessary, cars should be pre-booked in peak periods (December to February and on public holidays). Make bookings through any accredited travel agent, or directly by telephone or online:

Interislander *Second Floor, Wellington Railway Station, Wellington. Tel: (04) 498 3302, or toll-free 0800 802 802. www.interislander.co.nz*

Rail

Tranz Scenic is the country's main rail network and operates a number of long-distance services: Capital Connection (Palmerston North–Wellington), The Overlander (Auckland–Wellington), The TranzCoastal (Picton–Christchurch), and the award-winning TranzAlpine (Christchurch–Greymouth, *see pp124–5*). The Scenic Rail pass (for one week or one month) includes travel on the Interislander.

Tranz Scenic *Railway Station Bunny Street, Wellington. Tel: (04) 495 0775 or toll-free 0800 872 467. www.tranzscenic.co.nz*

For details of long-distance bus, ferry and rail services, consult the *Thomas Cook Overseas Timetable* (published bi-monthly) available at *www.thomascookpublishing.com* or from branches of Thomas Cook in the UK (*tel: (01733) 416 477*).

Travel passes

InterCity Coachlines and Newmans Coach Lines operate 120 services a day stopping at more than 600 towns and cities across New Zealand, and sell a variety of coach and travel pass options, which are worthwhile if you are planning on covering a lot of the country.

The most comprehensive passes are:

Flexipass: for coach travel nationwide. You buy travel time in blocks of 5 hours, starting at 15 hours and going up to 60 hours. You can top up your hours at any time.

Travelpass: for combination travel options throughout the country. The 2-in-One Travelpass includes unlimited coach travel with one ferry crossing. The 3-in-One Travelpass includes unlimited coach travel with one ferry crossing and a train journey. The 4-in-One Travelpass includes unlimited coach travel with one ferry crossing, a train journey and a domestic flight. You can buy any number of travel days from 5 to 15.

Passes are valid for 12 months from the date of first use, and can be bought before or after arrival in New Zealand, through travel agencies or online from InterCity Coachlines (*see opposite*).

Senior citizens

There are few limitations for senior citizens travelling in New Zealand; in fact, the Kiwis' innate sense of hospitality and general helpfulness mean that over-60s will probably find it an easier destination than many others. The main discounts are on the railways, with a saving of around 30 per cent on standard tickets for over-60s.

Student and youth travel

New Zealand is well geared up to cater for the needs of student and youth travellers. Young persons' discounts on internal travel are available through the Student Travel Agency (STA), which has branches throughout the country; it also issues International Student Identity Cards. YHA members also enjoy a wide range of travel, retail and activity discounts in New Zealand, including 15 per cent discount on InterCity and Newman Coachlines, 20 per cent discount on Tranz Scenic fares, and savings on car rental and the Kiwi Experience. You can purchase membership from your home country YHA office (only NZ residents can purchase YHA New Zealand membership), or get a Hostelling International Card for NZ$40 when in New Zealand. A VIP Backpackers Card (NZ$40) gives you similar discounts, and can be purchased from travel agents or online at *www.vipbackpackers.com*

STA Travel *187 Queen St, Auckland. Tel: (09) 309 0458. www.statravel.co.nz*
YHA New Zealand
Level 1, 166 Moorhouse Ave, Christchurch. Tel: (03) 379 9970, or toll-free 0800 278 299. www.yha.co.nz

Sustainable tourism

Thomas Cook is a strong advocate of ethical and fairly traded tourism and believes that the travel experience should be as good for the places visited as it is for the people who visit them. That's why we firmly support The Travel Foundation, a charity that develops solutions to help improve and protect holiday destinations, their environment, traditions and culture. To find out what you can do to make a positive difference to the places you travel to and the people who live there, please visit *www.thetravelfoundation.org.uk*

Telephones

Telecom New Zealand, still the major provider, offers both national and international services and operates two types of colour-coded payphones: phonecard booths – green; credit card booths – yellow. Most public phones now use phonecards, which are available from newsagents, supermarkets, petrol stations and other retail outlets. There are also around 200 credit card phones around the country. You can make direct-dial international calls from most phone boxes; hotels and motels will add charges for international calls.

Travellers can obtain Telecom calling cards which charge the calls to your home telephone bill.

Calls within New Zealand:
Emergencies *111*
Local Operator *010*
International Operator *0170*
Local Directory Assistance *018* (NZ$0.50 fee)
International Directory Assistance *0172* (NZ$1.50 fee)
International Access Code *00*
International Dialling Codes
Australia *(00) 61*; Canada *(00) 1*; Ireland *(00) 353*; UK *(00) 44*; USA *(00) 1*.

Please note: Toll-free numbers beginning with 0800 are free only within New Zealand.

Calls from Overseas:

International Dialling Code *+64*

Please note: Omit the *0* from the area code when calling from overseas, e.g. for Auckland, dial *+64 9 123 4567*, not *+64 09 123 4567*.

Time

Local time is GMT (Greenwich Mean Time) plus 12 hours; Australia plus 2–4 hours; Canada plus 15–20 hours; and USA plus 17–22 hours. New Zealand Summer Time runs from the beginning of October to the third Sunday in March, during which period local clock time is one hour ahead.

Tipping

It is a long-established part of the country's egalitarian culture that tips and gratuities are not expected.

Toilets

Public conveniences are found in information and visitor centres, tourist attractions, shopping malls, hotels, bars, petrol stations, libraries and urban parks.

Tourist offices

New Zealand has an official network of over 80 i-SITE Visitor Centres across the country, including those at Auckland and Christchurch international airports, where visitors can pick up a map listing i-SITE locations throughout New Zealand. Alternatively, the official website of Tourism New Zealand, *www.newzealand.com*, has the details and locations of all the centres. Some of the main centres are:

Auckland i-SITE Visitor Centre
137 Quay Street, Princes Wharf.
Tel: (09) 307 0612 or toll-free 0800 282 552. www.aucklandnz.com

Wellington i-SITE Visitor Centre
Corner of Victoria & Wakefield sts.
Tel: (04) 802 4860 or toll-free 0800 933 5363.
www.wellingtonnz.com

Christchurch i-SITE Visitor Centre
Old Chief Post Office, Cathedral Square.
Tel: (03) 379 9629.
www.christchurchnz.net

For New Zealand tourist information centres in other countries, contact the appropriate consulate (*see p181*).

Travellers with disabilities

New Zealand compares favourably with other countries in its provision of facilities for travellers with disabilities (you can even do a bungee jump in a wheelchair!). Most major attractions are accessible for wheelchair users. The *AA New Zealand Accommodation Guide* (*see p172*) lists accommodation options for wheelchair users.

The Disability Resource Centre
14 Erson Ave, Royal Oak, Auckland.
Tel: (09) 625 8069.
Fax: (09) 624 1633.
www.disabilityresource.org.nz

Index

Acknowledgements

Thomas Cook Publishing wishes to thank the following photographers, libraries and associations for their assistance in the preparation of this book.

DREAMSTIME 81 (FALK66), 143 (ROSSILLICON)
THOMAS COOK 1, 15, 25, 27, 29, 31, 63, 67, 68, 97, 106, 127, 141, 151, 153, 159
TRANZ SCENIC 125
PICTURES COLOUR LIBRARY 19, 21, 51, 72, 86, 95, 111, 113, 114, 116, 123, 145
WORLD PICTURES/PHOTOSHOT 43, 45, 69, 75, 79, 147, 155, 167, 171
WIKIMEDIA COMMONS 50 (Karora), 142 (Nomad Tales)

The remaining pictures are held in the AA PHOTO LIBRARY and were taken by PAUL KENWARD.

For CAMBRIDGE PUBLISHING MANAGEMENT LTD:

Project editor: Karen Beaulah
Typesetter: Paul Queripel
Proofreader: Jan McCann
Index: Karolin Thomas

SEND YOUR THOUGHTS TO BOOKS@THOMASCOOK.COM

We're committed to providing the very best up-to-date information in our travel guides and constantly strive to make them as useful as they can be. You can help us to improve future editions by letting us have your feedback. If you've made a wonderful discovery on your travels that we don't already feature, if you'd like to inform us about recent changes to anything that we do include, or if you simply want to let us know your thoughts about this guidebook and how we can make it even better – we'd love to hear from you.

Send us ideas, discoveries and recommendations today and then look out for your valuable input in the next edition of this title.

Emails to the above address, or letters to Travellers Series Editor, Thomas Cook Publishing, PO Box 227, Unit 9, Coningsby Road, Peterborough PE3 8SB, UK.

Please don't forget to let us know which title your feedback refers to!

TRAVELLERS

THE THOMAS COOK TRAVELLER TO NEW ZEALAND

comes from the world's leading travel expert and has everything you need to plan the perfect trip:

- The top sights and the less well-known ones
- Walks and tours with clear maps
- Places off the beaten track
- Special features on cultural background and other aspects
- Holiday hints and tips
- A-Z of essential information
- Advice on shopping, eating out, sport and nightlife

In Canada
$ 18.95

Thomas Cook Publishing
www.thomascookpublishing.com